THE e-POLICY HANDBOOK

OTHER BOOKS BY NANCY FLYNN

Blog Rules: A Business Guide to Managing Policy, Public Relations, and Legal Issues, Nancy Flynn (AMACOM)

Instant Messaging Rules: A Business Guide to Managing Policies, Security, and Legal Issues for Safe IM Communication, Nancy Flynn (AMACOM)

E-Mail Rules: A Business Guide to Managing Policies, Security, and Legal Issues for E-Mail and Digital Communication, Nancy Flynn and Randolph Kahn, Esq. (AMACOM)

The e-Policy Handbook: Designing and Implementing Effective E-Mail, Internet, and Software Policies, First Edition, Nancy Flynn (AMACOM)

Writing Effective E-Mail: Improving Your Electronic Communication, Second Edition, Nancy Flynn and Tom Flynn (Thomson Learning/ Crisp)

E-Mail Management: 50 Tips for Keeping Your Inbox Under Control (Thomson Learning/NETg)

The e-Policy Handbook: Rules and Best Practices to Safely Manage Your Company's E-Mail, Blogs, Social Networking, and Other Electronic Communication Tools, Second Edition, Nancy Flynn (AMACOM)

The e-Policy Handbook

Rules and Best Practices to Safely
Manage Your Company's E-Mail, Blogs,
Social Networking, and Other Electronic
Communication Tools

SECOND EDITION

Nancy Flynn

AMACOM

AMERICAN MANAGEMENT ASSOCIATION

New York • Atlanta • Brussels • Chicago • Mexico City • San Francisco
Shanghai • Tokyo • Toronto • Washington, D.C.

*Special discounts on bulk quantities of AMACOM books are
available to corporations, professional associations, and other
organizations. For details, contact Special Sales Department,
AMACOM, a division of American Management Association,
1601 Broadway, New York, NY 10019.
Tel: 212-903-8316. Fax: 212-903-8083.
E-mail: specialsls@amanet.org
Website: www.amacombooks.org/go/specialsales
To view all AMACOM titles go to: www.amacombooks.org*

Library of Congress Cataloging-in-Publication Data

Flynn, Nancy, 1956–
    *The e-policy handbook : rules and best practices to safely manage your company's
e-mail, blogs, social networking, and other electronic communication tools / Nancy
Flynn.—2nd ed.*
        p.   cm.
    Includes bibliographical references and index.
    ISBN-13: 978-0-8144-1065-3
    ISBN-10: 0-8144-1065-0
    *1. Electronic mail systems—Management.   2. Information technology—
Management.   3. Computer network resources—Management.   4. Computer
software—Management.   I. Title.*
HE7551.F58 2009
004.068—dc21

                                                                        2008044715

Printing number

10   9   8   7   6   5   4   3   2   1

This book is dedicated to my husband,
Paul Schodorf, and our daughter, **Bridget Flynn Schodorf.**
As always, thank you for your patience and support!

CONTENTS

ACKNOWLEDGMENTS

Sincere thanks to all those who contributed encouragement, support, expertise, information, time, and contacts to help make this book possible.

This book would not be possible without the generous gifts of time and encouragement from my husband, Paul Schodorf, and our daughter, Bridget Flynn Schodorf. As always, thank you for your support and patience!

Sincere thanks to the following professionals who generously contributed time and expertise to help make *The e-Policy Handbook*, Second Edition, a success: William T. (Todd) Gates, President and CEO, ArcMail Technology; Joseph Collins, Jr., CEO and Cofounder, VaporStream™ Confidential Messaging; Amit Shah, CTO and Cofounder, VaporStream Confidential Messaging; William Henneberry, Chief Marketing and Sales Officer, VaporStream Confidential Messaging; Robert Hall, Chief Brand Officer, VaporStream Confidential Messaging; and Susan Majerus, Principal, Intelec Group.

Thank you to American Management Association (AMA) for their ongoing support of my books and ePolicy Institute through joint programs including AMA/ePolicy Institute surveys, forums, and webinars.

I am grateful to AMACOM books for permission to excerpt material from my previous AMACOM titles: *The e-Policy Handbook*, First Edition; *E-Mail Rules; Instant Messaging Rules;* and *Blog Rules*. I am particularly grateful to Executive Editor Jacqueline Flynn for her belief in this updated second edition of *The e-Policy Handbook*, her patience, and her help in making it happen.

Finally, thank you to the clients, partners, members, and friends of ePolicy Institute, www.epolicyinstitute.com, for their ongoing support of our services and programs, including employee training programs, speaking services, expert witness services and litigation consulting, workplace surveys, and e-policy consulting services.

PART ONE

Electronic Business Communication Rules

Why Every Organization Needs Electronic Rules and Policies Based on Best Practices

Since the initial publication of *The e-Policy Handbook* in 2001, electronic business communication tools and technologies have taken the workplace by storm. Consequently, many employers find themselves drowning in risk as they struggle to manage the use—and curtail the abuse —of what were originally conceived as time-saving, productivity-enhancing technology tools.

Without question, e-mail has become the business world's communication tool of choice, forever altering the ways in which we exchange information and conduct professional and personal relationships. Meanwhile, new tools and technologies—instant messenger (IM), blogs, social networking and video sites, cell phones and camera phones, text messaging, "confidential" electronic messaging, and the BlackBerry Smartphone, to name a few—have joined the electronic business communication mix at a breakneck pace.

The good news: The ever-expanding universe of high-tech tools facilitates users' ability to quickly and conveniently transmit business-critical data and stay connected with colleagues and customers around the globe. The bad news: Emerging technologies dramatically increase employers' exposure to potentially costly and protracted risks including workplace lawsuits, regulatory fines, security breaches, and productivity drains, among others.

Fortunately, for savvy employers determined to manage technology use and minimize risks, there is a solution. Through the strategic implementation of a comprehensive e-policy program that combines written electronic rules with formal employee training supported by policy-based monitoring, management, and archiving tools, organizations can effectively minimize (and in some cases prevent) electronic risks while maximizing compliance with legal, regulatory, and organizational guidelines.

> **e-Policy Rule 1:** Through the implementation of a comprehensive e-policy program that combines written rules with employee education supported by discipline and technology tools, organizations can effectively minimize electronic risks and maximize compliance.

In the Electronic Office, Risks Abound

Even if your organization does not currently use IM, operate a business blog, or provide executives with BlackBerry Smartphones, you cannot afford to ignore new and emerging technology. If you fail to provide the hot, must-have technologies of the day, chances are your tech-savvy employees (particularly younger employees whose social lives revolve around IMing, texting, and social networking) will bring them in through the back door and load them onto your system without management approval or IT oversight. Left undetected and unmanaged, that's a recipe for disaster!

Manage Powerful, Popular Electronic Business Communication Tools Proactively

Considering that the average personal computer can hold 1 million pages of information, it's no surprise that 90 percent of the business documents we create and acquire are electronic, according to the Association of Records Managers and Administrators (ARMA) as reported by *Baseline* Magazine.[1]

Employers who are concerned about managing all that electronic information—and related risks—should act now to put written policies in place governing the use of established tools and new technologies at work during business hours and at home on employees' own time.

Old and new alike, all electronic business communication tools must be addressed by comprehensive, best-practices-based rules and policies as detailed in this book. Failure to establish and enforce written rules and e-policies puts the organization at risk of electronic disasters including, but not limited to: regulatory audits, security breaches, lost productivity, shattered stock valuation, negative publicity, lost credibility, and workplace lawsuits, which employers and legal professionals alike consistently identify as their number-one e-mail and Internet-related concern.[2]

> **e-Policy Rule 2:** You cannot afford to ignore new and emerging technology. If you fail to provide the hot, must-have technologies of the day, chances are your tech-savvy employees will bring them in through the back door. Left undetected and unmanaged, that's a recipe for disaster!

Employers Face Ever-Increasing Legal Liability

As early as 2001, when the first edition of *The e-Policy Handbook* was published, employers cited legal liability as their primary reason for monitoring employee e-mail and Internet use.[3] Since then, we have witnessed the expanding role of e-mail and other forms of electronically stored information (ESI) as evidence in civil lawsuits and criminal trials.

In 2006, 24 percent of organizations had employee e-mail subpoenaed, compared to just 9 percent in 2001. Another 15 percent of companies went to court to battle lawsuits specifically triggered by employee e-mail in 2006, according to the Workplace E-Mail, Instant Messaging, and Blog Survey from American Management Association and ePolicy Institute.[4]

Electronically Stored Information Plays an Ever-Expanding Evidentiary Role

There is no doubt that the evidentiary role of workplace e-mail and other electronically stored information will continue to expand. The United States Federal Court made clear this fact in December 2006, when the much-anticipated amendments to the Federal Rules of Civil Procedure (FRCP) were announced, affirming the fact that all electronically stored information is subject to discovery (which means it may be subpoenaed and used as evidence) in federal litigation.

When it comes to electronic evidence, it is the content that counts, not the tool or technology used. Whether created, transmitted, acquired, posted, downloaded, or uploaded via e-mail, IM, the Internet, a cell phone, or any other tool, ESI creates the electronic equivalent of DNA evidence. ESI can—and will—be subpoenaed and used as evidence for or against your company should it one day become embroiled in a workplace lawsuit. Will you be prepared?

> **e-Policy Rule 3:** Electronically stored information (ESI) creates the electronic equivalent of DNA evidence. ESI can–and will–be subpoenaed and used as evidence for or against your organization should it one day become embroiled in a workplace lawsuit.

Regulators Grow Increasingly Watchful

Over the years, government and industry regulators have turned an increasingly watchful eye to the content created and the business records generated by e-mail and other electronic business communication tools. For example, failure to comply with Security and Exchange Commission (SEC) rules governing written e-mail and IM content and record retention policies has cost brokerage firms hundreds of millions of dollars in fines.

The Health Insurance Portability and Accountability Act (HIPAA), Gramm-Leach-Bliley Act (GLBA), and Sarbanes-Oxley Act (SOX) are just three of the tens of thousands of regulatory rules with which workplace computer users must comply—or face consequences including monetary fines and possible jail time.

In spite of potentially costly penalties, regulated firms have been slow to adopt the type of business record–related rules and policies detailed in Chapter 3. Only 34 percent of organizations have e-mail record retention policies and schedules in place, and merely 13 percent of companies retain and archive business record IM, according to American Management Association/ePolicy Institute research.[5]

Among regulated employees, 43 percent either don't adhere to regulatory rules governing e-mail retention or they simply do not know if they are in compliance.[6] Overall, 43 percent of workers can't distinguish business-critical e-mail and IM that must be retained from insignificant messages that may be purged.[7]

It's no surprise that employees are confused and employers ill-prepared when it comes to the management of all-important ESI. Only 21 percent of companies provide employees with a formal definition of "electronic business record."[8]

This book is designed to educate employers and users about the importance of establishing and complying with rules and policies governing electronic business record retention, deletion, and archiving, as well as overall electronic risk management. Strategic business record retention and deletion rules and policies are essential for all employers, regardless of industry, size, or status as public or private entities.

Employ Tougher Rules to Combat Growing Risks

Along with increased risk, there has been growing awareness among employers of the devastating impact that inappropriate electronic content and unprofessional behavior—accidental or intentional—can have on users' careers and the corporate bottom line. Consequently, employers are increasingly putting teeth in their electronic policies.

In 2007, more than a quarter of employers (28 percent) fired employees for e-mail misuse. That's double the 14 percent reported just six years earlier in 2001. An additional 30 percent of bosses terminated workers for Internet violations in 2007, according to the 2007 Electronic Monitoring and Surveillance Survey from American Management Association and ePolicy Institute.[9]

No Employer Is Immune from Electronic Risk

Employee use of the company's electronic business communication system can open any organization to potentially costly and protracted risks including litigation, regulatory investigations, security breaches, malicious intruder attacks, lost productivity, wasted computer resources, viruses, business interruptions, loss of revenue, and public embarrassment should a workplace lawsuit be filed, the software police drop by for a visit, or the media get wind of a particularly salacious e-mail disaster.

You cannot be present in every office on every floor of every facility every hour of every day. You cannot rely on managers and staff to exercise sound judgment and good taste 100 percent of the time. And you should not discount the damage external intruders and internal saboteurs pose to your organization.

- If a female employee walks into the office of a male associate who is watching a pornographic video on his computer, you, the employer, could wind up on the wrong side of a sexual harassment lawsuit.

- If a former employee subpoenas company e-mail in the course of a hostile work environment lawsuit, your organization could face a lengthy and expensive search for messages, attachments, and other electronically stored information.

- If your employees are among the 78 percent of workers who have downloaded free IM software from the Internet to chat with colleagues, customers, the media, and other third parties via the public web, your business records, company secrets, and financial data are at risk.[10]

- If employees are illegally duplicating licensed software for business use, you could face six-figure fines, criminal charges, and negative publicity should a disgruntled ex-employee alert the software police to the piracy.

- If an employee-blogger posts defamatory comments about a competitor or supplier, you could be headed for a protracted lawsuit.

- If an employee uses Facebook, YouTube, or another social networking or video site to post racist or discriminatory content, your organization could face negative publicity, a public backlash, or worse.

- If a disgruntled ex-employee of your publicly traded company discloses confidential financial information via an online chat room, blog, discussion board, website, or social networking site, then you could face disciplinary action from regulators and scrutiny from the Wall Street investment community, individual shareholders, and the media.

- If a distracted driver, engaged in a business-related cell phone conversation, crashes and kills someone, your organization may be liable under the legal principle known as vicarious liability.

Keep Employees in Line While They're Online

Risks are as prevalent in the electronic office as e-mail is indispensable. For responsible organizations operating in the age of electronic business communication, written e-Policies are essential business tools. Clearly written and effectively communicated e-Policies can help employers maximize employee compliance and demonstrate to courts and regulators that the organization has made every effort to manage electronic use and content.

> **e-Policy Rule 4:** Clearly written and effectively communicated e-Policies can help employers demonstrate to courts and regulators that the organization has made every effort to manage electronic use and content.

Using This Book as a Best-Practices Toolkit

The best advice for employers who want to reduce electronic risks is: Take the initiative. Don't wait for electronic disaster to strike. Develop and implement comprehensive rules and written e-Policies governing old, new, and emerging technologies—*right now*.

This book is written to help employers of all sizes and industries navigate safely through the electronic workplace. It is written to help employers minimize electronic risks and maximize compliance by providing the tools needed, including:

- Content and usage policies

- Training tips

- Disciplinary rules

- Technology tools

Under the direction of your organization's legal counsel, feel free to adapt and use the fill-in-the-blank e-Policies in Appendix C. These sample policies are offered to help readers develop and implement successful electronic business communication policy programs for their own organizations.

RECAP & e-POLICY ACTION PLAN

1. Emerging technologies dramatically increase exposure to risks including lawsuits, regulatory fines, security breaches, and reduced productivity.

2. An e-policy program combining written rules with formal training supported by monitoring, management, and archiving tools can help minimize risks and maximize compliance with organizational, legal, and regulatory guidelines.

3. If you fail to provide the hot, must-have technologies of the day, tech-savvy employees may bring them in through the back door and load them onto your system without management approval or IT oversight.

4. Electronically stored information (ESI) creates the electronic equivalent of DNA evidence. ESI can be subpoenaed and used as evidence for or against your organization in civil lawsuits and criminal proceedings.

PART TWO

E-Mail Rules

CHAPTER 2

Legal Risks and Rules
E-Mail Creates Discoverable Evidence

Where does your organization stand on the matter of electronic evidence? Do you know the difference between business-critical e-mail that must be retained for legal or regulatory purposes versus insignificant messages that may be deleted in the ordinary course of business? Is your e-mail archive a dangerous mix of professional correspondence and personal conversations that could potentially embarrass your employees and sabotage your firm's legal position? Would you be able to locate and produce legally compliant e-mail messages and attachments quickly and responsively if ordered to do so by a court or regulatory body?

Struggling with E-Mail Business Record Retention? You Are Not Alone

In 2006, 24 percent of employers had e-mail subpoenaed by courts or regulators, up from 9 percent just five years earlier. And 15 percent of organizations went to court in 2006 to battle lawsuits specifically triggered by employees' smoking-gun e-mails, according to American Management Association/ePolicy Institute research.[1]

In spite of e-mail's growing evidentiary role, however, only 34 percent of U.S. companies have implemented written e-mail record retention policies and deletion schedules.[2] Of the 66 percent of businesses that do not formally preserve and systematically dispose of e-mail records according to written rules and schedules, some save all their messages, others purge everything, and still others approach record retention and deletion as hit-or-miss propositions.

A highly litigious business environment and heightened regulatory oversight have created new and potentially costly challenges to corporate e-mail systems. The business community's failure to strategically manage e-mail business records and other forms of electronically stored information is alarming.

Your ability to formally define, effectively retain, and successfully archive electronic business records is one of the most important jobs your organization can undertake. Your ability to separate business-critical e-mail from insignificant and personal messages can have an enormous impact on your organization's assets, reputation, and future should you one day find yourself battling a workplace lawsuit, responding to a regulatory inquiry, or searching for proof of a contested business transaction.[3]

> **e-Policy Rule 5:** Your ability to formally define, effectively retain, successfully archive, and quickly produce electronic business records is one of the most important jobs your organization can undertake.

E-mail disasters can include costly and protracted lawsuits, regulatory investigations and fines, and the loss of intellectual property and other confidential company information. Regardless of your organization's industry, size, or status as a public or private entity, the most effective way to prevent e-mail-related disasters is to develop and enforce a strategic e-mail management program that formally addresses record retention, archiving, and retrieval among other key issues.

What Is a Business Record?

Because the vast majority of business documents are created, acquired, and stored electronically, the effective management of e-mail and other electronic business records is a prerequisite for all businesses, regardless of industry, size, or regulatory status.

Unfortunately, for those who still struggle to manage electronically stored information, "business record" cannot be universally defined. Business records vary by organization, industry, and sometimes by department. Every organization must, therefore, develop its own clear and consistent definition of a business record.

In spite of the all-important nature of electronic data, only 21 percent of organizations have provided employees with a formal definition of "electronic business record." Consequently, 43 percent of e-mail users confess that they cannot distinguish business-critical e-mail that must be retained from insignificant nonrecords that may be purged, reveals American Management Association/ePolicy Institute research.[4] This is particularly disturbing, in light of the fact that 67 percent of companies allow individual users, rather than corporate policy, to determine e-mail retention periods, according to Osterman Research.[5]

Basically, a business record is a document (electronic or paper) that provides evidence of business-related activities, events, transactions, negotiations, purchases, sales, hiring, firing, and so on.[6] Not every message that enters or leaves your e-mail system is a business record. Not every electronic conversation you conduct rises to the level of a business record. Your organization's welfare depends on your ability to distinguish business-critical e-mail and other electronic records from personal and otherwise insignificant nonrecord messages.

> **e-Policy Rule 6:** There is no one-size-fits-all definition of a business record. Every organization must develop its own definition on a companywide or department-by-department basis.

Federal Court System Raised the Bar on Electronic Record Management in 2006

The business community's need for strategic electronic business record management intensified in December 2006, when the United States Federal Court system announced amendments to the Federal Rules of Civil Procedure (FRCP). The amended rules govern the discovery of electronically stored information (ESI), a newly minted phrase that refers to e-mail and other data that can be stored electronically. Mindful of new and emerging technologies, the court intends ESI to cover all current types of computer-based information plus future technology developments as well.

Enforced by the U.S. Supreme Court, the revised rules make it clear that all ESI—including but not limited to e-mail messages and attachments, IM chat, text messages, blog posts, history of Web surfing, backup tapes, voice mail, and all other forms of created, acquired, retained, and archived data—is subject to discovery in civil lawsuits. In other words, the information that is stored in your organization's computer system may be used as evidence—to support or sink your case—in the event of a workplace lawsuit.

> **e-Policy Rule 7:** E-mail and other electronically stored information is subject to discovery and may be used as evidence in litigation.

Focus on Content, Not Technology Tools

When it comes to ESI, it's the content that counts, not the tool used to create it. Whether written, transmitted, acquired, posted, downloaded, or uploaded via e-mail, IM, the Web, social networking sites, cell phones, or other electronic business communication tools, ESI creates the electronic equivalent of DNA evidence. ESI can and will be subpoenaed by opposing legal counsel, must be retrieved and relinquished in a timely and authentic manner, and may be used as evidence to support your case or sink your career should your company become embroiled in litigation.

More than a quarter (27 percent) of U.S. companies feel that the new FRCP amendments have made electronic discovery more challenging, according to the Fourth Annual Litigation Trends Survey from Fulbright & Jaworski L.L.P.[7] Is your organization up to the challenge?

Federal Law Outpaces State Data Discovery Rules

When it comes to electronic discovery in civil litigation, state court systems lag behind the federal system. As of January 2008, only 7 states had adopted the FRCP amendments in whole or part, with another 14 states still evaluating amendments to their own civil procedure rules governing the discovery of e-mail and other ESI.[8] Until all remaining states amend their electronic data discovery rules, be sure to assign your legal counsel the task of monitoring discovery-related rulings in every state in which your organization has a presence, or in which your workplace lawsuits are tried. To be safe, adhere to FRCP regardless of state jurisdiction.

The following list summarizes the FRCP Amendments.

1.   Within the federal court system and some state courts, ESI is discoverable. That means your organization's retained and archived

ESI, whether business records or not, may be subpoenaed by opposing counsel and used as evidence in workplace lawsuits.

2. Organizations that operate within the United States must manage their electronic data in a manner that allows them to produce it in a timely, complete, and legally compliant way in response to discovery requests during the evidence-gathering phase of litigation.

3. The FRCP amendments do not require organizations to retain *all* e-mail records and *all* other ESI *forever*. Within the ordinary course of business, and based on advice from your legal counsel, you may be free to purge your organization's system of electronic information that has reached the end of its life cycle, is not needed to fulfill regulatory requirements or business obligations, and is not relevant to current litigation, pending cases, or anticipated legal claims.

4. The courts appreciate consistency, especially when it comes to the preservation, purging, and production of e-mail and other ESI. The establishment and consistent adherence to formal retention policies, written deletion schedules, and comprehensive archiving practices will help your organization deflect claims that it has illegally destroyed or otherwise tampered with electronic evidence.

Five Compliance Tips for Effective Electronic Record—and Risk—Management

As part of your organization's comprehensive electronic business communication and electronic risk management programs, be sure to establish best practices–based rules, policies, and procedures governing the preservation, production, and purging of e-mail and other ESI.

To that end, best practices call for the adoption of five compliance tips:

1. Establish a clear definition of "business record" on a company-wide or department-by-department basis.

2. Know—and adhere to—ESI retention and production rules imposed by federal and state courts and government and industry regulators.

3. Communicate the company's "business record" definition clearly

and consistently to all employees. Make sure employees know the difference between business-critical e-mail and insignificant nonre-cords—and understand their individual roles, if any, when it comes to preserving records, purging nonrecords, and keeping their inboxes—and the company's archives—clear of potentially risky personal and nonbusiness-related e-mail.

4. Establish—and strictly enforce—written rules, policies, and proce-dures governing the retention and disposition of e-mail messages, attachments, and other ESI.

5. Take advantage of reliable, real-time archiving technology. As detailed in Chapter 5, an automatic archiving tool like ArcMail Technology's Defender solution helps ensure that incoming, outgoing, and internal e-mail messages and attachments are auto-matically captured, indexed, and stored in a legally compliant and tamperproof environment that facilitates the speedy search and responsive retrieval of electronic evidence.

RECAP & e-POLICY ACTION PLAN

1. Define the meaning of "business record" for your organization. If some of your employees are regulated, and others are not, consider establishing multiple definitions on a department-by-department basis.

2. Create a formal, written e-mail business record retention policy. At the same time, review—and as necessary adjust—the retention policies governing all the organization's other electronically produced, acquired, and stored information.

3. When it comes to the deletion of business record e-mail and other ESI, consistency is critical. Whether you never delete anything, always purge everything, or opt to "take out the trash" every seven years (the most commonly applied retention period),[9] the establish-ment of and strict adherence to a formal retention policy and written deletion schedule is essential. It will help strengthen your organiza-tion's position should you ever be accused of illegally destroying or otherwise tampering with electronic evidence.

4. Know and comply with the amended Federal Rules of Civil Procedure governing the preservation and discovery of business record e-mail and other ESI.

5. Know and comply with applicable state court rulings regarding electronic data discovery.

6. Know and comply with regulatory rules governing the content, retention, and production of business record e-mail and other ESI (see Chapter 4).

7. Educate employees about:

- electronic business records
- the company's retention policies and deletion schedules
- legal and regulatory compliance requirements
- the penalties individual users and the organization as a whole face for noncompliance

CHAPTER 3

Record Retention Risks and Rules

Courts and Regulators Take Seriously the Production *–and Destruction–*of Electronic Evidence

The retention of e-mail business records is fundamentally a legal issue, particularly for companies that are publicly traded and organizations that are heavily regulated. Although IT can certainly help the legal department understand retention challenges and archiving solutions from a technology perspective, it is essential for the organization's legal department to take the lead in determining *precisely* which e-mail messages and other data will be preserved, *exactly* how and where data will be stored, and *specifically* when—if ever—electronically stored information will be deleted.

> **e-Policy Rule 8:** The retention of e-mail business records is fundamentally a legal issue. Legal must take the lead in determining precisely which e-mail messages and other data will be preserved, exactly how and where data will be stored, and specifically when–if ever–electronically stored information will be deleted.

REAL-LIFE ESI DISASTER STORY: INSURANCE COMPANY AND LAWYERS FINED $1.25 MILLION FOR CONCEALING ELECTRONIC EVIDENCE

In 2007, Zurich American Insurance Company and two of its law firms were slapped with a $1.25 million fine for concealing electronic evidence related to a federal lawsuit. The missing ESI was important evidence in a hard-fought case to determine the insurer's liability for World Trade Center properties destroyed on 9/11.

Following the 9/11 terrorist attacks, Zurich American Insurance claimed to have evidence to support its position that neither the owner nor operator of the World Trade Center properties, nor its leasing agent, were entitled to insurance coverage. During the trial, however, it was discovered that Zurich American actually possessed—and intentionally had concealed—evidence that supported the opposition's claim.

Specifically, Zurich American withheld a copy of the plaintiffs' 62-page insurance policy, which the insurer had printed out on the day that the twin towers were destroyed, September 11, 2001. On that same day, Zurich American intentionally deleted an electronic version of the policy from its document library, replacing the plaintiffs' original insurance policy with one that was labeled "final corrected policy."

Zurich American's lawyers, who possessed and had made copies of the 9/11 policy as early as 2003, concealed the evidence from opposing legal counsel until 2005, when all the case-related depositions were completed.

According to the judge, Zurich American's guilt was established by its failure to produce the printed insurance policy, coupled with its intentional deletion of the electronic version. Fining Zurich American and its attorneys $1.25 million, the judge said the insurer either was dishonest or unreasonable when it insisted that there was no evidence to support the plaintiffs' claim that they were entitled to coverage following the 9/11 disaster.[1]

As Zurich American's ESI disaster story illustrates, the courts take seriously the production—and concealment or illegal destruction—of electronic evidence. Failure to manage e-mail and other electronically stored information can have a costly and otherwise devastating impact on your organization.

> **e-Policy Rule 9:** Failure to manage e-mail and other electroni-
> cally stored information can have a costly and otherwise devas-
> tating impact on your organization's bottom line, reputation, and
> future.

Litigation Hold Policies Help Prevent Spoliation Claims

While the courts typically won't punish a company for deleting e-mail in the course of a "routine, good-faith operation,"[2] spoliation—the accidental or intentional destruction or alteration of evidence—is another matter.

The courts and regulators frown upon and are free to impose sanctions for spoliation, including multimillion-dollar fines and instructions to jurors to assume the worst about a party and its legal position. It is, therefore, in your organization's best interest to systematically manage the production, preservation, and purging of e-mail and other electronic data.

One of the most effective ways to avoid a spoliation claim is to establish and consistently enforce a litigation hold policy. A litigation hold is designed to suspend the destruction of documents that would otherwise be purged in the ordinary course of business, thereby preventing the destruction (intentional or not) of electronic evidence. As soon as you receive word that a lawsuit or regulatory investigation is underway, or if you even suspect that a claim may be filed down the road, you must act immediately to implement your litigation hold.

That said, it is not enough simply to have a litigation hold policy in place as 89 percent of U.S. companies do, according to Fulbright & Jaworski research.[3] As the $10.4 billion insurance giant UnumProvident learned the hard way, litigation hold rules and timelines are useless—unless they are consistently applied.

REAL-LIFE RETENTION DISASTER STORY: LAX LITIGATION HOLD LEADS TO LOST EVIDENCE

In the course of a class-action lawsuit against UnumProvident, a U.S. District Court judge discovered that the company had continued deleting e-mail for two weeks after the court initially ordered its preservation. Because the insurer failed to promptly enforce a litigation hold, e-mail that was pertinent to the case was destroyed.

The judge didn't fine or otherwise sanction UnumProvident, but did issue this reprimand: "If UnumProvident had been as diligent as it should have been in complying promptly with the [court] order, maybe fewer tapes would have been inadvertently overwritten."[4]

REAL-LIFE SPOLIATION DISASTER STORY: MISSING E-MAIL EVIDENCE COSTS MICROSOFT $25 MILLION

In the case of *Z4 Technologies v. Microsoft*, the judge ordered Microsoft to pay damages of $25 million, plus $2 million in attorneys' fees, for litigation misconduct related to the company's failure to produce certain e-mail evidence and disclose the existence of a database in a timely manner during discovery.[5]

Need More Proof That the Courts and Regulators Take Spoliation Seriously?

During 2004 federal tobacco litigation, a U.S. District Court judge ordered Philip Morris USA to pay $2.75 million in fines when it was discovered that 11 managers had destroyed e-mail message printouts in violation of company policy.[6]

In the course of the lawsuit *William T. Thompson Co. v. General Nutrition Corp.* (GNC), the court ordered GNC to preserve all records maintained in the ordinary course of business. In spite of the order, management told employees that the judicial orders "should not require us to change our standard document retention or destruction policies or practices." Because GNC did not stop deleting files as ordered, electronic documents that were not otherwise available were deleted. The court ordered a default judgment (a ruling for the plaintiff and against GNC) and some $450,000 in monetary sanctions against GNC.[7]

The government is equally strict about the preservation and destruction of evidence. Title 26 of the Internal Revenue Code, for example, carries penalties of up to $500,000 and three years in prison for the destruction of records.[8]

REAL-LIFE SPOLIATION DISASTER STORY: UBS SLAPPED WITH $29.3 MILLION VERDICT

With locations around the globe, Zurich-based investment bank UBS in 2005 was hit with a $29.3 million verdict in a U.S. court for failing to produce subpoenaed e-mail in the course of an employment discrimination lawsuit.

In the lawsuit filed by ex-employee Laura Zubulake against her former employer UBS, it was discovered that backup tapes were missing and e-mail messages had been deleted.

Zubulake moved for sanctions against UBS for its failure to preserve the missing tapes and e-mails. The judge instructed the jury to "infer that the [missing] evidence would have been unfavorable to UBS."[9] In addition, the judge ruled that UBS should have known the e-mails would be relevant to future litigation and thus had a duty to preserve the missing evidence. "Almost everyone associated with Zubulake recognized the possibility that she might sue," the judge wrote.[10]

The judge also found that UBS failed to comply with its own retention policy, which would have preserved the missing evidence. The court ordered UBS to bear Zubulake's costs to redepose witnesses about the destruction of electronic evidence and any newly discovered e-mails.[11]

UBS denied discriminating against Zubulake and threatened to appeal the $29.3 million jury verdict. In 2005, however, UBS and Zubulake settled the case for an undisclosed sum.[12]

e-Policy Rule 10: Don't take chances with e-mail evidence. Combine formal retention rules and litigation hold policies with reliable archiving technology to ensure that electronically stored information is properly preserved and promptly produced.

How Long Should You Keep Old E-Mail?

There are different schools of thought on e-mail retention periods and deletion schedules. The retention and deletion of your electronic business records may be governed by laws or regulations. For example, the SEC dictates that brokerage firms be prepared to produce three years' worth of electronic records immediately upon request, and the Employee Retirement Income Security Act has a rule that e-mail and other correspondence related to employee benefit plans be kept indefinitely.[13] Unless your organization's e-mail and other electronic business records are governed by law or regulations, you are free to determine the retention periods and deletion schedules that are most appropriate for your organization.

As previously noted, the courts typically do not punish businesses for deleting e-mail in the ordinary course of business. Nonetheless, thanks to FRCP, SOX, HIPAA, and other widely publicized laws and regulations (see Chapter 4), many unregulated companies now opt to keep e-mail for increasingly long periods of time. Declining storage costs also have motivated more organizations to choose long-term archiving over quick-fix deletion.[14]

Destructive Retention Offers a False Sense of Security

In spite of e-mail's ever-expanding evidentiary role, many employers continue to engage in what the archiving experts at ArcMail Technology have termed "destructive retention." Destructive retention calls for the preservation of e-mail for a limited time, followed by its permanent deletion, manually or automatically, from the company network.[15]

When it comes to destructive retention, preservation periods can range from months to years:

- Nearly a quarter of all companies delete e-mail after 90 days, according to Osterman Research.[16]

- The real estate, technology, communications, and energy industries favor one-year or longer retention periods, Fulbright & Jaworski research reveals.[17]

- The most commonly applied corporate retention period is seven years, according to ArcMail Technology.[18]

"If your organization opts for destructive retention, bear in mind that e-mail never disappears completely. You may purge your system of messages and attachments, but e-mail always leaves an electronic footprint somewhere," notes William T. Gates, ArcMail Technology's President and CEO.

"Remember, your own employees file, print, copy, forward, and otherwise hold onto internal and external e-mail. Your workers' intended and unintended recipients and their employers retain incoming mail. Computer forensic investigators regularly recover long-lost e-mail messages—often incomplete, out of context, and potentially damaging to the sender's organization," said Gates.[19]

At the end of the day, a policy that calls for the purging of e-mail at regular intervals may render you the only party in the courtroom who is unable to produce copies of your own e-mail. That's a position you never want to be in!

> **e-Policy Rule 11:** A destructive retention policy that calls for the purging of e-mail on regular intervals may render you the only party in the courtroom who is unable to produce copies of your own e-mail. That's a position you never want to be in!

Be Strategic About the Deletion of Dead Records

Reliable archiving technology like ArcMail's Defender solution *guarantees* your ability to store, index, search, view, retrieve, and produce legally compliant, unaltered e-mail evidence. For some organizations, the strategic retention and automatic archiving of *all* company e-mail *forever* may be the most effective way to manage the fate of electronic business records. "In discovery, everything is a potential business record," said Gates. "You have no idea what will and won't be valuable down the road, which is why ArcMail recommends archiving everything."[20]

For other organizations, however, destructive retention may be deemed preferable to lifelong archiving. If so, the deletion process becomes a critical component of document management. As a first step, assign your e-policy team the task of determining when old records have outlived their usefulness and may be disposed of in a legally compliant fashion.

If your organization's e-mail retention periods are not specified by law or regulation, then consider keeping electronic business records for at least as long as you retain paper records. If, for example, you traditionally hold onto paper personnel records for three years, then keep electronic employment files for three years as well.[21]

The management of e-mail business records can be challenging, even for IT professionals. According to an Association for Information and Image Management (AIIM)/Association of Records Managers and

Administrators (ARMA) survey, 67 percent of records managers doubt that their IT departments really understand the concept of electronic records life cycle management. That's despite the fact that 70 percent of companies rely on IT professionals alone to manage their electronic records.[22]

Regardless of your approach to e-mail retention and disposition, do not assign your chief information officer sole responsibility for managing your organization's all-important electronic business records. Instead, have a team of legal, compliance, records management, and IT professionals work together to ensure that everyone responsible for the successful management of e-mail and other ESI really understands the concept of business records—and business record life cycle management—from all perspectives.

RECAP & e-POLICY ACTION PLAN

1. Electronic business record retention is an essential business, legal, and regulatory function for all organizations.

2. Advise employees to use e-mail and other electronic business communication tools primarily for legitimate business purposes. Instruct employees to save personal, nonbusiness-related e-mail for home—or risk embarrassment (or worse) should private messages go public in the course of a lawsuit, regulatory investigation, or Freedom of Information Act request.

3. Retention policies, deletion schedules, and archiving procedures should be driven by your legal and compliance departments. Records management and IT also should be involved in e-mail record management, under the clear direction of legal.

CHAPTER 4

Regulatory Risks and Rules
Government and Industry Watchdogs Guard
Content and Records

Over the years, government and industry regulators have turned an increasingly watchful eye to the content created and business records generated by e-mail messages and attachments. Overall, 36 percent of U.S. companies surveyed in 2007 reported an increase in regulatory inquiries or investigations. At the same time, approximately 50 percent of companies in the financial services, insurance, engineering, construction, technology, and communications fields saw an upswing in regulatory audits, according to Fulbright & Jaworski research.[1]

If your business is regulated, you cannot afford to take chances with e-mail record management. Consult with legal counsel to ensure that your organization is in compliance with regulators' e-mail-related rules, policies, and procedures. Regulations vary by industry, state, and country. Depending on the industry, U.S. jurisdictions, and foreign countries in which you operate, you must know and comply with all relevant laws and regulatory guidelines.

> **e-Policy Rule 12:** Consult with legal counsel to ensure that your organization is compliant with the e-mail-related regulations of the industries, states, and countries in which you operate.

Effective E-Mail Management Is Fundamental to SOX Compliance

For public companies and registered public accounting firms, inadequate e-mail management and lax security can lead to Sarbanes-Oxley Act violations. Designed by the SEC to thwart fraud in public companies, SOX requires regulated companies to implement internal controls for gathering, processing, and reporting accurate and reliable financial information. In other words, SOX requires businesses to demonstrate effective corporate governance and information management controls.

Effective e-mail management is fundamental to SOX compliance. The most common means of business communication, e-mail, is used to transmit financial information and related documents internally and externally. Consequently, e-mail security breaches—from intercepted messages, to corrupted files, to leaked, stolen, altered, or lost data—can put an organization at risk of noncompliance.

Just how tough is the SEC on SOX violators? Failure to retain e-mail related to audit work papers and financial controls for at least seven years—as mandated by SOX—can put your organization at risk of penalty for noncompliance. Knowingly altering or destroying records that are vital to an audit or investigation can net guilty parties 20 years in federal prison.

While SOX is somewhat vague about e-mail requirements and record keeping, employers are advised to review their e-mail management, content security, record retention, and archiving policies and procedures to ensure that financial data and related documents are safe from digital attacks, properly retained, safely archived, and otherwise SOX compliant.

Private Companies Share SOX Concerns, Too

While not regulated by SOX, private companies are coming under increasing pressure to comply with SOX provisions, which are recognized as industry best practices. A broad range of audiences can be satisfied by private companies' adoption of the SOX approach to financial oversight including lenders and insurers, prospective merger partners, disgruntled shareholders, federal regulators, and government agencies.

SOX Also Impacts EU Companies with U.S. Connections

An American law, SOX nonetheless applies to any company—including European-based enterprises—that is listed on the New York Stock Exchange (NYSE) or NASDAQ Stock Market. In fact, 81 percent of UK companies involved in regulatory matters in 2007 were subjected to SEC inquiries, according to Fulbright & Jaworski's Litigation Trends Survey.[2]

You may need to comply with SOX if:

- your UK-based operation is the subsidiary of a public company headquartered in the United States.

- your European organization supplies an NYSE-traded company.

- your English firm serves publicly traded clients that are listed on the NYSE or NASDAQ.[3]

Regardless of country of origin, all publicly traded companies listed on the NYSE or NASDAQ should assign a legal professional or compliance officer who is familiar with U.S. laws and regulatory rules the task of ensuring that the organization is compliant with SOX obligations.

HIPAA Ensures Patient Privacy and Record Retention

Companies in the health care industry are legally required by the U.S. Health Insurance Portability and Accountability Act (HIPAA) to safeguard e-mail messages and attachments that contain protected health information (PHI) related to a patient's health status, medical care, treatment plans, and payment issues. In addition, HIPAA retention rules require doctors and hospitals to save patient billing records and authorizations for six years, while preserving patients' e-mail conversations and other data for the life of the patient.[4]

In 2007, just over half of all health care companies surveyed by Fulbright & Jaworski reported an increase in regulatory investigations.[5] Like the courts and other regulators, HIPAA takes compliance seriously. HIPAA violations can result in seven-figure regulatory fines, civil litigation, criminal charges, and jail time.

Organizations that are governed by HIPAA are advised to apply policy, training, and technology through monitoring, blocking, security, encryption, and archiving tools. This will ensure the safe and compliant transmission and storage of HIPAA-regulated patient information.

GLBA Safeguards Customer Privacy

The Gramm-Leach-Bliley Act (GLBA) is to the financial industry what HIPAA is to health care. Under GLBA, financial institutions are legally obligated to protect the privacy of customers and their nonpublic personal information. In spite of Congress' attempts to protect customer privacy and regulate corporate accountability, however, many organizations remain challenged by GLBA.

Employee education is essential to regulatory compliance. You cannot expect untrained employees to be familiar with GLBA rules and regulations, appreciate the importance of compliance, or understand their individual roles in the compliance process. Support written e-mail policy with formal training and stress the fact that regulatory compliance—GLBA and otherwise—is 100 percent mandatory.

> **e-Policy Rule 13:** To ensure regulatory compliance and safeguard protected data, implement an e-mail management program that addresses content, security, retention, and archiving.

SEC and FINRA Rules and Regulations

Brokerage firms, investment banks, and other regulated financial services companies that fail to manage e-mail content and record retention according to SEC and Financial Industry Regulatory Authority (FINRA) regulations can face lengthy investigations, multimillion-dollar fines, embarrassing headlines, unhappy customers, and disgruntled shareholders.

Eager to promote accuracy, longevity, and access to trustworthy electronic records, the SEC and FINRA (created in 2007 through the consolidation of NASD and the regulation, enforcement, and arbitration operations of the New York Stock Exchange) provide specific requirements for the media and process used to archive e-mail and other ESI. SEC and FINRA regulated firms also are required to protect confidential business information and customers' personal data.[6]

REAL-LIFE E-MAIL RETENTION DISASTER STORIES: REGULATORS CLOBBER NONCOMPLIANT FINANCIAL SERVICES FIRMS

The list of investment banks and brokerage firms that have been penalized for e-mail record mismanagement reads like a who's who of the financial services industry.

Merrill Lynch paid a $2.5 million fine in 2006 to settle SEC charges that the brokerage firm had inadequate ESI retention policies and procedures in place and had delayed turning over e-mail records during a government investigation into its business practices.[7]

JPMorgan paid $2.1 million in 2005 to settle an e-mail retention dispute with the SEC, NYSE, and NASD.[8]

Banc of America Securities paid a $10 million fine in 2004 to settle SEC claims that the brokerage "repeatedly failed promptly to furnish" e-mail, gave "misinformation" about its records, and turned over incomplete and unreliable data.[9]

Deutsche Bank was clobbered with an $87.5 million fine in 2004 by then–New York Attorney General Eliot Spitzer for failing to have in place effective e-mail retention policies and retrieval procedures.[10]

Goldman Sachs, Smith Barney, Morgan Stanley, Deutsche Bank, and U.S. Bancorp Piper Jaffray were fined a combined $8.25 million in 2003 by the SEC, NASD, and NYSE for what were deemed to be inadequate e-mail preservation and production policies and procedures.[11]

Know—and Comply with—Every Regulatory Body Governing Your Business

ARMA reports that 90 percent of documents created or acquired by business are stored electronically.[12] All that electronic data requires consistent oversight. Regulated organizations (and nonregulated companies alike) are obliged to put rules, policies, and technology tools in place to ensure the legally compliant retention, trustworthy archiving, and responsive retrieval of e-mail records and other electronically stored information—or face potentially expensive and otherwise disastrous consequences.

SOX, GLBA, HIPAA, SEC, and FINRA aren't the only regulations and agencies that employers need to worry about. The Food and Drug Administration (FDA), Environmental Protection Agency (EPA), Internal Revenue Service (IRS), Occupational Safety and Health Administration (OSHA), state insurance regulators, and other federal and state agencies regularly request access to e-mail for audit or review.

If you are unsure which government regulators or industry regulations oversee your business and your employees' use of e-mail, now is the time to find out. Assign a team of legal, compliance, records management, and IT professionals to determine where e-mail fits into your organization's regulatory puzzle, and how an e-mail management program that combines written policy, employee education, and management technology tools can help maximize compliance and minimize e-mail-related disasters.

RECAP & e-POLICY ACTION PLAN

1. As part of the discovery process, government and industry regulators can demand the production of authentic, trustworthy, and legally compliant e-mail and other ESI.

2. If you are unclear about which regulators and regulations govern your business and industry, find out. Then develop and implement written rules and a formal compliance policy—immediately.

3. Regulators are concerned about privacy, and you should be, too. Incorporate e-mail rules, policies, and technology tools into your organization's e-mail management program to help safeguard protected health information, customers' financial data, and other nonpublic personal information.

4. Don't expect regulated employees to know or understand regulatory rules governing e-mail content and retention. Educate all regulated employees about your organization's e-mail and other ESI-related risks, rules, and regulatory requirements.

CHAPTER 5

Archiving Rules, Tools, and Best Practices

How great a stranglehold does e-mail and other electronically created, acquired, and stored information have on business? Consider the facts:

- A whopping 90 percent of business documents produced and acquired by companies today are electronic, according to ARMA.[1]

- Corporate e-mail users averaged 126 incoming messages daily in 2006, a 55 percent increase over 2003. At that rate, employees in 2009 likely will spend 41 percent of the workday just managing their e-mail, estimates the Radicati Group.[2]

- In terms of archived data, there are 13.4 million terabytes of magnetically stored information, 255,000 terabytes on film, and 1,956 terabytes on paper and optical disks worldwide, reports *Baseline* Magazine. One terabyte equals 1 trillion characters, which works out to 13,656,965 trillion letters and numbers just waiting to be discovered and used as evidence—for your organization's legal benefit or its detriment.[3]

Given the depths of the electronic evidence pool, it is particularly alarming that one-third of IT managers confess to being incapable of locating and retrieving e-mail that is more than one year old, according to Osterman Research.[4] That finding is in sync with research conducted by Cohasset Associates for ARMA and the Association for Information and Image Management (AIIM), in which 33 percent of record managers say they are "not confident at all" that their organizations could prove their electronic records are accurate, reliable, trustworthy, and therefore legally compliant, years after they were created.[5]

Where does your organization stand when it comes to the long- and short-term management of e-mail and other electronic data? In the event of a lawsuit, could you quickly search, retrieve, and produce 12-week-old, 12-month-old, or even 12-year-old e-mail? If not, you had better get to work putting your electronic record management house in order—right now!

REAL-LIFE DISCOVERY DISASTER STORY: MISMANAGED E-MAIL COSTS MORGAN STANLEY $1.6 BILLION

Thanks to e-mail mismanagement, a Florida jury awarded $1.6 billion to Coleman Holdings Inc. in the company's 2005 fraud suit against investment bank Morgan Stanley.

Morgan Stanley repeatedly failed to turn over electronic evidence during the state court trial. One of the bank's technology workers intentionally concealed knowledge of 1,423 backup tapes, which were later located. On at least three other occasions, Morgan Stanley lost or mislaid backup e-mail tapes.

Fed up with Morgan Stanley, the judge informed the jury of the bank's missteps, which included overwriting e-mail messages and using inadequate search tools to locate e-mail records. The judge also instructed the jury to assume that Morgan Stanley had approached its discovery obligations with "malice or evil intent."

The mismanagement of e-mail evidence cost Morgan Stanley a record-setting $1.6 billion. The bank is appealing the jury award.[6]

---

e-Policy Rule 14: The effective management of e-mail business records is an essential business task. Your ability (or inability) to preserve, protect, and produce electronic evidence can make (or break) your case, your company, and your career in the event of a workplace lawsuit or regulatory investigation.

Five Qualities of Reliable E-Mail Evidence

Not all e-mail rises to the level of admissible legal evidence. Not all e-mail meets the compliance standards set forth by regulators. When it comes to e-mail management, every decision you make, every policy you set, and every technology tool you employ is open to attack from opposing legal counsel.

To enjoy legally compliant business record status, e-mail must embody five characteristics.

1. *Authenticity:* To be accepted as legal evidence, e-mail must be authentic. You must be able to demonstrate the origin of a business record including who wrote the original message and who may have added to or edited it.

2. *Integrity:* A good e-mail business record has integrity. You can prove that its content and meaning have not been altered since its creation.

3. *Accuracy:* To be legally acceptable, e-mail must be accurate about the facts originally documented, and it must remain accurate throughout its life. In other words, you must be able to prove that the message has never been tampered with.

4. *Completeness:* It is essential that an e-mail message and its metadata or parts (body, header, attachments, and log files relating to its transmission and receipt) remain intact as part of a complete record.

5. *Repudiation:* In business and contract situations, it's easy for a party to claim he or she did not receive a message, or that he or she is not responsible for promises made via e-mail. Unless properly managed and securely archived, e-mail opens your organization to repudiation, the legal term for a variety of claims ranging from "I never received your message," to "That's not what the attachment said."[7]

Protection against repudiation is a component of legally compliant e-mail records. Written retention policies that are supported by real-time automatic archiving technology like ArcMail's Defender solution can help ensure the authenticity, integrity, accuracy, and completeness of business record e-mail—and help protect your organization against false claims.

Whether you operate a small, midsized, or large organization, best practices call for the installation of an archiving appliance like ArcMail Defender to ensure your ability to successfully accomplish the following:

- Maintain a secure, legally valid record of business-critical e-mail communications, transactions, and intellectual property.

- Resolve—and in some cases prevent—business disputes and workplace litigation.

- Comply with the courts' and regulators' rules governing the retention and production of authentic and tamperproof electronic evidence.

REAL-LIFE ELECTRONIC EVIDENCE DISASTER STORY: LAWYER ALTERS E-MAIL EVIDENCE

In 2007, a lawyer for Best Buy acknowledged falsifying two e-mails and a memo before handing the evidence over to the plaintiffs in a nationwide class-action lawsuit. The lawsuit alleges that Best Buy signed up some 100,000 customers for a trial subscription to Microsoft's MSN Internet service, often without the customer's knowledge, resulting in unapproved credit card charges after the trial period ended.

The Superior Court judge previously had reprimanded Best Buy for not being forthcoming about documents related to the case. The intentional altering of evidence by Best Buy's legal counsel "could prompt the judge to find the company liable for tens of millions of dollars in damages."[8]

Automatic Archiving Protects the Integrity of E-Mail

Unbeknownst to many users, e-mail can be changed—and rendered legally invalid—by any recipient who is intent on harming your company's legal position or future. With just a few keystrokes, an e-mail recipient can change text, alter metadata, edit attachments, adjust the time sent, and otherwise tamper with the sender's original message.

To prevent evidence tampering and help ensure the forensic compliance of your e-mail, you can apply a technology solution to what is essentially a people problem. Specifically, you can protect the integrity of corporate e-mail by implementing an archiving solution that automatically completes three essential e-mail evidence management tasks:

1. Capturing all inbound and outbound, internal and external e-mail messages and attachments.

2. Indexing captured e-mail to simplify and speed up data searches.

3. Preserving e-mail in a single location, where it remains secure and tamperproof until litigators or regulators call on you to locate, restore, and relinquish it.

> **e-Policy Rule 15:** Safeguard your organization's e-mail records and ensure their forensic compliance with automatic archiving technology that guarantees your organization's ability to produce *precisely* the e-mail messages and attachments you need, *exactly* when you need them, *specifically* to courts' and regulators' specifications.

Best Practices to Help Boost the Evidentiary Value of Corporate E-Mail

The archiving experts at ArcMail Technology and the policy professionals at ePolicy Institute offer tips to help organizations prepare today for the eventuality of a workplace lawsuit—and e-mail-related discovery—tomorrow.

1. Take steps, through written retention rules and archiving technology, to demonstrate that your e-mail records are authentic and reliable. Remember, if you can demonstrate that your stand-alone network archiving appliance is reliable and your archived e-mail records are legally valid and tamperproof, then your organization will be on more solid footing with courts and regulators.

2. Define "business record" for your organization on a company-wide or department-by-department basis. Establish formal policies to govern the retention and archiving of your organization's e-mail and other electronic business records.

3. Know—and consistently adhere to—the retention and archiving rules and procedures mandated by each regulatory body that governs your business and industry.

4. Educate employees about e-mail risks, rules, and regulations. Make sure all employees understand what a business record is and why business-critical e-mail is so significant. Stress the fact that the organization's e-mail system is intended for business use. With the exception of limited amounts of approved personal use, employees should limit workday e-mail to business-related matters.

5. Keep e-mail for as long as possible. Your ability to search your archive and retrieve electronic evidence may just save the day in court. You never know what will be important down the road, or what information may one day be involved in a lawsuit. Someone always has a copy of any given e-mail message, and that someone should be you. There is nothing worse than walking into court empty-handed—especially if your legal opponent is holding altered or out-of-context copies of *your* corporate e-mail.

6. Take advantage of the comprehensive and automatic features of real-time archiving technology. ArcMail's archiving solution, Defender, for example, provides immediate access to preserved data; automatically captures and stores internal and external e-mail in one central location; protects against malicious intruders intent on altering, deleting, or stealing your files; and guarantees your ability to promptly produce legally compliant, authentic evidence in the event of a lawsuit or regulatory investigation.

Discovery Obligations Are Inescapable

Given e-mail's ever-expanding evidentiary role, it is no longer a matter of *if* your organization's e-mail will one day become part of court proceedings or a regulatory audit. The question is *when* will you be required to produce legally valid e-mail evidence as part of the evidence pool?

When it comes to data recovery and e-mail discovery costs, the courts have yet to establish a consistent definition of "unduly burdensome." That said, courts and regulatory bodies tend to be unsympathetic when employers claim that they cannot fulfill their discovery obligations because they lack the financial, human, or technical resources to retrieve, restore, or otherwise produce e-mail and other ESI. A computer system that is good enough to operate your business, after all, should be up to the task of preserving and producing e-mail.[9]

Best advice: Protect your organization from potentially costly discovery costs and obligations by implementing a retention policy and installing archiving technology that is designed to support your organization's legal, regulatory, and business-related discovery needs.

REAL-LIFE DISCOVERY DISASTER STORIES: COMPANIES SMALL AND LARGE MUST MEET FRCP REQUIREMENTS

In the case of *Williams v. Taser International,* Taser, a small company with just 245 employees, argued that it had made a significant effort to meet its discovery obligations by hiring and training a technology employee specifically to manage discovery related to the case. The judge, however, didn't accept Taser's claim of limited resources as an excuse. In spite of its relatively small size, the court ordered Taser to make "all reasonable efforts . . . including . . . retaining additional IT professionals to search electronic databases and adding additional attorneys."[10]

In the case of *Best Buy v. Developers Diversified Realty*, publicly traded real estate investment trust Developers Diversified was ordered by a court to meet its discovery obligations—in just 28 days and in spite of an anticipated six-figure price tag. Despite the company's argument that the e-mail and other ESI sought by Best Buy were not "reasonably accessible" from the company's backup system, the judge ordered the restoration and review of e-mail and other data from 345 backup tapes. According to Law.com, the final price tag was $500,000, excluding legal fees.[11]

Ten Legal, Regulatory, and Business Reasons to Archive E-Mail[12]

1. When it comes to legal proof, many people incorrectly assume that e-mail creates only damaging evidence with smoking gun messages that point to corporate wrongdoing or criminal activity. On the contrary, e-mail often produces supportive evidence that may help "save the day" by providing valuable legal proof and performing essential business functions.

2. E-mail records may provide the evidence necessary to help shelter your company from false claims and unfounded lawsuits.

3. E-mail evidence that is uncovered by your organization in the course of legal discovery may motivate your opponent to settle a weak claim out of court, saving you from a costly and protracted lawsuit.

4. E-mail may provide your organization with the all-important evidence it needs to successfully defend—and win—a lawsuit.

5. E-mail provides a written record that can "speak" for witnesses who may be unwilling or unable to testify.

6. E-mail records can fill in the blanks when human memory falters.

7. For regulated companies, e-mail archiving is a fundamental business task. Some 40 percent of companies cite SOX alone as their primary reason for archiving more e-mail.[13]

8. E-mail provides the written records that all organizations need in order to operate on a day-to-day basis. Formal documentation of transactions, decisions, personnel matters, and business operations is essential to efficient company management. No entity of any kind can function without reliable records.

9. E-mail helps keep the courts happy. The concealment, destruction, or failure to produce e-mail during discovery may lead to charges of spoliation, monetary fines, and instructions to the jury to draw a negative inference about your company or your case.

10. E-mail archiving saves resources that otherwise would be wasted on time-consuming data searches. A company that employs 1,000 information workers, for example, can expect to lose more than $5 million in annual salary costs as the result of employees wasting time on unproductive e-mail searches, according to International Data Corp (IDC).[14] By automating the process of capturing inbound, outbound, and internal e-mail, employers eliminate the need for individual users to create personal archives or spend time trying to locate and restore e-mail messages and attachments.[15]

Don't Confuse Backup with Archiving

If your organization relies solely on backup systems for record retention, then you are putting your e-mail records—and your legal position—at risk. A backup system is no substitute for automatic archiving technology. Designed solely for the recovery of critical data in the event of a man-made or natural disaster, backup is nothing more than the mass storage of electronic information in a known location.

An archive, on the other hand, is a strategic record management tool that not only preserves corporate e-mail, but also facilitates the speedy search and reliable retrieval of the specific records you need, exactly when you need them.[16] An archive with quick and easy search capabilities also allows you the flexibility to search beyond the scope of discovery requirements, notes ArcMail's William T. Gates. This process can be arduous, perhaps even impossible, when your search is limited to stored backup tapes.[17]

REAL-LIFE BACKUP TAPE DISASTER STORY: BEST PRACTICES CALL FOR SAFE AND SECURE STORAGE

A backup computer tape was stolen from the car of a state of Ohio intern in 2007. The tape contained Social Security numbers, bank account information, and other sensitive data for some 1.3 million individuals, businesses, school districts, and other entities. The data has never been recovered.[18]

Backup tapes should be kept only long enough to recover data and restore operations following a system-related disaster. Typically, an IT department will maintain a schedule that calls for the creation of backup tape on a daily, weekly, monthly, or quarterly basis. Used tapes are written over and recycled regularly, which is fortunate since, as the following real-life disaster story illustrates, backups may contain a treasure trove of information that your organization could be ordered to search, reformat, and turn over in the course of litigation.[19]

REAL-LIFE BACKUP TAPE DISASTER STORY: RESTORATION OF 2.3 MILLION E-MAILS COSTS $6.2 MILLION

During a 2002 breach of contract suit, Murphy Oil USA, Inc. sought to compel Fluor Daniel, Inc. to produce backup tapes containing e-mail messages. Because Fluor Daniel had failed to adhere to its own destructive retention policy, which called for the deletion of e-mail every 45 days, the company was sitting on

93 backup tapes, each of which recorded some 25,000 e-mail messages, for the 14-month period in question.

The court ordered Fluor Daniel to restore the backup tapes, convert some 2.3 million e-mail messages to TIFF files, and print them out. Fluor Daniel estimated the job would take six months and cost $6.2 million.[20]

Had Fluor Daniel consistently adhered to its 45-day e-mail deletion schedule, the backup tapes would have been recycled and rotated in the ordinary course of business, leaving no e-mail evidence to be discovered. Remember, e-Policies are only as effective as your willingness to enforce them.

Prohibit Underground Archiving

As part of your organization's strategic retention and archiving program, prohibit employees from engaging in time-consuming and counterproductive "underground archiving." In other words, don't allow individual users to move personal e-mail to electronic folders or store messages on the hard drive or disks, in metal file cabinets, or anywhere else inside the company.

Organizational risks increase when employees behave like e-mail filing clerks. Self-managed e-mail can result in the deletion of electronic records, alteration of e-mail evidence, time-consuming searches for back-up tapes, and failure to comply with legal discovery demands. Even if a destructive retention policy is in place, the "desktop discovery" of an employee's underground archive can prove to be prohibitively expensive and potentially damaging.[21]

Take advantage of archiving technology to block underground archiving. By automatically providing complete, centralized archiving, with ArcMail Defender, for example, you eliminate the need for employees to self-manage their mailboxes, messages, and attachments—while supporting the organization's legal and regulatory needs. With ArcMail, users can independently locate and restore e-mail, but they cannot edit content or delete messages. Even after employees are long gone from the company, archiving technology enables IT to quickly find and produce e-mail messages and attachments that might otherwise be lost without a time-consuming search through backup tapes.

Keep Your Company's Virtual File Cabinet Clean and Compliant

Just a few decades ago, permanent business records were handled in one of two ways on an organizational level. Either records were physically printed on paper and locked away in metal file cabinets, or they were saved and stored on removable floppy disks.

Today, e-mail serves as a virtual file cabinet for the vast majority of business records. When it comes to e-mail evidence, it is the content (written words and images), not the tool (desktop, laptop, or Black-Berry), that counts.

Public or private, regulated or nonregulated, large or small—no organization can afford to take a hit-or-miss approach to the management of e-mail records and risks. In today's highly litigious, heavily regulated business environment, employers are obligated to keep their electronic file cabinets clean and compliant, safe and secure.

To that end, best practices call for the adoption of a 3-E approach to e-mail risk and record management:

1. Establish formal rules and written policies governing e-mail usage, content, records, retention, and archiving.

2. Educate all employees, from the summer intern to the CEO, about e-mail- and evidence-related risks, rules, and regulations.

3. Enforce e-Policies with a combination of disciplinary action, up to and including employee termination. Choose technology that includes tools that are designed to monitor usage, filter content, block bad behavior, and archive all-important e-mail records. Make sure it accomplishes this securely, compliantly, and in real time.

RECAP & e-POLICY ACTION PLAN

1. Ninety percent of business documents produced and acquired by companies are electronic.

2. The effective management of e-mail business records is an essential business task. Your ability (or inability) to preserve, protect, and produce electronic evidence can make (or break) your case, your company, and your career in the event of a workplace lawsuit or regulatory investigation.

3. Unbeknownst to many users, e-mail can be altered—and rendered legally invalid—by any recipient who is intent on harming your legal position or company.

4. Given e-mail's ever-expanding evidentiary role, it is no longer a matter of *if* your organization's e-mail will one day become part of the evidence pool. The question is *when* will you be required to produce legally valid e-mail evidence as part of court proceedings or a regulatory audit?

5. An automated archiving appliance like ArcMail Defender can help control search costs and enhance overall e-mail management by reducing the human and financial resources needed to locate and produce e-mail in compliance with court orders, regulatory requests, and day-to-day business operations.

PART THREE

Privacy, Confidentiality, and Data Security Rules

CHAPTER 6

Online Privacy Risks, Rights, and Rules

Do you employ young people in their 20s or even in their teens? If so, you may face a stiff challenge when attempting to impose privacy rules and confidentiality guidelines that are designed to help protect company secrets and employees' personal business as well.

While older employees tend to view technology as a means to transmit, store, and access information, younger workers rely on electronic communication tools for relationship building, networking, and socializing. Seventy percent of 18- to 19-year-old students access social networking sites daily, compared to just 4 percent of those over 30, according to the EDUCAUSE.[1]

Instant messaging, texting, and social networking are standard tools in the Internet generation's electronic communication arsenal. Young people are so accustomed to communicating online that many think nothing of expressing their most personal thoughts, provocative opinions, and private images with their "closest online friends," who may number in the hundreds, thousands, or even millions in the case of wildly popular blogs and social networking sites.

There Are No Secrets in Cyberspace

The youngest members of an organization are much more likely to spread business-related gossip than older employees, who still tend to place a premium on privacy. Only 9 percent of the workforce's youngest employees (18- to 24-year-olds) keep company news quiet, compared to 48 percent of older employees (55- to 64-year-olds), who have no trouble safeguarding organizational secrets, according to a 2007 Steelcase Workplace Index Survey.[2]

Online Gossip Sparks Lawsuits, Sinks Careers, Savages Corporate Reputations

Thanks to e-mail, IM, and texting, gossip that once was spread verbally (and relatively slowly) around the watercooler, now can be transmitted to millions of readers worldwide in a matter of seconds. In fact, 10 percent of employees say they rely on e-mail or IM for workplace gossip, according to an Equisys survey, as reported by *USA Today*.[3]

Overall, 64 percent of employees say their coworkers regularly gossip about company news. In offices lacking a consistent means of communicating news, such as regular staff meetings or internal newsletters, 28 percent of employees report that they rely on gossip as their primary source of company information.[4]

REAL-LIFE PRIVACY DISASTER STORIES: RUMOR-MONGERING SPARKS STOCK SLIDES

The NASD fined a Fulcrum Global Partners securities analyst $75,000 in 2002 for circulating a "false and sensational rumor" about RF Micro Devices Inc. via instant messages and phone calls to at least eight institutional clients. Thanks to the rumor, the company's stock dropped about 10 percent, according to the NASD. This was the first time the NASD disciplined an analyst for rumormongering. Just two years earlier, however, the NYSE had fined a banking analyst $75,000 for spreading a false rumor.[5]

Brokerage firms must ensure that brokers do not make misrepresentations to potential investors. Use policy, training, and monitoring technology to ensure compliance with SEC and FINRA (formerly NASD and NYSE) rules. Don't let irresponsible electronic leaks sink your corporate ship.[6]

No One-Size-Fits-All Privacy Policy: Conform Rules to Jurisdictional Laws

As part of your organization's electronic business communication program, combine written policy with formal education to notify employees of privacy rules and laws.

Because privacy laws vary by jurisdiction, there is no such thing as a one-size-fits-all privacy policy. If you operate in multiple jurisdictions, ask your legal counsel or compliance officer to investigate the privacy-related laws and regulations of every state and country in which you employ workers or have a facility. Then adjust privacy policy accordingly to meet the needs of each jurisdiction.

The federal Electronic Communications Privacy Act allows U.S. employers to monitor computer use and review all electronic transmissions. While only two states, Delaware and Connecticut, require employers to notify workers of monitoring, all organizations are advised to join the 84 percent of bosses who opt to notify employees that their computer activity is being monitored, according to American Management Association and ePolicy Institute research.[7]

Best practices call for employers to inform users that the computer system is intended primarily for business use, that it may be monitored, and that employees have no reasonable expectation of privacy when it comes to e-mail, IM, the Internet, and other technology tools—regardless of whether they are using the organization's resources and systems or their own personal accounts and tools.

One U.S. court has ruled, "Employers can diminish an individual employee's expectation of privacy by clearly stating in the policy that electronic communications are to be used solely for company business, and the company reserves the right to monitor or access all employee Internet or e-mail usage."[8]

Follow the court's lead and extend your organization's privacy policy to cover Web surfing, e-mailing, instant messaging, blogging, texting, social networking, and all other forms of electronic business communication.

> **e-Policy Rule 16:** Notify employees that they have no reasonable expectation of privacy when it comes to computer use—regardless of whether they are using the organization's resources and systems or their own personal accounts and tools.

U.S. Employees Have No Reasonable Expectation of Privacy

Why notify employees of monitoring if the law doesn't require you to do so? Generally, employees who know that computer content and use are monitored will be less inclined to misuse the system. U.S. courts generally accept the fact that informed employees neither would nor should consider corporate computer systems their own. Even in situations in which employers have told users that their electronic communications are *not* monitored, the courts have ruled that employees still should *not* expect privacy when using the company's system.[9]

That said, a U.S.-based multinational corporation might not be able to apply this same policy to employees stationed in other countries. In the United Kingdom, for example, a premium is placed on employee privacy. English law allows organizations to monitor Web surfing and e-mail transmissions, but employers are legally required to alert employees to monitoring and must use the least intrusive surveillance methods possible.[10] UK employers also must comply with the Data Protection Act, which is designed to protect consumer privacy and personal information.[11]

Before implementing domestic privacy policies abroad, seek the counsel of a lawyer who is familiar with the legal, regulatory, and privacy requirements of each country in which your organization operates.

Caution Employees to Guard Their Own Privacy, Too

As part of your electronic privacy program, suggest that workers protect themselves, their families, and friends by strictly separating their business and personal lives. When it comes to e-mail and the Internet, it's best to keep personal business personal. In other words, wait until you get home to engage in nonbusiness-related e-mail and Internet activity.

Of the 28 percent of bosses who fired employees for e-mail violations in 2007, more than a quarter (26 percent) cited excessive personal use of the company system as the reason for dismissal, according to the 2007 Electronic Monitoring & Surveillance Survey from American Management Association and ePolicy Institute.[12]

To keep terminations at a minimum and compliance at a maximum, institute clear personal use rules in conjunction with your organization's privacy policy. Let employees know exactly how much personal e-mail and Internet use they are allowed to engage in, when, why, with whom, and under what circumstances.

> **e-Policy Rule 17:** Institute personal use rules in conjunction with your organization's privacy policy. Let employees know exactly how much personal e-mail and Internet use they are allowed to engage in, when, why, with whom, and under what circumstances.

Inform employees that they are never to use the company computer system to transmit a message that could harm the user or embarrass loved ones were it made public. Remind employees that e-mail simply is not a secure way to communicate sensitive or private information. Stress the fact that you never know where a message may land, thanks to forwarding, copying, mistyped addresses, monitoring, and human error.

REAL-LIFE PRIVACY DISASTER STORY: THE E-MAIL LOVE NOTE READ AROUND THE WORLD

A twentysomething woman in England sent her boyfriend an e-mail love note complimenting his romantic performance the night before (and recounting her own). The woman's message was so graphic and flattering that her lawyer-boyfriend decided to forward it to a half-dozen male friends employed by London-based law firms and banks. His friends—all employed by international firms—in turn forwarded the saucy message to their friends and colleagues around the globe.

That very personal e-mail message ended up traveling to 10 million computer screens in London, Australia, Hong Kong, and the United States. An international media sensation followed, with the *New York Times*, NBC's *Today Show*, and other media outlets around the world covering the story. The relentless London tabloids, intent on pursuing the embarrassed e-mail writer, eventually drove the mortified woman into hiding.[13]

A cautionary tale for anyone who uses e-mail to communicate. Keep your personal life off-line, or risk reading about yourself in tomorrow's news.

Personal E-Mail Accounts and Public IM Tools Create a False Sense of Security

Most employees are surprised to learn that it is possible for corporate IT departments to track e-mail sent via employees' personal accounts (Gmail, AOL, etc.) and to search the system for unauthorized IM downloads (AIM, Yahoo! Messenger, for example). Employers are advised to combine technology with policy and training in order to enforce a strict ban on all personal e-mail accounts and any Web-based IM tools that are not supported by IM gateway/management software (see Part 5).

Because personal e-mail accounts and IM tools transmit messages across the public Web—outside the organization's secure firewall—they pose tremendous and potentially costly risks to the organization. When transmitted via the public Internet, messages can be intercepted by thieves, infected by viruses, or tampered with by hackers. If customers' financial data or patients' health records are stolen, altered, or otherwise tampered with, you could face regulatory fines and criminal penalties. If your organization's intellectual property or other proprietary data is accessed, the negative impact on your assets, reputation, and future could be staggering. If business records travel outside the organization's system, then retention and archiving processes are sidestepped and all-important electronic evidence may be lost forever.

> **e-Policy Rule 18:** Personal e-mail accounts and IM tools transmit messages across the public Web, outside the organization's secure firewall. Reduce risks by enforcing a strict ban on all personal e-mail accounts and any Web-based IM tools that are not supported by IM gateway/management software.

Don't Allow Employees to Use E-Mail Inboxes as Ad Hoc Filing Systems

In spite of formal policy and training, some employees may still insist on using the organization's e-mail system for personal reasons. As a precautionary measure, instruct all employees to empty their inboxes of all nonbusiness-related e-mail at the end of each business day. Instruct employees to forward personal messages to their home accounts or simply delete them at the end of the workday. Prohibit employees from engaging in "underground archiving," moving personal e-mail to electronic folders or storing messages on the hard drive or disks, in metal file cabinets, or anywhere else inside the company.

While it's true that e-mail never disappears completely, there's no point making it easy for a computer forensic investigator to locate and read potentially damaging and embarrassing private correspondence, should the organization's e-mail one day be subpoenaed as part of a workplace lawsuit.

RECAP & e-POLICY ACTION PLAN

1. Use your written policies and employee training program to advise employees that the computer system is company property. All transmissions and content that is sent, received, viewed, downloaded, uploaded, forwarded, copied, saved, printed, or stored belongs to the organization.

2. Use your e-Policies to explain that the theft of the organization's proprietary or confidential information may result in termination and could be punishable in criminal or civil court.

3. Notify employees that they have no reasonable expectation of privacy when using the company's computer system.

4. Research and draft privacy policies to meet the relevant laws and regulations of the states and countries in which employees and offices are located.

5. Advise employees to guard their own privacy, and the privacy of their families and friends, when using e-mail, IM, and other electronic business communication tools.

CHAPTER 7

Confidential Messaging
Rules and Tools

When it comes to employee e-mail and IM transmissions, employers have far more to worry about than the spread of petty office gossip, the posting of personal pictures, and the distribution of electronic love notes, as discussed in the previous chapter.

As embarrassing as the distribution of personal text, photos, and videos can be, the potential damages are dwarfed by the losses suffered by and costs associated with the accidental and intentional transmission of confidential company information, trade secrets, and intellectual property. According to the U.S. Department of Commerce, the loss of intellectual property rights alone costs business $250 billion and 750,000 jobs annually.[1]

Left unmanaged, e-mail and instant messaging can result in the rapid-fire transmission of company secrets, confidential financial data, personal health information, executive memos, eyes-only internal correspondence, and other proprietary and protected content that can pose a threat to the organization, its people, products, reputation, and future.

> **e-Policy Rule 19:** Left unmanaged, e-mail and IM can result in the rapid-fire transmission of proprietary and protected content that can pose a threat to the organization, its people, products, reputation, and future.

E-Mail Can Compromise Confidences, Reveal Trade Secrets, and Expose Proprietary Business Information

Twenty percent of outbound e-mail messages transmitted by U.S. companies in 2007 posed a legal, financial, or regulatory threat to the organization. Thirty-four percent of employers investigated a suspected leak of confidential or proprietary business information via e-mail, and an additional 26 percent of organizations suffered the exposure of embarrassing or sensitive information during the same 12-month period, according to Proofpoint/Forrester research.[2]

That's no surprise, considering that the standard arsenal of electronic business communication tools, most notably corporate e-mail, makes it *so easy* for employees to compromise corporate confidences, reveal trade secrets, and expose proprietary business information—accidentally or intentionally.

Simply by committing thoughts to writing and clicking *send*, an employee can quickly and quietly transmit trade secrets to competitors, share embarrassing internal documents with reporters, and hand valuable intellectual property over to third parties who may not have the organization's best interests at heart.

While it's easy to sneak business-critical data and confidential material out of the e-mail system, it is almost impossible to erase the evidence. E-mail leaves behind an electronic footprint that never disappears completely. Whether retained and archived intact by your own organization, tampered with and then saved by your recipient, or purged and later pieced together by a computer forensic expert, e-mail messages and attachments live on forever—in your system, the networks of your intended recipients, and the systems of everyone else who, intentionally or accidentally, receives copies of your transmissions.

That's a deep pool of potentially damaging information—from business records and confidential executive correspondence to intellectual property and trade secrets—just waiting to be discovered by litigators, regulators, competitors, criminals, employees, disgruntled ex-employees, and the media among others.

> **e-Policy Rule 20:** E-mail leaves behind an electronic footprint that *never disappears completely*. Messages and attachments live on forever—in your system, the networks of intended recipients, and the systems of everyone else who, intentionally or accidentally, receives copies of your transmissions.

Loss of Confidential Data Tops
Compliance Concerns

When it comes to outbound e-mail, employers have good reason to worry. Fully 80 percent of compliance and security violations are e-mail related, according to a 2006 Aberdeen Messaging Security Benchmark Report.[3] Leading compliance concerns include fears that employees will transmit inappropriate and potentially damaging content including confidential or proprietary business information (30 percent); adult, obscene, or otherwise offensive content that can trigger harassment and hostile work environment claims (25 percent); personal health information or financial and identity data in violation of HIPAA, GLBA, and breach notification laws (21 percent); and intellectual property and trade secrets that should never leave the company without permission from management (17 percent), according to Proofpoint's 2007 survey, Outbound Email and Content Security in Today's Enterprise.[4]

Increasingly, employers' security concerns are translating into disciplinary action against policy violators. Of the 28 percent of employers who terminated employees for e-mail policy violations in 2007, 22 percent cited a confidentiality breach as the reason for dismissal, according to American Management Association and ePolicy Institute research.[5] Employers who are eager to protect company secrets and keep confidential conversations under wraps are advised to follow the lead of these organizations by putting some teeth in corporate e-policy programs.

REAL-LIFE CONFIDENTIAL E-MAIL DISASTER STORY:
TOP SECRET $1 BILLION SETTLEMENT TALKS
EXPOSED BY MISADDRESSED E-MAIL

Need proof that e-mail is the worst way to transmit confidential information? Eli Lilly and its outside legal counsel learned that lesson the hard way in January 2008, when the *New York Times* broke the story of Lilly's confidential settlement talks with the U.S. government—thanks to a misaddressed top-secret e-mail message.

Eli Lilly and federal prosecutors were in settlement talks related to civil and criminal investigations into the marketing of the antipsychotic drug Zyprexa. With negotiations over Lilly's alleged marketing improprieties reaching more than $1 billion (in addition to the $1.2 billion Lilly had already paid to settle 30,000 individual lawsuits), the pharmaceutical giant was eager to keep the settlement talks under wraps.

Given the secrecy surrounding the negotiations, company officials were understandably shocked when contacted by a reporter preparing to publish an in-depth article exposing the Zyprexa settlement details on the front page of the *New York Times*. Lilly initially accused federal prosecutors of leaking the news. As it turns out, the source of the leak was much closer to home.

One of Lilly's lawyers at the Philadelphia-based firm Pepper Hamilton had intended to e-mail a confidential settlement document to attorney *Bradford* Berenson, her cocounsel at Lilly's Chicago law firm Sidley Austin. Unfortunately, she mistakenly sent the top-secret document to *New York Times* reporter *Alex* Berenson, whose name was the first to pop up on the sender's e-mail autocomplete feature when she began typing "Berenson."[6]

Click.

Eli Lilly's private, closed-door negotiations went public on the front page of the *New York Times,* thanks to a misaddressed top-secret e-mail message.

Confidentiality Risks Compounded for Public and Regulated Companies

Unmanaged confidential content could land a publicly traded company in hot water with the SEC, exposing the company to liability for violations of federal securities laws. From securities fraud, to jumping the gun, selective disclosure, and forward-looking statements, public companies must ensure that employees do not use e-mail to disclose proprietary insider information, transmit untrue content, or otherwise violate securities laws.[7]

For public companies and regulated firms, it is particularly important that e-mail be managed in accordance with written policy; that government and industry regulatory rules are strictly complied with; and that electronic business records are retained, archived, and readily accessible in the event of a regulatory audit.

In some industries and situations, the creation and archiving of business records is mandatory. In the financial services arena, for example, financial analysts are prohibited from communicating with investment bankers without recording their conversations.

Alternatively, there are times when recordless conversations are perfectly legal and appropriate. In those situations, it may be best to avoid e-mail altogether and opt instead for a more confidential and recordless form of communication—if your organization's legal counsel deems it appropriate to do so.

REAL-LIFE EYES-ONLY IM DISASTER STORY: STOCK TANKS WHEN GOSSIP GOES PUBLIC

In 2001, a San Francisco–based hedge fund manager sent several associates an instant message about the software company PeopleSoft. In his message, the fund manager suggested that regulators were looking into accounting irregularities at a publicly traded PeopleSoft subsidiary, and that the company might be sued by a customer for breaking a contract.

When news of the instant message leaked out, PeopleSoft's stock tumbled 27 percent, from $42 to $30. The hedge fund manager later retracted his statement.[8]

Like e-mail, IM creates a written record that can be copied, forwarded, printed, saved, and shared. Although your instant message may be intended solely for one reader's eyes, you never know where it will end up, or who ultimately will read it.

Don't let thoughtless leaks or irresponsible content sink your corporate ship. Institute written polices that clearly spell out what material may, and may not, be communicated via e-mail, IM, and other forms of recorded electronic conversation.

Internal E-Mail Doesn't Always Stay Internal

As part of your organization's confidential electronic communication policy and program, remind employees that *all* e-mail—including internal messages that are never intended to be read by outsiders—creates a written record, the electronic equivalent of DNA evidence.

Internal e-mail can pose a significant risk to business. Some employees tend to play it fast and loose with content and language when writing messages that are intended for their colleagues' eyes only. In internal e-mail, executives and employees sometimes express controversial opinions and discuss confidential business matters that should never be committed to writing, and which can prove devastating if exposed to outside readers.

Compounding the problem is the fact that employers often turn a blind eye to internal e-mail. While 96 percent of companies monitor external (incoming and outgoing) e-mail, only 58 percent monitor the internal e-mail conversations that take place among employees, according to the 2007 Electronic Monitoring & Surveillance Survey from American Management Association and ePolicy Institute.[9] When it comes to the protection of confidential company data, management's failure to track internal e-mail is a potentially costly oversight. As the following disaster story illustrates, there simply is no guarantee that internal e-mail will stay internal.

REAL-LIFE INTERNAL E-MAIL DISASTER STORY: INTERNAL E-MAIL CRACKS KICKBACK CASE

In 2004, the world's largest insurance broker, Marsh & McLennan, was accused by then–New York Attorney General Eliot Spitzer of taking kickbacks from insurance companies to steer business their way. According to prosecutors, e-mail evidence "cracked the case,"[10] and helped prove that Marsh was engaged in a pattern of bid-rigging.

Deemed to be "the functional equivalent of eavesdropping,"[11] prosecutors relied on e-mail evidence to build their case. Presumably, Marsh executives never expected their damning internal e-mail messages would be read by outsiders.

Included among the evidence were these gems: "I will give you clear direction on who [we] are steering business to and who we are steering business from," and "We need to place our business in 2004 with those that have superior financials, broad coverage and pay us the most."[12]

The fallout from the bid-rigging scandal was enormous: Marsh & McLennan settled the lawsuit for $850 million, the largest single settlement in Spitzer's battle against corporate wrongdoing. Marsh's disgraced CEO was replaced, and 3,000 employees saw their jobs slashed in an effort to reduce expenses.[13] The brokerage firm lost nearly half its market value as its stock declined 42 percent after the investigation was announced.[14] Legal expenses related to Spitzer's suit were projected to cost the firm $46 million in 2007, three years after the investigation began.[15]

Leaving aside the issue of Marsh's wrongdoing, the lesson here is that internal e-mail cannot be guaranteed to stay internal. If you cannot risk being overheard by outsiders or unintended and uninvited readers, then don't use e-mail.

Internal E-Mail Can Be Forwarded, Copied, Printed, Saved, and Shared Just as Easily as Outbound Messages

There are countless examples of confidential and compromising internal e-mail messages that have been forwarded to reporters and other third parties by employees who are intent on short-circuiting a colleague's career, embarrassing an executive, or damaging the company's reputation.

As illustrated by the following real-life internal e-mail disaster story, caustic and critical comments about the company, its customers, or the communities in which it operates have no place in e-mail, internal or external.

REAL-LIFE INTERNAL E-MAIL DISASTER STORY: ECONOMIST'S E-MAIL SLAMS SINGAPORE

Morgan Stanley's chief Asia economist, Andy Xie, was forced to resign in 2006 after colleagues circulated a caustic internal e-mail that Xie had intended strictly for readers inside Morgan Stanley. Xie's e-mail was so highly critical of Singapore that it incited the wrath of the city-state, a Morgan Stanley client.

In his internal message to colleagues, Xie sniped, "Singapore's success came mainly from being the money-laundering centre for corrupt Indonesian businessmen and government officials," and "Singapore isn't doing well. To sustain its economy, Singapore is building casinos to attract corrupt money from China."[16]

In addition to terminating Xie and the two staffers who leaked his internal e-mail, Morgan Stanley was forced to smooth over relations with the sensitive Singaporean government and endure a public relations nightmare culminating in worldwide publicity about the fallout from Xie's inflammatory internal e-mail.[17]

The Law Does Not Require E-Mail Use: Confidential, Recordless Communication Is Completely Legitimate

Regardless of whether your organization is public or private, regulated or unregulated, you can limit the untimely and risky exposure of executive musings, financial data, confidential negotiations, and other proprietary information by steering clear of e-mail on those occasions when you are not required by law or regulators to maintain formal records of conversations and transactions.

As detailed in Chapter 2, in 2006, the amended FRCP governing the discovery of ESI were announced. Conversely, information (even electronically created, transmitted, or acquired information) that is *not* retained and archived electronically does *not* constitute ESI.

The amended rules make clear the fact that ESI is discoverable and may be used as evidence—*for or against your company*—in litigation. However, the new rules *do not* require employers to conduct *all* business communication via e-mail. Nor are employers legally obligated to retain and archive *all* employee e-mail *forever*. Your company's retention policy and deletion schedule dictate what e-mail is preserved and when electronic business records that have reached the end of their life cycles may be purged.

With the exception of those situations in which you must create and save a formal record for business, legal, or regulatory reasons, you *are still allowed* to hold confidential, recordless business-related conversations in person (over a meal or on the golf course, for example), or on the phone (provided the call is not taped by either party), or online via VaporStream Confidential Messaging, a new secure technology that is designed to send electronic messages that are not stored on either the sender's or recipient's systems and are not retained by VaporStream after transit.

VaporStream Confidential Messaging Facilitates Recordless Electronic Communication

An alternative to e-mail and IM, VaporStream Confidential Messaging leaves "absolutely no trace of ever being sent," according to industry analyst Michael Osterman, writing in *NetworkWorld*. "This can be a major boon to people who need to send confidential [messages] for which no record of communication is required, and also those who want to send non-business [messages] using corporate resources."[18]

Considering that nearly half (47 percent) of employers have expressed fears that employees will transmit confidential data, proprietary information, intellectual property, and trade secrets via outbound e-mail,[19] VaporStream Confidential Messaging offers concerned organizations a technology solution to what essentially is a people problem.

Employers who are eager to keep secrets safe and eyes-only conversations under wraps are advised to take advantage of the law and limit e-mail use to situations in which a business record is required. When your legal counsel or compliance officer agrees that the need for secrecy outweighs the need for a permanent record, then take advantage of your right to communicate in a confidential, recordless fashion via telephone, face-to-face meeting, or confidential electronic messaging technology.

> **e-Policy Rule 21:** Business is not required to communicate via e-mail. Unless the law or regulators demand a record of your discussion or transaction, private recordless communication—conducted in person, on the phone, or via electronic confidential messaging—is legal and may be the most appropriate form of business communication.

Use E-Mail When the Law or Regulators Require a Business Record

As detailed in Chapter 2, a business record provides evidence of a company's business-related activities, events, and transactions. Not every message that enters or leaves your e-mail system is a business record. Not every conversation you engage in rises to the level of a business record. Your organization's welfare depends on your ability to distinguish business records, which must be retained and archived, from non-business records, which may be transmitted via the telephone, one-on-one conversation, VaporStream Confidential Messaging, or another form of private and recordless communication.

As a first step, assign your legal counsel the task of determining what you need—or want—to retain as permanent electronic business records. From a legal perspective, the process of formally defining, properly identifying, and effectively retaining and archiving business records is one of the most important e-mail management activities your organization can engage in. Your ability to separate electronic business records from non-business records can have an enormous impact (positive or negative) should you one day find yourself battling a workplace lawsuit or regulatory investigation.

Merely 34 percent of employers have an e-mail retention policy in place. No wonder 43 percent of employees don't know the difference between an electronic business record that must be retained versus a non-business record that may be purged.[20] Even among regulated employees who are required to adhere to record retention rules, 43 percent either don't comply or are unsure if they are in compliance, according to American Management Association and ePolicy Institute research.[21]

Could your organization survive a multimillion-dollar verdict or regulatory fine—on top of the six- or seven-figure professional fees charged by your legal defense team? Don't wait to find out. Get your ESI house in order now before discovery disaster strikes.

Big Brother Is Reading over Your Electronic Shoulder

Despite its undisputed business communication benefits, e-mail is a terrible way to transmit confidential, proprietary, or personal information. You simply never know who might be reading over your electronic shoulder.

- Forty-three percent of employers monitor employee e-mail, according to American Management Association and ePolicy Institute research.[22] Your recipient's employer and the employers of anyone to whom your message is forwarded or copied are likely to have access to your e-mail, confidential or not.

- The amended FRCP make e-mail and other ESI available to the courts, lawyers, investigators, jurors, witnesses, the media, and the public in the course of litigation.

- State and federal Freedom of Information statutes give the media and taxpayers access to government employees' e-mail.

- The PATRIOT Act authorizes law enforcement agencies to seize corporate e-mail.

- SOX, GLBA, HIPAA, SEC, FINRA, FDA, EPA, and IRS are just a few of the federal and state regulations and regulators that audit e-mail.

- Copied, forwarded, and improperly addressed eyes-only e-mail can land in the inboxes of competitors, the media, and other unintended internal and external readers.

Telephone, Voice Mail, and Face-to-Face Meetings Do Not Guarantee Privacy, Either

If you think the telephone guarantees a confidential alternative to e-mail, think again. According to the 2007 Electronic Monitoring & Surveillance Survey from American Management Association and ePolicy Institute, 16 percent of organizations record employee phone conversations, and another 10 percent monitor workers' voice mail.[23]

Your employer may not be taping calls and reviewing voice mail, but you have no idea who is listening in at the other end of the line. Employers who monitor voice mail often save and store those messages, too. When voice mail records are entered into evidence in the course of litigation, courtroom participants—judge, jury, witnesses, lawyers, reporters, and the public—get to eavesdrop on private messages that originally were intended for just one set of ears.

Even if you opt for a face-to-face meeting, there is always the chance that someone will accidentally overhear or intentionally eavesdrop on your conversation. At the end of the day, electronic confidential messaging technology may be the only way to guarantee that you will not be overheard.

Use Electronic Confidential Messaging When You Cannot Risk Being Overheard

Some electronic conversations—discussions about business strategies, employees and clients, intellectual property, research and development, human resources, or mergers and acquisitions, for example—call for privacy.

If you simply cannot risk being overheard by uninvited internal and external parties, and if you are committed to keeping your secrets safe and your privacy intact, then consider integrating VaporStream Confidential Messaging into your organization's electronic business communication mix.

Confidential messaging technology is not intended as a replacement for e-mail or IM. When you need or want to create a permanent electronic record, e-mail and IM remain the go-to tools. On the other hand, when your lawyer determines that a business record is unnecessary and privacy is mandatory, VaporStream Confidential Messaging delivers an electronic solution.

One of *NetworkWorld*'s "Top 10 Security Companies to Watch in 2006,"[24] VaporStream Confidential Messaging combines the passivity of e-mail (readers control when messages are opened and acted on) and the speed of IM (once a message is opened, writers engage in immediate confidential conversations).

Unlike e-mail and IM, however, confidential messages transmitted via VaporStream are not permanently stored on the computers and servers of senders and recipients. The technology also ensures that messages cannot be forwarded, edited, copied, cut, pasted, retained, or archived by senders or recipients. Once a VaporStream confidential message is read, it is gone for good.

Because VaporStream Confidential Messaging runs on a closed system, it creates no records and leaves no trails. By the time a confidential message has been read, it has already been deleted from VaporStream's servers. Because confidential messages never exist on writers' or readers' servers, desktops, laptops, or BlackBerry devices, ESI is not created like it is with e-mail and IM. There simply is no electronic evidence to be found in the event of a lawsuit or regulatory investigation.

How Does the Law View Confidential Electronic Messaging?

As discussed in Chapter 3, it is illegal to destroy evidence, including electronic business records, once a lawsuit is underway or if you even suspect a claim may be filed down the road. *Spoliation* is the legal term that is used when evidence is destroyed—accidentally or intentionally. *Litigation hold* is a record retention policy designed to prevent spoliation by overriding deletion schedules and preserving records that are relevant to current or expected litigation.

There is no precedent to suggest that employers are expected to create new types of records in situations where records otherwise do not exist. For example, a company that is embroiled in litigation is not expected to suddenly start recording telephone conversations in order to create records that might be subject to a litigation hold. Similarly, because VaporStream Confidential Messaging does not involve the creation of business records, litigation holds may not apply.

Before integrating VaporStream Confidential Messaging into your company's electronic communication mix, be sure to consult with your company's legal counsel. Your lawyer can help you define "electronic business record," determine when to use e-mail for recorded conversations, assess when the private and recordless use of VaporStream is most appropriate, and establish formal policies governing employee and executive use of VaporStream Confidential Messaging and e-mail.

Because the courts appreciate consistency, always use Vapor-Stream Confidential Messaging in conjunction with formal rules and written policies backed by comprehensive employee training and disciplinary action for policy violators. There is no guarantee that consistent compliance with written policies and procedures will grant you safe harbor in the event of a lawsuit or regulatory investigation. But strict adherence to formal policies and procedures may help demonstrate that your organization has made every effort to identify, record, and retain ESI when legally required to do so, while exercising your legal right to conduct confidential, recordless electronic conversations when records are not required.

Seven-Step Strategy to Integrate VaporStream Confidential Messaging into the Electronic Communication Mix

1. Work with your legal counsel to define "business record" for your organization on a companywide or department-by-department basis. Establish written record retention policies, deletion schedules, and litigation hold rules. Support your retention policy with a proven archiving solution like ArcMail Defender, which is guaranteed to facilitate the preservation and quick production of the type of legally authentic and trustworthy records the courts and regulators demand (see Chapter 5).

2. Work with your legal counsel to determine when, how, why, and with whom VaporStream Confidential Messaging is the most appropriate, effective—and legally compliant—way to hold recordless, eyes-only business discussions when permanent records are not required.

3.   In order to preserve attorney-client privilege, a phone call or confidential electronic messaging may be preferable to e-mail. Have your attorney spell out the manner in which executives and employees should communicate with lawyers when discussing business, seeking legal advice, or asking questions related to specific litigation.

4.   Define key terms for employees. Don't assume employees understand what management means when using terms like "confidential," "proprietary," "intellectual property," "top secret," "eyes-only," "private," "copyright," "trademark," "patent," etc. You can't expect employees to comply with confidentiality rules if they don't understand them.

5.   Implement written rules and policies governing the use of e-mail and VaporStream Confidential Messaging (see sample policies in Appendix C). Electronic communication policies should be clearly written and easy for employees to access, understand, and adhere to. Avoid vague language that may leave the organization's VaporStream Confidential Messaging policy, e-mail policy, or any other employment policy open to individual employee interpretation. Integrate VaporStream rules and policies into your organization's overall, strategic electronic business communication program and procedures.

6.   Distribute a hard copy of your confidential messaging policy, e-mail policy, and every other company employment policy to all employees. Insist that every employee sign and date a copy of each policy, acknowledging that they have read the policy, understand it, and agree to comply with it or accept disciplinary action up to and including termination.

7.   Educate employees to ensure that everyone knows the difference between business record e-mail and recordless VaporStream Confidential Messaging—and when, how, and why each tool is to be used. Make sure employees understand that compliance with all company policies including e-mail, IM, confidentiality, and VaporStream is mandatory, not an option. Topics to cover in training:

  • What is a business record? What is the organization's retention policy and deletion schedule? What is each employee's individual role (if any) in the retention and deletion process?

  • What constitutes confidential messaging? When, how, why, and with whom is confidential and recordless electronic messaging advisable?

- Business record e-mail versus recordless VaporStream Confidential Messaging: Under what circumstances may each tool be used—or not used?

- VaporStream technology: How does it work? How does it differ from traditional e-mail?

- Review e-mail and other electronic business communication risks and liabilities facing the industry, organization, and individual users.

- Discuss ownership and privacy concerns. Review the organization's monitoring rights versus employees' privacy expectations.

- Review industry and governmental regulations.

- Discuss penalties—up to and including termination—awaiting those who violate organizational rules and policies.

RECAP & e-POLICY ACTION PLAN

1. Left unmanaged, e-mail and IM can result in the rapid-fire transmission of proprietary and protected content that can pose a threat to the organization.

2. Unmanaged confidential content could land a publicly traded company in hot water with the SEC and other regulators, exposing the company to liability for violations of federal securities laws.

3. There are times when recordless conversations are perfectly legal and appropriate. In those situations, it may be best to avoid e-mail altogether and opt instead for a more confidential and recordless form of communication—if your organization's legal counsel deems it appropriate to do so.

4. To reduce the risk of being overheard by an uninvited reader, consider using a recordless, secure form of communication—a phone call, face-to-face meeting, or VaporStream Confidential Messaging—to keep your secrets safe and your privacy intact.

CHAPTER 8

Data Security Risks and Rules

The accidental loss or intentional theft of personal and financial information, including credit card data and Social Security numbers, reached unprecedented levels in 2007, with financial fraud surpassing virus attacks as the greatest source of financial loss for business, according to the annual CSI Computer Crime and Security Survey.[1]

Forty-six percent of organizations surveyed by the Computer Security Institute (CSI) experienced a security incident in 2007.[2] In the United States alone, some 79 million records were reported compromised, a fourfold increase over the previous year, according to the Identity Theft Research Center.[3] Worldwide, more than 162 million electronic records were lost or stolen in 2007, reports Attrition.org.[4]

**REAL-LIFE DATA BREACH DISASTER STORIES:
LOSSES DRAIN BUSINESSES, DEVASTATE
CONSUMERS**

Lost and stolen electronic data added up to big losses in 2007:

- When hackers broke into the computer systems of TJX Companies, the parent company of discount retailers T.J. Maxx and Marshalls, the credit-card data of some 46 million customers was grabbed and at least 94 million electronic records were stolen.

- A check-authorizing subsidiary of Fidelity National Information Services reports that a former employee stole financial information related to 8.5 million consumers.

- Contact information for more than 6.3 million customers was stolen when hackers accessed the database of online brokerage firm TD Ameritrade Holding Corporation.

- The privacy of 1.3 million job seekers was violated when con artists grabbed contact information from résumés submitted to online job site Monster Worldwide Inc.[5]

Breach Notification Laws Protect Consumers, Punish Corporate Violators

In 2007, 69 percent of organizations expressed concern for the safety of personal identity and financial privacy information, according to Proofpoint.[6] Employers aren't alone in their concern for the security of electronic records and the impact data theft can have on individuals. Legislators are taking steps to combat data theft, too. As of 2007, 39 states had enacted breach notification laws, requiring companies to notify customers and other affected parties in the event of a data breach.[7]

The law takes data theft—and corporate compliance with security laws and procedures—seriously. For example, it cost Chicago-based claims management company CS Stars LLC $60,000 to settle a security breach claim with the state of New York in 2007. In addition to paying the first settlement under the state's new security breach notification law, CS Stars agreed to implement security procedures and comply with New York's notification law in the event of any future security breaches.[8]

Comply with best practices and the law. If your company touches credit cards, Social Security numbers, private health information, financial data, or other sensitive and private consumer information, then you must adopt policies and procedures to ensure compliance with data breach notification laws.

REAL-LIFE DATA BREACH DISASTER STORY: CHOICEPOINT PAYS $15 MILLION TO SETTLE SECURITY BREACH CLAIM

Consumer data broker ChoicePoint Inc. agreed to pay $15 million to settle Federal Trade Commission (FTC) charges that the company failed to protect consumers' personal information. The largest data-security-related civil penalty in FTC history, the 2006 settlement, stemmed from ChoicePoint's sale of information concerning 163,000 consumers to an alleged crime ring. At least 800 cases of identity theft resulted from the company's data breach.[9]

e-Policy Rule 22: If your company touches credit cards, Social Security numbers, protected health information, financial data, or other sensitive and private consumer information, then you must adopt policies and procedures to ensure compliance with data breach notification laws.

Battle Breaches with Policy, Training, and Technology

With nearly half (46 percent) of organizations suffering a security incident in 2007,[10] you cannot afford to leave data security to chance. Unfortunately, the majority of employers are woefully ill-prepared to manage data security risks. According to a Vontu/Harris Interactive survey, 32 percent of managers and employees with access to sensitive customer data are unaware of internal company policies to protect customer data. Twenty-eight percent of managers report that they don't have a written security policy, nor do they know if their employers have written security policies in place.[11]

Best practices call for the development of a strategic data security protection program that combines written policy with employee education supported by technology tools. Don't leave your employees in the dark. Data protection rules and security policies serve no purpose unless your staff is aware of them and understands the individual roles they play in keeping organizational information safe and customer data secure.

Control Access to Buildings and Data Centers

From smart card technology and fingerprint scans to facial recognition and iris scans, there are a broad range of technologies available to help organizations control access to buildings and data centers where sensitive company data and customer information is stored.

In 2007, more than half of all employers (52 percent) relied on smart card technology to manage physical access to company facilities as a means to counter theft. Other organizations employed video surveillance (48 percent), fingerprint scans (2 percent), facial recognition (0.4 percent), and iris scans (0.4 percent) to try to keep thieves at bay and maintain the integrity of data, according to American Management Association and ePolicy Institute research.[12]

In addition to keeping malicious intruders out, employers who are intent on protecting data are obligated to keep an eye on their own employees. Of the 43 percent of employers who monitor employee e-mail and the other 43 percent who store and review computer files,[13] many do so as a means to prevent employees from transferring proprietary content and customer files out of the system—accidentally or intentionally.

Curtail Internal Theft of Proprietary Information

In the age of electronic business communication, just about any document can be attached to an e-mail or instant message and transmitted outside the organization.

Twelve percent of employees surveyed by American Management Association and ePolicy Institute in 2006 confessed that they had sent or received confidential information about their companies, coworkers, or themselves via IM. An additional 26 percent admitted to transmitting attachments, which could potentially contain confidential company and customer files, via IM.[14] A whopping 79 percent of employees have confessed to using e-mail to share company secrets with others—innocently or not.[15]

Compounding the problem is the fact that internal data theft often goes undetected. Because electronic transmission is completed instantly, and data remains intact within the company system, employers often don't know security has been breached—until it is too late.

Combine technology, rules, and training to prevent employees from:

- E-mailing confidential company information and business secrets to competitors.

- Stealing customer lists, marketing plans, business proposals, and other proprietary information as they leave your employment to set up shop on their own.

- Selling customers' credit card data and employees' Social Security numbers to identity thieves.

- Selling trade secrets to competitors and foreign governments.

- Posting photos or videos of products in development, the company's R&D department, floor plans, computer rooms, and other secret sites and materials on blogs and social networking or video sites (see Part 6).

Protect Outbound Information with Policy-Based Content Monitoring and Filtering Tools

Best practices call for the use of policy-based monitoring and filtering technology to audit employees' e-mail transmissions. Monitoring and filtering tools allow management to track content as it leaves or enters the system. Using an automated search tool, employers can seek out target words and phrases including the names of company executives, products, trade secrets, competitors, customers, or patients. In addition, the organization can use the same technology to capture and block obscene, harassing, discriminatory, or otherwise offensive or objectionable content that could potentially trigger a hostile work environment, harassment, or discrimination claim. Monitoring technology also can be used to spot and stop transmission of particularly large attachments, which may contain valuable data and always warrant a review.

Combine Policy, Training, and Disciplinary Rules to Safeguard Data

Reduce the likelihood of external data theft and internal security breaches, accidental or intentional, by combining written policies with employee education supported by disciplinary rules.

Use written policy to spell out clear rules governing company, customer, or patient data. Conduct formal training programs to ensure that employees understand the risks and rules governing the transmission of confidential or proprietary information via corporate e-mail or Vapor-Stream Confidential Messaging (see Chapter 7). Enforce your policy with consistent disciplinary action, up to and including the termination of policy violators. Notify employees that data theft also may be punishable by criminal or civil penalties.

RECAP & e-POLICY ACTION PLAN

1. Take advantage of technology tools to monitor external and internal e-mail. Review particularly large or otherwise suspicious e-mail attachments.

2. Require employees to sign an acknowledgment form, attesting that they understand the organization's data security policy and acknowledge that all electronic and paper records are the property of the organization.

3. Ban the use of personal e-mail accounts or IM tools, which transmit data via the public Web, leaving business records and confidential data vulnerable to thieves and other malicious third parties.

4. If your company touches credit cards, Social Security numbers, protected health information, financial data, or other sensitive and private consumer information, then you must adopt policies and procedures to ensure compliance with data breach notification laws.

PART FOUR

Content, Personal Use, and Netiquette Rules

CHAPTER 9

Content and Personal Use Risks and Rules

When it comes to inappropriate content, offensive language, and excessive personal use, employers have little tolerance. Of the 30 percent of bosses who terminated employees for Internet misuse in 2007, 84 percent cited the viewing, downloading, or uploading of pornography and otherwise offensive or inappropriate material as the reason. That's a 65 percent increase over the 19 percent of employers who dismissed employees for the same reason in 2001, according to American Management Association and ePolicy Institute research.[1]

Similarly, of the 28 percent of managers who fired workers for e-mail violations in 2007, more than half (62 percent) cited inappropriate content or off-color language as the termination-worthy offense—up from just 8 percent six years earlier.[2]

Employees who want to keep their jobs should know and adhere to company rules and policies governing electronic usage and content. Generally, that means no obscene, pornographic, sexual, harassing, discriminatory, defamatory, menacing, or threatening language. Don't transmit gossip, rumors, jokes, or disparaging remarks about executives, coworkers, or outside parties. Don't violate confidentiality rules, expose trade secrets, or share valuable intellectual property with anyone outside the company. If you are surfing the Web, steer clear of sites— porn, gambling, auctions, sports—that your employer has ruled off-limits.

If you don't want your online activity singled out for review, simply adhere to your employer's electronic content rules and usage policy.

Stop and Think Before You Write and Send

Ninety percent of U.S. companies reported "at least one litigation matter in their home jurisdiction" in 2007, according to Fulbright & Jaworski's Litigation Trends Survey.[3] You simply never know when you will be hit with a workplace lawsuit that requires you to turn over electronic evidence—e-mail or otherwise.

To help control e-mail risk—including the possibility of the wrong people receiving, retaining, and retrieving messages that could harm you and your organization—stop and think before you write and send.

REAL-LIFE ESI DISASTER STORY: UNMANAGED CONTENT TRIGGERS $570 MILLION VERDICT

The retention of too many electronic business records–and the deletion of too few–contributed to a $570 million jury award against medical manufacturer Medtronic Sofamor Danek Inc. in its breach of contract suit against spine surgeon Gary Michelson, MD.

Medtronic was ordered by the court to produce 124 backup tapes at a cost of $5,000 per tape, or $620,000–a fraction of the $16 million to $22 million that Medtronic estimated it ultimately would cost to process and review electronic evidence related to the case. Michelson's law firm, Jeffer Mangels Butler & Marmaro LLP, spent six months reviewing 44 million pages of electronic data.

"The sheer volume of data that [Medtronic] retained, including vast amounts of e-mail stored on backup tape" created a discovery nightmare for the company, according to Michelson's attorney Stanley Gibson.

Medtronic's failure to strategically manage its own e-mail and other electronic records provided opposing legal counsel with the evidence it needed to prove that the company had engaged in a "knowing pattern of contract breaches and patent infringement" against Dr. Michelson.

Following a four-month trial, the jury awarded Dr. Michelson $170 million in compensatory damages, plus $400 million in punitive damages, for a total award of $570 million.[4]

> **e-Policy Rule 23:** To help control e-mail risk, stop and think
> before you write and send.

Personal E-Mail Use: Risks, Rules, and Retention Concerns

The 58 percent of employers who dismissed employees in 2007 for computer violations combined cited excessive personal e-mail use (26 percent) and Internet use (34 percent) as their reasons.[5]

To help minimize employee terminations and maximize compliance, use written e-Policies to spell out rules governing personal e-mail and Internet use. That said, be realistic about personal computer use. While the company computer system is intended primarily for business use, it is unrealistic to ban personal use entirely.

E-mail and IM may be the only means for some employees to stay in touch with children, spouses, teachers, babysitters, doctors, and other important personal contacts during the workday. Working parents who are prohibited from communicating with and about family via e-mail or IM may seek out a more family-friendly employer.

Personal Use Heightens Organizational Risk

- Personal use takes a toll on employee productivity and eats up valuable system space and bandwidth. According to American Management Association and ePolicy Institute research, 86 percent of employees engage in personal e-mail at work. With all that personal communication taking place, it's no surprise that 10 percent of workers spend more than half the workday (four or more hours) engaged in writing, reading, and responding to e-mail.[6]

- Personal content tends to be more relaxed—thus, potentially more risky—than business-related content.

- Personal e-mail messages that are retained and archived alongside business records may become part of the evidence pool during litigation, possibly disgracing employees and derailing the organization's legal position in the process.

- Personal Web surfing leaves electronic footprints that computer forensic experts will happily follow in the course of legal discovery.

Manage Personal Use with Clear Rules

If you allow personal use of electronic business communication tools, be sure to let your staff know when personal e-mail or other electronic communication is allowed, for how long, during what periods of the day, with whom, and under what circumstances.

Remember, clear guidelines are always easier to understand and adhere to. If "some" personal use is allowed, employees will have to individually interpret where the line is drawn, and you may not be comfortable with their conclusions.

REAL-LIFE E-MAIL DISASTER STORY: PROSECUTOR'S LOVE LIFE EXPOSED BY COURT

Texas's most powerful prosecutor, the district attorney of Harris County (population 4 million), faced public embarrassment, family strife, media scrutiny, and political disaster when private e-mail correspondence was inadvertently made public by a federal court in December 2007.

District Attorney Charles A. Rosenthal Jr. used his office e-mail system to send hundreds of personal messages including racist jokes, pornographic images, and what the *New York Times* called "professions of love and longing" to his executive secretary.

The married DA's private e-mail messages, which were revealed as part of a federal civil rights lawsuit against Harris County, initially had been sealed to prevent public exposure. When a court mix-up inadvertently unsealed the messages, Rosenthal's personal dirty laundry was exposed, placing him under intense government, media, family, and public scrutiny for misusing his county e-mail account.[7]

Rosenthal's electronic disaster escalated when he admitted to a federal judge that, in violation of two subpoenas and a court order, he had deleted as many as 3,500 e-mail messages related to the civil rights lawsuit. In the process, Rosenthal opened himself to possible perjury charges. Ultimately, Rosenthal's e-mail disaster led to his resignation from office.[8]

Best practice: Save your personal correspondence for your home computer.

REAL-LIFE E-MAIL DISASTER STORY: PERSONAL E-MAIL HAUNTS EMPLOYEES YEARS AFTER TRANSMISSION

The employees of fallen energy giant Enron made the company e-mail system an extension of their own personal lives. Like workers in many other offices, Enron employees thought nothing of using the company's e-mail system to discuss personal matters and air dirty laundry.

Because those private (and in some cases highly confidential) messages were mixed in with Enron's electronic business records, they were gathered as evidence during the Federal Energy Regulatory Commission (FERC) investigation of Enron's alleged energy-market manipulation.

In March 2002, FERC posted online 1.6 million Enron e-mails from 2000 through 2002. At no charge, the public could surf the e-mail inboxes of 176 current and former executives and employees, some of whom had thousands of business and personal messages on display.

Romances, affairs, and gossip were discussed. Complaints were lodged against in-laws and managers alike. Executive salary packages and employee performance reviews were transmitted. Employees' bank records and Social Security numbers were displayed—all with senders' and receivers' names attached.

Two days after the e-mails were posted, Enron petitioned FERC to remove the most sensitive and confidential messages. FERC agreed to remove 8 percent of the database (141,379 documents), including a payroll document that listed the Social Security number of every Enron employee. In the end, only 5,128 e-mails containing Social Security numbers and employee performance evaluations were permanently removed.[9]

The Enron e-mail disaster was covered by the *Wall Street Journal*, CNBC, and National Public Radio, among other national business media outlets. Millions of curious readers (and potential data thieves) jumped online to sort through the goldmine of Social Security numbers, personal dirt, and other "goodies," crashing the site in the process.

A cautionary tale for all e-mail users, the Enron e-mail disaster drives home an important lesson for employees. Never use your employer's e-mail system to transmit personal, sensitive, or confidential information that would embarrass or otherwise harm you or your loved ones were it made public.

RECAP & e-POLICY ACTION PLAN

1. The easiest way to control electronic risk is to control written content.

2. To help maximize compliance and minimize terminations, use written e-policy to specify rules governing personal use of e-mail, the Web, and other electronic business communication tools.

3. When retained alongside business record e-mail and other ESI, employees' personal—and potentially embarrassing—correspondence may become part of the evidence pool in litigation, may be accessed by the media in accordance with the Freedom of Information Act, or could otherwise be exposed to unintended readers who may not have the best interests of the user or the company at heart.

CHAPTER 10

Netiquette Rules

Every e-mail message transmitted by an employee reflects on the organization's credibility and the professionalism of the writer. E-mail that is badly written and filled with typos can turn off readers and stall careers. Messages that betray confidences, reveal trade secrets, or disclose financial information can trigger lawsuits and regulatory investigations. E-mail that is menacing, harassing, pornographic, defamatory, discriminatory, or otherwise inappropriate can lead to terminations, litigation, and negative publicity.

An effective e-mail policy should incorporate a discussion of the rules of netiquette, or electronic etiquette. By addressing and enforcing the rules of netiquette, employers can maximize civil business behavior while minimizing the likelihood that employees will write inappropriate messages or attach offensive content that could harm the organization.

> **e-Policy Rule 24:** Incorporate netiquette, or electronic etiquette, rules into your organization's e-policy program to help maximize civil business behavior.

Mind Your Electronic Manners

Use your organization's e-mail policy to provide employees with formal rules for acceptable and effective electronic business communication. By its nature, e-mail is a "cold" medium. Messages written and conversations held on-screen lack the warmth of face-to-face discussions and telephone calls, which benefit from body language or intonation.

Couple its coldness with the tendency of many writers to type messages quickly and thoughtlessly, and it's easy to see how e-mail can result in hurt feelings, misunderstandings, and liabilities. Adherence to the basic rules of netiquette can alleviate problems and help cast your employees and organization in a favorable light.

Netiquette Guidelines for Employees

1. ***Beware of Hidden Readers.*** If confidentiality is an issue, don't use e-mail. It's simply not secure. You may intend to send a message to one person, but an inaccurate keystroke or the recipient's decision to forward your message could land your e-mail on dozens, hundreds, or thousands of unintended readers' screens. Never use e-mail to communicate trade secrets, proprietary information, or any news that could damage the organization or its employees were it read by unintended readers.

2. ***Write as Though Mom Were Reading.*** Write your message as if your boss, the media, or your mom were reading. People treat e-mail too casually, sending electronic messages that they would never record on paper. Don't write anything you would not be comfortable saying in an elevator crowded with colleagues, customers, and competitors.

3. ***Keep All the Organization's Employment Policies in Mind.*** A policy is a policy. Employees are obligated to adhere to all company policies when corresponding via e-mail, including the company's ethics guidelines, code of conduct, harassment and discrimination rules, and language or content rules.

4. ***Don't Use E-Mail to Let Off Steam.*** Upset or angry? Compose yourself before composing your message. Once you hit "send," your e-mail is on its way and probably can't be retrieved. Don't take the chance of sending a hastily written message that could worsen an already difficult situation. If communication is urgently needed, ask a trusted colleague to read a questionable message before you transmit it.

5. ***Control the Urge to Flame.*** An e-mail flame is a message that is hostile, blunt, rude, insensitive, or obscene. Flames are unique to e-mail, as the slow pace of snail mail does not accommodate immediate heated reactions. Flames, and the obscene and abusive language that feed them, have no place in a business environment.

6. ***Respect Others' Time.*** Do not use the company system to send or forward spam, nonbusiness-related messages, or personal correspondence. An inbox stuffed with jokes, vacation photos, and gossip can be more than a time-consuming annoyance. Violate your employer's spam policy, and you may find yourself out of work, or incarcerated if you work in a state that outlaws spamming.

7. ***Never Reply to Spam.*** If you are on the receiving end of spam, do not reply to the "unsubscribe" option. Your reply merely confirms your e-mail address and encourages the sender to sell your address to other spammers. Replying to spam also can be a waste of time, as senders sometimes use one-time-only addresses to blast spam. Your irate reply could land in a black hole. So why bother? Simply delete unsolicited messages. Deletion is the easiest, most effective way to control spam. Be sure to download all antispam software updates provided by the company's IT department. Also, be sure to check your junk folder regularly. Spam filters may inadvertently send legitimate messages to your junk folder. If you delete without checking, you may trash legitimate, business-related e-mail along with junk mail.

8. ***Don't Post Your Business E-Mail Address on a Personal Website.*** Computerized "spambots" automatically and continuously search the Web for e-mail addresses. Post your company e-mail address on a personal site today and watch your spam intake explode overnight.

9. ***Don't Mail to the World.*** Send e-mail only to readers with a legitimate need for your information. Mail to your group list only when it is appropriate for everyone on the list to receive the message. Do not reply to a message unless you have something to contribute.

10. ***Copy with Care.*** Sending a carbon copy (CC) or blind carbon copy (BCC) to a recipient who doesn't need to read your message wastes everyone's time. As a rule, address your message to the person you want to motivate to act, and send carbon copies strictly as a courtesy. Carbon copy recipients are not required to reply to messages. So don't get upset when a response is not forthcoming.

11. ***Don't Oversell Your Message.*** Just because you have the ability to mark messages "urgent," doesn't mean you should. Reserve the urgent classification for messages that demand immediate action.

12. ***Ask Permission to Forward Material.*** Do you subscribe to an electronic publication that would interest an associate or customer?

Don't forward it without first asking permission of the original sender. Otherwise, you may be in violation of copyright law.

13. ***Treat Others as You Would Have Them Treat You.*** If you receive someone else's e-mail by mistake, don't trash it. Hit "reply" to redirect it back to the sender, along with a brief note about the mix-up.

14. ***Consider E-Mail's Limitations.*** E-mail may be the best way to deliver news fast, but it's not necessarily the best route to a quick reply. Unless company policy requires employees to download and respond to e-mail regularly, your reader is under no obligation to read or reply to incoming messages. For an immediate response to a pressing issue, don't rely on e-mail. Instead, pick up the phone or schedule a face-to-face meeting.

Special Netiquette Considerations for Managers

Executives and managers should, of course, adhere to the basic rules of netiquette. In addition, there are a handful of special netiquette guidelines that apply solely to those who supervise employees.

1.   On a regular basis, remind employees that the organization has the right to monitor e-mail and the Internet. Also remind users that they have absolutely no reasonable expectation of privacy when using the company's computer system. Address invasion-of-privacy complaints by explaining exactly how monitoring works, what the company is looking for, and why compliant employees have nothing to fear from surveillance.

2.   Adhere to the organization's e-mail policy yourself. If, for example, the e-mail policy limits personal use to a certain amount of time or specific periods of the day, then adhere to that prohibition yourself. Do not allow yourself any special rights other employees do not enjoy equally.

3.   Enforce the organization's termination rules consistently. If the organization's e-mail rules state that policy violations will result in termination, then managers must follow through by firing *all* violators regardless of title, tenure with the company, or friendships with management. The only way the organization's e-mail policy will be effective at reducing liability risks is through consistent enforcement. No exceptions.

4.   Be realistic about personal use policies. E-mail may be the only way for some employees to keep in touch with spouses, children, and

other important personal contacts during working hours. If all personal e-mail use is banned, then some employees may start looking for a more accommodating, family-friendly employer.

5. Never use e-mail to fire employees or deliver bad news. Without the benefit of body language, facial expression, or intonation, e-mail is the worst way to deliver bad news. Whether your objective is to terminate an employee or notify a department head of budgetary cutbacks, demonstrate respect for your employees by delivering bad news in person. A one-on-one meeting will give the employee the opportunity to ask questions and absorb the shock of bad news. And, should a wrongful termination lawsuit follow, personal notification may help cast management in a better light than electronic notification would.

6. Don't use e-mail to discuss an employee's performance. As a manager, you are obligated to treat every worker with professional courtesy. If you need to discuss an employee's professional short-comings with the human resources director or instruct a department head to terminate an employee who just isn't working out, do so in person and behind closed doors.

7. Don't rely on e-mail to the exclusion of personal contact. To varying degrees, your employees, customers, and suppliers all crave human interaction. While some people may be content to communicate electronically 100 percent of the time, others may feel slighted or unappreciated without ongoing personal contact. Even in the age of e-mail, relationship skills remain at the heart of long-term business success. Supplement your e-mail communication by holding regular meetings with your staff, customers, and important suppliers.

8. Avoid e-mail if there is any chance your message will be misunder-stood or misconstrued. If your message is complex, technical, or in any danger of being misinterpreted, opt for a phone call or personal meeting instead.

RECAP & e-POLICY ACTION PLAN

1. An effective e-mail policy should incorporate a discussion of the rules of netiquette, or electronic etiquette.

2. By addressing and enforcing the rules of netiquette, employers can maximize civil business behavior while minimizing the likelihood that employees will write inappropriate messages or attach offensive content that could turn off readers, trigger litigation, or otherwise harm the organization.

PART FIVE

Instant
Messaging Rules

CHAPTER 11

IM Is Turbocharged E-Mail
All the Risks, Rules, and Regulations Apply[1]

Long popular with teens and college students, 84 percent of whom use IM on a daily basis,[2] IM now is gaining a solid foothold in the workplace. More than a third (35 percent) of workers reported using IM at work in 2006, according to American Management Association and ePolicy Institute research.[3] We can safely assume that number will continue to grow as more organizations adopt IM for internal and external communication.

Business Struggles to Define Instant Messaging

As IM sweeps through the workplace, employers, lawyers, compliance officers, and IT professionals wrestle to define and manage it in light of myriad business, legal, and regulatory concerns.

Think of IM as a combination of the telephone, which facilitates conversations with multiple people in real time, and e-mail, which combines the speed of online communication with a written record of your conversation.

The hybrid nature of IM has created confusion among organizations that can't decide whether to interpret IM traffic as e-mail or phone chat. Some (incorrectly) think of IM chat as an extension of a casual telephone call—a conversation that ends when all parties hang up. Others (correctly) define IM more formally as a type of e-mail—electronic communication that produces a written record that may be discoverable in the course of a regulatory audit or lawsuit.

When the NASD in 2003 joined the SEC and NYSE in announcing

new IM retention regulations, the definition of IM was clarified for broker-dealers, investment bankers, and those who choose to follow the lead of the financial services industry in the adoption of IM technology. Industry and governmental regulators helped the financial services industry clarify the fact that, from the standpoint of content and retention, IM is a form of written correspondence that creates an electronic business record, just as e-mail does.

That definition was solidified in 2006 when the U.S. federal court system announced the amended FRCP, clarifying the fact that all electronically stored information—including IM chat—is discoverable and may be used as evidence in litigation. (See Chapter 2.)

Instant Messenger Creates Written Business Records

IM is nothing more than turbocharged e-mail. Like e-mail, IM creates business records, which employers are obliged to retain, archive, and produce in the event of litigation or a regulatory investigation. Failure to manage workplace IM also can result in regulatory fines, court sanctions, and costly legal settlements.

> **e-Policy Rule 25:** IM is nothing more than turbocharged e-mail. Like e-mail, it is written correspondence that creates an electronic business record.

Don't Get Left Behind by Tech-Savvy Employees

The message to employers is clear. You cannot allow employees to engage in unauthorized or unmanaged IM chat. IM use must be governed by rules, policies, and procedures, just as e-mail usage is.

Unfortunately, in many offices, the strategic management of IM lags well behind its actual use. Only 31 percent of organizations have in place a policy governing IM use and content, versus 76 percent that have implemented formal e-mail policy, according to American Management Association and ePolicy Institute research.[3]

Instant Messaging Is Being Used—With or Without Your Knowledge

Of the 35 percent of employees who IM at work, half use company-provided, enterprise-grade IM. The other 50 percent have downloaded free IM software from the Internet—a fact that 53 percent of employers are unaware of, according to the 2006 Workplace E-Mail, Instant Messaging & Blog Survey from American Management Association and ePolicy Institute.[4]

In any given office, half of all employees who are instant messaging are doing so without management's knowledge, without written rules and policies to guide usage, and without IT-approved technology to help prevent security breaches, retain business records, and control overall risk.

> **e-Policy Rule 26:** Assume that your employees are already using instant messaging—without your knowledge, authorization, rules, or policies.

All across the country, in offices large and small, employees are downloading free consumer-grade IM software from the leading public network players—AOL Instant Messenger, Yahoo! Messenger, and MSN Messenger Service—directly onto their desktop computers. The most avid instant messagers download every available IM product, or "client," so they can communicate internally and externally with any other IM user, minus software compatibility concerns. Industry insiders estimate that some 66 percent of active IM users have more than one IM client installed—and in use—on their desktop computers.[5]

Management Is Oblivious to Rogue IM Use

Rogue employees spend the workday engaging in risky online behavior without technology in place to prevent security breaches, monitor content, or retain and archive IM business records. Oblivious to the behavior and out of touch with the technology, some employers simply allow high-risk IM to occur, absent of written rules and policies to govern employee behavior and protect the organization from risk.

REAL-LIFE IM DISASTER STORY: BROKERS USE IM WITHOUT REGARD FOR REGULATORY RULES

An internal survey revealed that more than half of the 1,300 employees of regional stock brokerage firm Stifel Nicolaus had downloaded free IM software from the Web, without management's knowledge or approval.

Brokers were using IM without the authorization of the firm's compliance department, which is charged with ensuring that the firm adheres to SEC and FINRA regulations covering the management, monitoring, and retention of instant messages.[6]

The government and industry regulators who oversee financial services firms are serious about IM and e-mail compliance. Securities firms that violate regulators' IM rules, intentionally or accidentally, should expect to be hit with the type of six- and seven-figure financial penalties that e-mail abusers have suffered for years, as detailed in Chapter 4.

Security Concerns: Instant Messaging Tops the List of IT Risks

Instant messaging security challenges stem from the fact that half of all corporate use takes place across public networks,[7] which lack built-in protections against Trojan horses, worms, viruses, and other destructive intruders.

Unlike corporate e-mail systems, which typically use networks and servers controlled by the organization, consumer-grade IM moves outside the organization's firewall, across public networks, and through servers controlled by AOL, Yahoo!, or Microsoft. That makes sensitive business information vulnerable to malicious hackers, data thieves, and eavesdroppers. It also opens the door to viruses and IM spam, known as "spim."

Employers who allow IM use must be sure they have a secure IM solution in place. The consumer-grade IM products that most employees have adopted on an ad hoc basis are only appropriate for business use if you invest in management technology. To integrate public IM networks into your private system and manage IM as a business asset, install management technology that guards against security breaches, monitors internal and external communications, purges content that violates policy, blocks attachments, and archives business record messages.

Software Compatibility Issues: Instant Messagers Can't Chat Universally

Software compatibility is not a concern for e-mail users. One e-mail user can communicate with any other e-mail user anywhere in the world, regardless of the software used by either party.

IM, on the other hand, poses significant compatibility challenges. Because each IM product uses its own proprietary technology, instant messagers can communicate only with those who are using the same IM client or system. In other words, if you use AOL Instant Messenger (AIM), the only people you can chat with are other AIM users.

IM also doesn't allow for the encryption of confidential messages unless the sender and receiver both use the same IM tool.

Software incompatibility creates headaches for business users who seek to instant message a broad range of clients, colleagues, and friends—all of whom may use different IM tools. To overcome compatibility issues, some employees simply download multiple IM tools—with or without management's knowledge.

The widespread use of multiple IM clients creates challenges for employers eager to manage all aspects of IM use. Employers who allow IM use must make a strategic decision about the type of IM system they adopt, and then make an investment in technology products that are designed to help manage that system as a business asset.

Retention and Archiving Challenges: IM Must Be Retained as a Business Record

The consumer-grade IM clients many workers use don't provide built-in tools for central administration and control. Like e-mail and most other electronic communication tools, IM creates written documents that must be managed as business records according to clear business rules. Without proper management of IM business records for legal and regulatory purposes, the organization faces enormous risk.

According to the 2006 E-Mail, Instant Messaging & Blog Survey from American Management Association and ePolicy Institute, only 13 percent of organizations retain and archive IM business records. That leaves 87 percent of businesses vulnerable to charges that they have improperly, perhaps illegally, destroyed evidence.[8]

Content Challenges: Instant Messagers Tend to Play It Fast and Loose

Because of its instantaneous nature, many users think IM is a throw-away medium that permits casual off-the-cuff content. Unsupervised use of IM, coupled with a lack of language rules and training, can lead to the type of inappropriate content that triggers lawsuits, embarrasses employees, and haunts employers as evidence of possible wrongdoing.

WHAT TYPE OF CONTENT DO EMPLOYEES TRANSMIT VIA IM?	
Attachments of any kind	26%
Jokes, gossip, rumors, disparaging remarks	24%
Confidential information about the company, coworkers, or users themselves	12%
Sexual, romantic, pornographic content	10%[9]

Confidentiality Breaches: You Can Lose Intellectual Property in an Instant

Instant messaging compounds the risk of confidentiality breaches, which may be triggered when employees use IM to chat about proprietary or personal matters that would be more safely discussed on the phone, in person, or via VaporStream Confidential Messaging technology, as discussed in Chapter 7.

Allowing employees to access public IM networks opens the organization to huge security risks. Confidential information and intellectual property can flow out in an instant, and there's always a risk of interception.

If your organization allows IM, you must address confidentiality concerns and rules in your policy. In particular, heavily regulated public companies must hold employees accountable for conversations conducted via IM.

Productivity Problems: Are Your Employees Chatting the Day Away?

Eighty-six percent of employees engage in personal e-mail at work, and another 10 percent of employees spend more than half the workday (four-plus hours) reading, writing, and replying to e-mail, according to American Management Association and ePolicy Institute research.[10]

Critics argue that e-mail's toll on workplace productivity will be dwarfed by instant messaging. IM users tend to chat often, setting aside legitimate business tasks in the process. Unlike easily overheard phone calls, supervisors really can't tell what's going on with IM unless they're standing over an employee's computer screen.

Some employees may find it hard to concentrate when messages are continually popping up onscreen. Some managers may use IM to brainstorm ideas and make decisions while on the road at all hours. Employees who fear being left out of the loop may feel compelled to stay glued to their computer screens—at the office and at home.

Employers who allow workplace IM use should develop and enforce written rules and policies to battle productivity challenges. Use your policy to drive home the point that the organization provides IM to augment business productivity, not as a diversion from work.

RECAP & e-POLICY ACTION PLAN

1. Think of IM as turbocharged e-mail—written communication that must be managed as a business record.

2. Take control of workplace IM by establishing written rules and policies, conducting employee training adhering to regulatory and legal requirements, and managing IM use with technology tools controlled by your IT department.

CHAPTER 12

IM Management Rules and Tools

Employers cannot afford to ignore IM. They have an obligation to discover whether or not employees are using IM, under what circumstances they are using it, with whom they are chatting, and what type of content they are transmitting. The risks inherent in unmanaged IM use range from lawsuits and loss of confidential data, to security breaches and lost productivity—risks that are too costly to ignore.

Go High-Tech to Uncover Employees' Unauthorized IM Use

To help get a grip on unauthorized IM use, you may want to take advantage of technology. A number of vendors including Akonix and FaceTime provide tools that enable employers to test their networks for the presence of consumer-grade IM clients. These products reveal what screen names employees are using, and whether or not they are using IM to transfer files, and if so, what files.[1] Don't stop with a one-time check of your system. Have your IT department conduct regular IM screenings. Your findings will help you develop a comprehensive strategic plan for effective IM management.

Conduct an Internal Audit to Determine How Widespread IM Use Is

In addition to using technology to detect the presence of personal IM, you may want to conduct an internal IM survey among employees. Your survey will reveal how many employees are accessing public IM networks, and will help you design IM policy and training to meet the specific needs of your staff, organization, and industry.

To maximize employee participation in the internal survey and ensure honest responses, guarantee anonymity. Assure employees that management will make no attempt to identify respondents or penalize employees who, prior to the development and implementation of formal IM rules and policies, may have downloaded and used personal IM tools without authorization.

What's the Best Way to Manage IM Use?

Once you've screened your computer system and surveyed staff to determine the extent of your employees' IM use (and misuse), it's time to decide how to manage all that IM activity. When it comes to IM management, you have three choices:

1. Ban workplace use altogether.

2. Exercise control over the situation by installing an in-house enterprise-grade solution to replace users' personal IM software.

3. Take a middle-ground approach and support employees' use of personal IM clients with technology that helps control content, monitor use, retain business records, purge nonrecords, enhance security, and reduce risks.

Don't Rush to Ban Instant Messaging

Once executives and IT managers discover that unauthorized IM use is taking place, a common reaction is to ban it entirely. Although banning IM may appear to be a simple and effective solution to IM risk, it may not be so easy to enforce. In spite of IT's objections, employees want IM, and have demonstrated that they won't hesitate to sneak it in through the back door.

**REAL-LIFE IM DISASTER STORY: IT CONSULTANT
CIRCUMVENTS INSTANT MESSAGING BAN**

You can impose rules that forbid employees from using personal
IM software for external communications, but that won't necessarily stop tech-savvy workers from doing so anyway.

Take the case of the IT consultant who was assigned to
brokerage firm Morgan Stanley for several months. Undeterred
by the brokerage's ban on external IM, the consultant simply
programmed his way around the firewall in order to chat with his
outside buddies on company time.[2]

Don't assume a ban on IM will result in a workplace that is
100 percent clean. Some IM fans will continue to download free
software, in spite of your policy and the potential for disciplinary
action or termination.

IM users may be reluctant to part with IM, particularly those who
work in competitive sales environments, where seconds can make the
difference between making the sale and losing the lead. Try banning IM
across the board, and you may just trigger a revolt among your employees and the clients they are instant messaging regularly.

Impose a strict no-exception ban on IM use, and you're likely to
find yourself in an uphill battle against computer-savvy scofflaw employees who continue downloading free IM products, regardless of how
many times your scanning software detects and removes them. You may
even lose valuable employees to competitors who are more tolerant of
workplace IM use.

**REAL-LIFE IM DISASTER STORY: 50,000 EMPLOYEES
PROTEST INSTANT MESSAGING SHUTOFF**

When a global investment bank tried to shut off IM, the IT department was flooded by support calls from staff. With over 50,000
employees, management's attempt to manage IM risk was a
nightmare.

That said, if you opt to join the 20 percent of companies that, according to Gartner research, are reconsidering their once open-minded

policies toward employee IM use,[3] take steps to prevent rogue use once your ban goes into effect.

Tips for Enforcing an Instant Messaging Ban

1. Use your written IM policy to clearly forbid all employee use.

2. Configure desktop computers so employees cannot download free IM software.

3. Do not install IM technology on your employees' computers.

4. Configure firewalls and networks to block instant messages.

5. Use IM management software to automate your IM policies.

6. Limit use of personal cell phones, Smartphones, and other devices that offer IM capabilities.

7. Conduct periodic scans of your system to detect the presence of personal IM software.

Standardization Offers Risk Management Benefits—and Some Big Disadvantages

While 35 percent of employees are using some form of IM, only half of them use a standardized corporate solution.[4] Instant messaging standardization occurs when the organization adopts an enterprise-grade IM tool that is designed for business use, versus more widely used consumer-oriented IM products.

Closed to external communication, enterprise IM systems are designed for internal use only. No other IM clients, including free downloads, are allowed. Messages written on unauthorized, unrecognized IM tools are prevented from leaving the network.

Enterprise IM tools come equipped with antivirus software, encryption capabilities, and other security features that personal products don't offer. Another benefit to rolling out your own IM solution is control. Employees' IM connections, passwords, and conversations stay inhouse and are not transmitted over the public Web. Enterprise IM also enables IT to monitor content and retain and archive messages.

Those are some of the positives of standardization. Topping off the list of negatives is the fact that standardization restricts IM communication to internal chat only. Your employees can use your enterprise IM solution to chat only with other employees using the same IM software.

Because the use of public IM networks is banned, employees are blocked from instant messaging clients and other outsiders. In the minds of some users, standardization may help manage risks, but it defeats the primary purpose of IM—efficient and effective real-time communication. Expect defiant employees to disregard policy and download personal IM clients from the Internet, even after your enterprise-grade software is installed.

If you opt for standardization, be sure to use written IM rules to help stop renegade behavior. Inform staff that the unauthorized downloading and use of personal IM clients is a violation of company policy, which will result in disciplinary action, up to and including termination.

Flexibility Is One Way to Control Use and Manage Risks

Another option is to meet employees halfway by permitting the use of free IM downloads, and installing server-based gateway, or management, technology through which all messages must pass. FaceTime, Akonix, and Websense, for example, offer gateway products that manage public IM traffic at the discretion of corporate IT. These products enable management to test the network to find out what consumer IM clients are being used, control user IDs, monitor use, filter content, save and store messages, and detect viruses, among other features.[5]

Another feature available with gateway/IM management products is the ability to block the use of buddy names that have a sexual, suggestive, or otherwise offensive tone. With IM, it's not just the message, it's also an employee's user name that could embarrass or create risk for the organization.

User ID is one of the biggest problems facing the IM industry and users. With consumer-grade IM, users are free to establish their own IM name and to use any domain they wish. Using AOL Instant Messenger, for example, a competitor could use your corporate domain to create an IM user name that reads JDoe@YourCompany.com. Another problem arises when employees using personal IM clients select inappropriate user IDs ("HotMamma"). The misuse and misappropriation of user names and domains raises concerns over authenticity, among other challenges. How do you really know who a message came from? Employers are advised to combine written user ID policy with technology products that give the IT department some control over user IDs, enabling you to reserve your domain name and kick imposters off the system.

Gateway/IM management software also can be used to block the use of IM attachments. Unlike e-mail attachments, IM attachments are not checked by the typical antivirus search engine. Consequently, IM attachments create legal, compliance, and security threats. Reduce your risks by combining a gateway/IM management technology solution with written policy that prohibits employee use of IM to transmit attachments.[6]

Gateway/IM management technology creates a win-win scenario. Employees maintain the ability to chat with customers and other outside parties. The organization gains the ability to manage IM use through the automated enforcement of rules and policy.

This flexible approach may appeal to organizations that are reluctant to invest in a standard enterprise product until IM vendors work out their compatibility issues. These users may prefer to wait until enterprise IM users are able to communicate with buddies on other IM systems.

RECAP & e-POLICY ACTION PLAN

1. No organization can afford to allow employees to engage in unmanaged IM—the potential risks and costs are too great. Take strategic, preventive action now.

2. Combine screening technology with an internal audit to uncover the extent and nature of employees' IM use and misuse.

3. There is no one-size-fits-all approach to strategic IM management. Each organization must balance risks with business needs to determine the most appropriate approach.

4. Banning IM may not be right for all organizations. A ban may lead to rogue use, employee outcry, and customer complaints.

5. Enterprise system standardization reduces risks, but limits communication to internal chat.

6. If you opt for flexibility, be sure to select a gateway/IM management technology tool that enables you to control risks and manage use within policy and regulatory guidelines.

PART SIX

Internet Rules

Web, Blog, Social Networking,
and Video Site Risks, Rules,
Policies, and Best Practices

CHAPTER 13

Internet Risks and Rules

When employees make inappropriate use of the Internet, the result is waste. Productivity is wasted when employees log on and slack off. Money is wasted when management must divert resources to defend copyright violation claims and other Web-related lawsuits. Corporate reputations are wasted when the media get hold of particularly salacious tales of online intrigue.

Internet Content and Web Surfing Create Written Evidence and Legal Exposures

As detailed in Chapter 2, the 2006 amendments to the FRCP state that all electronically stored information—including corporate website content and employees' history of Internet surfing—can be subpoenaed and used as evidence in the course of federal litigation. Best practices call for the strategic management of Web use and content through the implementation of written policy, employee training, Internet monitoring, and URL blocking tools.

Video Snacking Devours Space, Security, and Productivity

Do you allow employees' to surf the Web for personal reasons during their lunch breaks? A common practice within some organizations, unrestricted personal lunchtime surfing is an increasingly risky proposition for employers.

Web content providers are well aware that employees' Internet usage spikes at midday. Short on time and hungry for entertainment, many employees engage in lunchtime "video snacking," tuning in to video snippets on computers, cell phones, and PDAs.

Video snacking is such a popular workday pastime that sites like ComedyCentral.com are splitting full-length shows into short segments, while PoliticalLunch.com and other sites are producing short webcasts for midday broadcast. Mindful of the power and popularity of lunchtime video snacking, the advertising community has gotten into the act, charging higher ad rates for spots that accompany video snacks.[1]

Video snacking opens the organization up to bandwidth waste and other risks as employees download and file large, nonbusiness-related videos. Systems can be damaged and security breached as spyware, viruses, and other malicious intruders enter your system via infected content. Employee productivity may be diminished as video snackers, hungry for more content, stretch the lunch hour into the afternoon.

As part of your organization's Internet policy and personal use rules, be sure to address video snacking. If you decide to allow video snacking, use policy to spell out what type of sites or what specific URLs are permitted and which are prohibited. Inform employees of any limits on time (the 60-minute lunch hour, for instance) or periods of the day (lunchtime and approved work breaks, for example) that may include video snacking.

If you want to outlaw video snacking altogether, support your anti-snacking rule with a technology tool that blocks access to banned URLs.

> **e-Policy Rule 27:** Video snacking opens the organization up to bandwidth waste, security breaches, and lost productivity. Apply written policy, monitoring technology, and URL blocks to manage video snacking risks.

Thirteen-Point Strategy for Reducing Web-Related Risks

1. *Conduct a legal review of your corporate website.* Don't take chances with posted content. Assign a member of the legal team or another responsible individual to review all website content including but not limited to text, white papers, book excerpts, surveys, news articles, photos, videos, cartoons, and links to

external sites. Avoid copyright infringement claims by securing the written permission of copyright holders before publishing third-party content on your business site. Avoid defamation claims by eliminating negative comments about competitors and their products.

2. ***Establish a written Internet policy.*** Effective Web management begins with a clear and comprehensive Internet policy that focuses on content, use, and other key issues.

3. ***Address personal Web use.*** Notify employees that the company's Internet system is a business tool that is intended primarily for authorized commerce, communication, research, and other business-related purposes. Spell out exactly how much personal Web surfing is allowed, when, and for what purposes. Address video snacking as part of your Web use policy.

> **e-Policy Rule 28:** Use written Internet policy to notify employees that the company's Internet system is a business tool that is intended primarily for authorized commerce, communication, research, and other business-related purposes.

4. ***Review and update all company policies.*** While developing your comprehensive Web policy, take time to review and update all the company's employment policies. Notify employees that all employment policies apply to the Internet, regardless of whether employees are surfing at work or posting content at home on their own personal websites.

5. ***Provide formal Internet policy training.*** The courts appreciate, and tend to respond favorably to, policy and training when it is consistently applied.[2] Don't leave Internet policy compliance to chance. Educate employees about Web-related risks and rules, policies and procedures. Require all employees to sign and date an acknowledgment form, confirming that they have participated in formal Internet policy training. Retain all employee acknowledgement forms. One day, you may need to demonstrate to a court that you have done everything possible to ensure Internet policy compliance.

6. Inform employees that Web content and usage rules apply, regardless of whether they are viewing, forwarding, downloading, uploading, transmitting screen shots, copying files, storing files, or otherwise engaged in Internet-related activity.

7. Notify employees that they are prohibited from using company computer resources to create, view, print, copy, download, upload, transmit, file, or forward content that is offensive or otherwise in violation of *any* company rule or policy.

> **e-Policy Rule 29:** Use written Internet policy to notify employees that they are prohibited from using company computer resources to create, view, print, copy, download, upload, transmit, file, or forward content that is offensive, objectionable, or otherwise in violation of *any* company rule or policy.

8. Prohibit employees from mentioning (in words or images) the company, its people, products, services, secrets, suppliers, or customers on personal or third-party websites without first securing written permission from management.

9. Prohibit employees from identifying themselves as employees of the company, in words or images, on personal or third-party websites, including LinkedIn and other social networking sites designed for business people, without first securing written permission from management.

10. Prohibit employees from posting business e-mail addresses on personal and third-party websites, including business-related social networking sites, without first securing written permission from management. Thanks to automated spambots that troll the Internet for e-mail addresses, violation of this rule will increase the amount of spam hitting the violator's e-mail inbox and the company system as a whole.

11. Inform employees that they have no reasonable expectation of privacy when using the company's Internet system. Combat resentment and invasion of privacy claims by taking time to explain why you monitor, how monitoring works, what management is looking for, why policy compliance is mandatory, and what type of penalties await policy violators.

**REAL-LIFE INTERNET DISASTER STORY:
GOVERNMENT EMPLOYEES PREFER
PORN TO PRODUCTIVITY**

An investigation into District of Columbia government agencies revealed that nine employees had each surfed at least 20,000 porn sites (about 200 hits per workday) during 2007. In addition, another government employee had visited more than 48,000 pornographic sites during the same 12-month period. Prompted by an employee's complaint about the pervasive browsing and downloading of pornographic images, the investigation led to disciplinary action, ranging from two-week suspensions to terminations, against 32 employees from a dozen District agencies.[3]

12. ***Don't forget the company intranet.*** Use policy and training to make clear the fact that Internet rules and all other employment policies, including but not limited to electronic usage and content rules, apply to the organization's internal intranet system, too.

13. ***Discipline policy violators.*** If monitoring unearths a violation, act immediately to discipline the violator. In 2007, 30 percent of employers terminated employees for misusing the Internet.[4] Follow their lead and put some teeth in your Internet policy. Let one violation slide today, and you may find yourself battling a department full of Internet policy scofflaws tomorrow.

RECAP & e-POLICY ACTION PLAN

1. Risks associated with inappropriate Internet use include lost productivity, security breaches, and workplace lawsuits.

2. Corporate website content and employees' history of Internet surfing create electronically stored information that can be subpoenaed and used as evidence in litigation.

3. Video snacking threatens productivity, security, and company resources. It should be addressed within Internet policy and personal use rules.

4. Best practices call for the strategic management of Internet content and use through the implementation of written policy, employee training, and technology tools.

CHAPTER 14

Blog Rules[1]

With a new blog created every second,[2] the hype and hoopla surrounding blogging is understandable. From the millions of individuals with a conviction or cause they are eager to share with like-minded readers, to the thousands of corporations that are looking for a more effective and reliable way to polish reputations and build trust-based relationships with customers, to the bands of citizen journalists who are challenging the mainstream media by offering an alternative news source—everyone, it seems, is blogging.

In spite of the fact that 62 percent of Internet users don't even know what a blog is,[3] blogging has become wildly popular among enthusiasts at home and at the office. Without doubt, the blog is an electronic communications powerhouse that could have more impact on business communications and corporate reputations than e-mail, instant messaging, and traditional marketing-oriented websites combined.

> **e-Policy Rule 30:** The blog is an electronic communications powerhouse that could have more impact on business communications and corporate reputations than e-mail, instant messaging, and traditional marketing-oriented websites combined.

What Differentiates a Blog from a Website?

A blog is a website that is updated frequently (44 percent of bloggers write new posts at least once a day[4]), and on which bloggers post personal opinions, feelings, and commentary. Unlike websites, which are primarily intended as marketing tools and usually are written in the "company voice" by public relations and marketing professionals, blogs are almost always written in the first-person ("I") voice, and are almost always produced by people who possess no formal writers' training, but (ideally) possess a knack for writing in a conversational, reader-friendly tone.

Business Can't Afford to View Blogs as "Emerging" Technology

Far from an "emerging" technology that doesn't yet warrant employers' time and attention, blogging is here now; it's here to stay; and it is rapidly—and profoundly—changing the voice of business communications.

With 89 percent of corporations already blogging or planning to do so,[5] the phenomenon has infiltrated all types of businesses in all industry sectors around the globe. Among professionals, lawyers have been early and enthusiastic adopters of blogging. That's fitting, given the tremendous legal liability—including workplace lawsuits alleging copyright infringement, defamation, sexual harassment, and other claims—inherent in business blogging.

Business Blogs Are Not Right for Every Organization

A skillfully written, consistently updated, content-rich business blog can be an extremely effective way for organizations to position executives as industry thought leaders, gain the trust of prospective clients and business partners, facilitate productive two-way communication with customers and other important constituencies, enhance media relations, build brand awareness, and nurture valuable relationships with influencers in the blogosphere and beyond.

That does not mean, however, that a blog is a necessary or appropriate tool for every organization. On the contrary, the blogosphere is an extremely risky environment for business, full of potentially costly legal liabilities and other disasters. Before rushing to establish a business blog, it is essential to consider whether a blog is really right for your organization.

Two-Way Communication Compounds Risks

Unlike websites, which facilitate the one-way consumption of information, blogs are interactive, featuring the blogger's post and often encouraging comments from readers who are interested in weighing in on topics to keep the online dialogue going.

According to a Pew Internet & American Life Project survey, it is the interactive nature of blogs that appeals to the 12 percent of Internet users who post comments or other material on blogs.[6] Ironically, it is precisely the casual, conversational, back-and-forth nature of blogging that makes it both so appealing to blog writers and readers—and so potentially dangerous to business.

> **e-Policy Rule 31:** The casual, conversational, anything-goes nature of the blog makes it appealing to blog writers and readers—and potentially dangerous to business.

Slash Risks by Managing Commenters

Everyone (including customers and other third parties) who contributes to a blog's comment section has a voice—a voice that employers should consider silencing to preserve the organization's reputation and future. This can be done by deactivating or modifying the comment function, editing comments pre-post, or requiring readers to register before posting comments.

This recommendation is likely to spark outrage among blog enthusiasts who oppose efforts to edit or constrain the unfiltered, transparent, "honest" nature of blogs. Understood. Bear in mind, however, that the purpose of this book is to provide business readers with an understanding of the risks, policies, and procedures that will help organizations manage (and perhaps prevent) online disasters, while making the most of an important electronic business communications tool.

That said, while it may be standard operating procedure for blog publishers to allow anyone—customers, anonymous posters, vengeful former employees, competitors, and industry critics to name a few—to write freely in response to blog posts, the publishing of unmanaged comments is simply a bad business practice.

The publication of unedited third-party content is just one of many dangers blogs pose to business. Chapter 15 details a few of the other, significant blog-related risks that employers must address—through policy, training, and technology—before incorporating blogging into the organization's electronic business communication mix.

RECAP & e-POLICY ACTION PLAN

1. The blog is an electronic communications powerhouse that is likely to have more impact on business communications and corporate reputations than e-mail, instant messaging, and traditional marketing-oriented websites combined.

2. Employers cannot afford to dismiss the blog as an "emerging" technology that doesn't yet warrant consideration. Blogging is here now, and it's here to stay.

3. A skillfully written, regularly updated, content-rich business blog can be an extremely effective way for organizations to position executives as industry thought leaders, gain the trust of customers, and facilitate productive two-way communication with colleagues, customers, and other important constituencies.

4. Consider whether a blog is really right for your organization—or whether the legal liabilities and other risks associated with blogging simply outweigh the potential benefits.

5. The conversational nature of blogging makes it appealing to writers and readers—and potentially dangerous to employers. Take control of business blogging through the establishment of written rules and policies backed by employee training and technology tools.

CHAPTER 15

Blog Risks

The strategic management of blogs begins with the establishment of written rules and policies governing usage and content. Unfortunately, when it comes to blogging, rules and policy have not yet caught up with ease of use and popularity.

While the majority of employers (76 percent)[1] apply policy to help manage employees' e-mail use and content, and another 67 percent install technology to monitor Internet activity,[2] the same cannot be said of workplace blogging. Only 7 percent of organizations use formal policy to control business blogging,[3] and merely 12 percent monitor the blogosphere to see what is being written about the company, its people and products.[4]

The likelihood that some of your employees, customers, suppliers, former employees, shareholders, competitors, industry influencers, and other members of your corporate community are blogging is very real. In spite of the boom in blogging and the potentially costly risks associated with unmanaged content, employers have been slow to implement policies and procedures designed to control what employee-bloggers may—and may not—write about the organization, its people, products, and services.

FEW EMPLOYERS USE POLICY AND TECHNOLOGY TO MANAGE BLOG RISKS	
Policy governing the retention of blog business records	3%
Antiblog policy banning blog use on company time	5%
Policy governing personal postings on corporate blogs	6%

Policy governing business blog use and content	7%
Rules governing content employees may post on their own personal, home-based blogs	7%
Policy governing the operation of personal blogs on company time	9%
Monitor the blogosphere regularly to see what's being written about the company	12%
Use technology to block employee access to external blogs	18%[5]

Allowing employees free rein over corporate communications puts the organization at tremendous risk. Some blogs attract hundreds of thousands of readers a day—day after day. Do you really want your employees communicating with an audience that large without the benefit of comprehensive rules, clearly written policy, and formal training? Are you willing to risk having unmanaged and untrained employee-bloggers talk about your business, engage your customers, and accidentally (or intentionally) reveal top-secret company information?

It is important for organizations to maintain control over employees' blog content because blogs (whether business blogs or employees' personal blogs) can open the organization up to potential disasters including the loss of trade secrets, confidential information, and intellectual property; negative publicity, damaged reputations, and public embarrassment; workplace lawsuits alleging copyright infringement, defamation, sexual harassment, and other claims; court sanctions, legal settlements, and regulatory fines; lost employee productivity; and comment spam and splog (spam blog) attacks.

Before Rushing to Establish a Business Blog, Consider the Risks

Blogging poses risks to employers, employees, and even individual bloggers. Thousands of employees have been dooced (fired) for blogging, often on their own time using their own computers in the privacy of their own homes. A few high-profile personal bloggers have been the targets of embarrassing media coverage when their extremely private blogs have unintentionally gone public. Now we are starting to see individual bloggers being hit with lawsuits stemming from the content they and their readers are posting.

While an employee who has just been dooced for publishing catty comments about the boss may not agree, the fact is that the dangers blogging poses to individuals do not compare to the risks faced by employers who opt to host company blogs—particularly if they do so without written rules, policies, and procedures in place.

Consider the Risks Blogs Pose to Business

Litigation Risks: Copyright Infringement, Invasion of Privacy, Defamation, Sexual Harassment, Hostile Work Environment, Among Others

Bloggers' posts and readers' comments open the organization up to a broad range of legal risks and create a new pool of electronic evidence for prosecutors and litigators to dive into. Once you begin accepting commentary from customers and other third parties on your business blog, your organization becomes a publisher. As a publisher, you may be liable for defamation, slander, libel, and other claims triggered by the inappropriate content posted by outsiders in the comment section of your business blog.

An employer could face a "false light" defamation claim if an employee were to post a doctored image on the company's blog, falsely depicting a third party engaged in a crime. If injured by the doctored photo, it's possible that the third party could file a claim against both the blogger and the blogger's employer.[6]

If an employee were to intercept an e-mail message or other document and then post it to the organization's blog, the employer might face an invasion of privacy suit. Even if the employee were to do this at home on a personal blog, the employer might be held responsible if a reasonable person could assume that the employer was aware of the employee's actions.[7]

Vicarious liability (and the related legal concept of *respondeat superior*) is the legal term that is used when an organization is held responsible for the bad acts of its employees.[8] That said, an employer might be held responsible for the offensive, hostile, or illegal blog postings of a rogue employee on the organization's business blog, or perhaps even on the employee's personal, home-based blog.

Security Breaches: Loss of Trade Secrets, Confidential Information, Intellectual Property

Employees may be privy to the trade secrets and confidential information of business partners, customers, patients, and other third parties. If an employee were to post confidential information on the company's blog or on a personal blog that is hosted by the company's system, the company might be open to claims of trade secret violation and breach of contract. At the end of the day, once a trade secret becomes public knowledge, it holds no value as proprietary information.[9]

More than half of all employers surveyed (57 percent) are concerned about employees exposing sensitive company information on blogs, according to Forrester/ Proofpoint research.[10] No wonder 18 percent of companies surveyed by American Management Association and ePolicy Institute use technology to block employees' access to external blogs,[11] where they could easily post comments that disclose confidential company information.

Discovery Disasters: Mismanagement of Electronic Business Records

The amended FRCP make clear the fact that all electronically stored information—including posts and comments on company-sponsored blogs—is subject to discovery in federal lawsuits. While nearly a third of bloggers surveyed (32 percent) report that their primary reason for blogging is to "create a record of my thoughts,"[12] a scant 3 percent of organizations have in place a policy governing the retention of blog business records.[13]

Failure to manage blog-related business records is a potentially costly oversight for the 97 percent of organizations that, faced with a subpoena, will be in no position to produce the electronic evidence courts and regulators demand.

Public Relations Nightmares: Blog Storms Sink Corporate Reputations

Anyone with a computer or cell phone with Internet access can create a blog and start posting commentary within minutes. More than 50 percent of bloggers surveyed report that they write about companies, their products, or employees at least once a week.[14]

Orchestrated attacks in the blogosphere have tarnished corporate reputations, defamed individuals, disabled corporate operations, cost millions in lost revenues, and terrified the employees and families of scapegoats. According to one legal expert, at least half of all blog attacks are sponsored by competitors eager to destroy business rivals by unleashing the fury of the blogosphere.[15]

Loss of Control

Fear of losing control of the company message has stopped 22 percent of employers from adopting business blogs. Another 22 percent report that they steer clear of business blogs because of their concerns about what employees might say.[16]

The permalink, a unique Web address that can be created for every posting on a blog, adds to employers' concerns. Thanks to the permalink, blog posts typically remain accessible forever—unlike Web pages, which are subject to change and removal. The permalink creates a double-edged sword for business, giving blogs "a viral quality, so a pertinent post can gain broad attention amazingly fast—and reputations can get taken down just as quickly."[17]

Productivity Lost: Bloggers Log On and Slack Off

Whether blogging for business or personal reasons, employees are devoting (and often wasting) a tremendous amount of time reading, writing, and commenting on blogs. About 35 million workers, or one in four employees, spend 3.5 hours, or 9 percent of the work week, in the blogosphere, according to an *Advertising Age* "best-guess" analysis of blog-related surveys and data.[18]

In dollars and cents, what does all that nonwork-related blogging actually mean to employers? According to an employee productivity survey conducted by America Online and Salary.com, the average American worker wastes two hours a day on nonwork-related activities, with 45 percent of slackers reporting that their number-one goof-off activity is surfing the Web for personal reasons. The cost of all that slacking (online and otherwise) is a whopping $759 billion in lost productivity annually.[19]

Regulatory Violations: Risks to Publicly Traded and Regulated Companies

Unmanaged blog content could land a publicly traded company or regulated firm in hot water with the SEC, FINRA, or other federal, state, local, and industry regulators.

RECAP & e-POLICY ACTION PLAN

1. The strategic management of business blogs begins with the estab-
    lishment of written rules and policies governing professional and
    personal use, along with the type of content employees, customers,
    and other third parties may post.

2. Giving employees free rein over corporate communications—without
    strategic blog-related rules, policies, procedures, training, and tech-
    nology in place—opens the organization up to potential disasters
    including the loss of trade secrets, confidential information, and intel-
    lectual property; negative publicity, damaged reputations, and public
    embarrassment; workplace lawsuits alleging copyright infringement,
    defamation, sexual harassment, and other claims; court sanctions,
    legal settlements, and regulatory fines; and lost employee produc-
    tivity.

CHAPTER 16

Blog Policies and Best Practices

When it comes to employee blog use, there simply is no way to guarantee a completely risk-free environment. Whether blogging at the office or at home, even the most conscientious employees are prone to accidents and missteps. And there is always a chance that a rogue employee will intentionally publish blog content that creates problems for the organization.

That said, you can limit liability somewhat by developing and implementing comprehensive blog rules and policies that address issues including content, language, confidentiality, copyright, defamation, privacy, monitoring, compliance, personal use, retention, regulatory rules, and disciplinary action among other key issues.

Blog policies may not be required by law, but they certainly can help keep your organization out of legal hot water. To date, employers have spent millions of dollars defending and settling lawsuits related to the improper use of e-mail, IM, and the Internet. Blogging is certain to exacerbate an already litigious business environment.

Put Best Practices to Work with the 3-Es of Blog Risk Management

Employers are advised to put best practices to work by focusing on the 3-Es of blog risk management to comply with government regulations, prevent accidental misuse and intentional abuse, and reduce the risk of litigation and other blog-related disasters. The 3-Es are:

1. Establish policy.

2. Educate employees.

3. Enforce policy with discipline, coupled with blog content management and monitoring technology.

Establish Policy

Establish comprehensive, clearly written blog rules, policies, and procedures to govern blog use, content, and retention. Develop written blog policies keeping the following issues in mind:

- regulatory compliance

- litigation concerns

- security challenges

- productivity issues

- overall business needs

Be sure that your company's blog policy addresses all the risks and regulations facing your business and industry.

Blog policies should be clearly written and easy for employees to access, understand, and adhere to. Avoid vague language that may leave the organization's blog policy open to individual employee interpretation. Update written blog policies annually to ensure that your organization has rules, policies, and procedures in place to maximize compliance with changing regulations or laws, and to address any new risks that may arise.

Distribute a hard copy of the organization's written blog policy to all employee-bloggers, including the CEO and other senior executives who may be blogging. Insist that every employee sign and date a hard copy of the policy, acknowledging that they have read the policy, understand it, and agree to comply with it or accept disciplinary action up to and including termination.

Remember, employers are responsible for maintaining a lawful and compliant business environment that is harassment-free, discrimination-free, crime-free, and based on civil business behavior. Developing, implementing, and enforcing a comprehensive blog policy are steps toward ensuring that environment.

Educate Employees

Support written blog rules and policies with company-wide employee training conducted on-site by an in-person trainer or via online webinar or video. If your organization's CEO or members of senior management are blogging, be sure they participate in blog-related risks and rules training, too. Make sure employees understand that blog policy compliance is mandatory, not optional. Thanks to blog policy training, employees will better understand the risks, rules, and responsibilities of blogging. Consequently, employee-bloggers will be more likely to comply with policy, and the courts may be more accepting of the fact that your organization has made a reasonable effort to remain free from discrimination, harassment, hostility, and other objectionable behavior. A strategic blog policy and formal employee training program may one day help your organization defend itself against blog-related litigation.

Based on the legal principle known as vicarious liability, an employer may be held responsible for the accidental or intentional misconduct of employees. That should serve as a wake-up call to the 98 percent of employers who do not provide formal training to employee-bloggers, according to American Management Association and ePolicy Institute research.[1]

Enforce Policy

Enforce your organization's written blog rules and policy with a combination of disciplinary action, content management tools, and monitoring technology. If you have any doubt about your employees' willingness to adhere to the organization's blog usage and content rules, consider applying a technological solution to what essentially is a people problem. Consider utilizing a blog content management tool to review and aggregate employee posts, block banned or inappropriate content, and stay on top of employees' overall blogging activity.

Be sure to take advantage of technology tools that automatically monitor the blogosphere, including employees' business and personal blogs. Subscribe to blog search engines including Google News Alerts, PubSub, DayPop, Technorati, Feedster, IceRocket, or BlogPulse to find out just what your employee-bloggers have to say.

If monitoring reveals that an employee is violating the organization's blog policy, then it is essential for management to take immediate disciplinary action. Consistently apply discipline to show employees that management is serious about blog policy compliance. Failure to discipline one employee for blog-related misconduct may encourage other employees to violate the organization's written rules and policies and could create liability concerns for the organization. While fewer than 2 percent of employers have terminated employees for violations committed on business or personal blogs,[2] that number is certain to grow as workplace blogging becomes more prevalent.

Best Practices to Maximize Compliance and Minimize Risk

Consider incorporating the following best practices into your organization's blog policy program to help maximize employee compliance while minimizing organizational risk.

Establish a Written Policy Governing Your Organization's Business Blogs

If you operate internal or external blogs on which employees are free to post commentary (business and/or personal), then you must establish and enforce clear rules governing language, content, and usage.

Use your written policy to make sure employees know what type of language and content are allowed and what is banned from the organization's blogs. Join the 6 percent of organizations that have policies in place governing the publication of personal posts on corporate blogs.[3] Decide how you are going to handle the issue of business versus personal posts, and let employees know what the rules are.

Remind employees that blog content also must be in compliance with the organization's harassment and discrimination policies, confidentiality agreements, ethics rules, code of conduct, and other employment policies. To help prevent smoking-gun blog content from triggering a workplace lawsuit, stock slide, regulatory investigation, or media feeding frenzy, prohibit employees from posting critical opinions or defamatory comments about the organization, its products, services, employees, executives, competitors, partners, suppliers, customers—or anyone else for that matter.

Establish Policy Governing Employees' Personal Blog Use

Make sure employees understand that all the organization's written rules and policies apply, regardless of whether employees are operating business blogs from their cubicles at work or personal blogs from their bedrooms at home.

If you allow personal blogging on office computers, notify employees that the computer system is the property of the company, and employees have no reasonable expectation of privacy when using it to operate a personal blog. Also consider setting limits on the amount of time employees may devote to personal, non-business-related blogging. According to American Management Association and ePolicy Institute research, 9 percent of organizations already have implemented policies governing employees' personal blogging on company time.[4]

Instruct employees who operate personal nonbusiness-related blogs outside the office that they are prohibited from:

- discussing the organization, employees, clients, business partners, suppliers, or other third parties associated with the organization; posting company-related content.

- using the organization's logo, trademarks, advertising slogans, and other copyright-protected material.

- otherwise violating the organization's blog rules and corporate policies.

Make sure employees understand that the concept of free speech doesn't protect bloggers, and that violation of the organization's rules and policies—at work or at home—may result in the blogger's termination.

Guard Professional (and Personal) Secrets

Protect your organization's trade secrets and your employees' privacy by enforcing rules governing the posting of confidential information on employees' business and personal blogs. Do not allow employee-bloggers to post any content that could embarrass or otherwise harm the organization and its executives, employees, clients, partners, or suppliers. Do not allow employees to violate copyright law by posting copyright-protected material without written permission from the copyright owner.

Support your blog policy with employee training that's designed to educate employees about trade secrets, confidentiality, copyright, and privacy, among other issues that are important to your organization. Make sure employees understand what information the organization classifies as confidential data, trade secrets, intellectual property, etc., and what penalties await policy violators, up to and including termination.

Prohibit Anonymous Blogging

Do not allow employees to post anonymously by using pseudonyms or fake screen names. Anonymity creates an atmosphere in which some people might be tempted to write in an irresponsible, offensive, harassing, defamatory, or otherwise inappropriate manner. It also runs counter to the blogosphere's honest and transparent nature.

If employees are writing about business on a business blog, they should identify themselves as employees of the company. When employees write about business on personal blogs (strictly in compliance with the organization's rules and policies), their identities and affiliations with the company should be disclosed.

The courts have not responded consistently to organizations that have attempted to force Internet service providers to disclose the identities of anonymous bloggers who have posted allegedly defamatory statements.[5] Until the courts weigh in formally on this issue, it is in the organization's best interest to use policy to outlaw the use of pseudonyms on business blogs, as well as personal blogs that can adversely affect the organization in any way.

Instruct Bloggers to Use a Disclaimer

Require employees who operate personal blogs or post personal comments on the organization's business blog to incorporate a legal disclaimer stating that their views and opinions are their own, and are not necessarily representative of the organization's views and opinions. It is unclear how much protection a legal disclaimer would give the organization in the event of a workplace lawsuit, but it certainly cannot hurt your situation.[6]

Tell Bloggers How to Handle Media Inquiries

Your organization's business blog program may lead to increased inquiries from the media. According to the Annual Euro RSCG Magnet and Columbia University Survey, 28 percent of journalists rely on blogs for their daily reporting. Another 70 percent of reporters who use blogs do so to find story ideas, research, and uncover breaking news.[7]

Knowing that employee-bloggers are likely to be contacted directly by reporters, be sure to use your blog policy to instruct bloggers how to handle media calls. Some organizations, for example, want employee-bloggers to route all media inquiries to the organization's public relations department. To be safe, consider putting all bloggers through formal media training, so they are prepared to properly handle any media inquiries that may come in as a result of their posts.

Impose Financial Rules

Publicly traded companies must be careful that employee-bloggers do not disclose confidential financial material at the wrong time to the wrong audiences. Make sure employees with access to financial data and investor relations information are thoroughly informed, through written policy and formal training, about what may and may not be revealed to external audiences—and what penalties await organizations and employees who violate regulatory and organizational content and disclosure rules.

Require Bloggers to Keep Retention Policy in Mind

Blog posts and comments can create written business records that the organization must retain and archive for business, legal, and regulatory purposes. Use your organization's blog rules and retention policy to remind employees that, when writing blog posts and comments, they should be mindful of the fact that their written content may be retained, archived, and turned over to the courts or regulators one day. Stress the fact that business blogs call for professional, business-oriented content that will not harm the organization (or the individual blogger) in the event that it one day becomes part of a litigator's evidence pool.

Notify Employees of Your Corporate Blog Policy

There is no point having a policy if no one knows about it. According to one survey, 94 percent of workers in the United Kingdom report that they have not been informed of their employers' policies on blogs. Another 64 percent believe that employers should not be allowed to fire employees for blogging about their companies.[8] Perhaps if employers did a more effective job of explaining blog-related risks, rules, policies, and procedures to their employees, then employee-bloggers would have a clearer understanding of their rights, along with employers' responsibilities. The introduction of your organization's blog policy program is a good time to remind employees of all the organization's employment policies.

Use Technology to Help Manage People Problems

If you are monitoring employees' business and personal blogs, use your policy to inform them of that. Be sure to secure signed and dated consent forms from employees, acknowledging that they have given management permission to monitor their business and personal blog activity.[9] Sometimes just the knowledge that Big Brother is reading over their electronic shoulders is enough to keep employees in line when they are online.

Require Employees to Formally Acknowledge Blog Rules and Policy

Require all employees to sign and date an acknowledgment form, attesting to the fact that they have read the organization's blog policy, understand it, and agree to comply with it or accept the consequences. Ideally, the acknowledgment process should take place at the conclusion of formal employee training. Keep hard copies of all employee acknowledgment forms on file with the compliance officer or human resources manager. In the event of a workplace lawsuit, you may need signed and dated employee acknowledgment forms to demonstrate the fact that the organization takes blog policy and employee compliance seriously.

RECAP & e-POLICY ACTION PLAN

1. Whether your organization operates blogs internally (for employees' eyes only) or externally (for customers and the world to read), it is essential that you establish written rules and policies to support and enforce your strategic blog management program.

2. Limit liability somewhat by developing and implementing comprehensive blog rules and policies that address issues including content, language, confidentiality, copyright, defamation, privacy, monitoring, compliance, personal use, retention, regulatory rules, and disciplinary action among others.

3. Put best practices to work by focusing on the 3-Es of blog risk management: (1) establish policy, (2) educate employees, and (3) enforce policy with discipline and monitoring technology.

4. Distribute a hard copy of the organization's written blog policy to every employee-blogger, including the CEO and other senior executives who may be blogging. Insist that all employees sign and date a hard copy of the policy, acknowledging that they have read the policy, understand it, and agree to comply with all the organization's blog-related rules, policies, and procedures or accept disciplinary action up to and including termination.

CHAPTER 17

Social Networking and Video Site Risks and Rules

Once the domain of college students, social networking sites now are targeting older audiences—including the business community. While Facebook remains "the online hangout of just about every college student in the nation," the company is expanding its reach into the adult world, too. Growing at a rate of 3 percent a week, Facebook added 100,000 new registrations every day in 2007. MySpace, twice Facebook's size and the biggest player in terms of raw numbers, boasts 70 million users.[1]

Video sites are growing right along with social networking. Traffic to YouTube and other video sites doubled between 2006 and 2007. On an average day in 2007, the number of people accessing video sites was nearly twice that reported 12 months earlier, according to a Pew Internet & American Life Project survey. Average daily visits to video sites rose 100 percent among 30- to 49-year-olds in 2007, Pew reports.[2]

Facebook, MySpace, YouTube, and other popular social networking and video sites are likely to count some of your employees (and possibly a few vengeful ex-employees) among their users. Are you prepared to handle the potentially damaging fallout that can result when your business is publicly exposed?

Social Networking and Video Sites Expose Your Employees—and Company Secrets—Directly to the Public

Unlike mainstream news sites that authenticate information and vet sources before posting content, social networking and video sites allow anyone to post anything—without regard to fact checking or potential fallout.

Social networking and video sites increase the risk of confidentiality breaches and information leaks when employees and ex-employees— caught up in the unstructured, unfiltered, anything-goes culture of on-line sharing—discuss proprietary or private matters in words, pictures, and videos for all the world to see. Employers need to face some simple facts.

- Anyone with a computer and Internet access can establish a social networking page and start sharing harmful comments about your people, products, financials, and future in minutes.

- Anyone whose cell phone has a camera or video recorder can capture and upload potentially embarrassing or otherwise damaging photos and videos of employees, facilities, and secrets.

- Should dissatisfied workers or angry ex-employees post confidential company information on social networking or video sites, the devastating results can range from media expo-sure and public scrutiny to regulatory investigations and declining stock valuations.

> **e-Policy Rule 32:** Unlike mainstream news sites that authenti-cate information and vet sources before posting content, social networking and video sites allow anyone to post anything— without regard to fact checking or potential fallout.

REAL-LIFE SOCIAL NETWORKING DISASTER STORY: EX-EMPLOYEE REVEALS ZYPREXA MARKETING SECRETS ON YOUTUBE[3]

Facing civil and criminal investigations into the marketing of the antipsychotic drug Zyprexa®, and having already paid $1.2 billion to settle 30,000 Zyprexa-related lawsuits,[4] the last thing Eli Lilly needed was to have an insider disclose information about the company's alleged marketing improprieties to the world on YouTube.

That's exactly what happened when former Eli Lilly sales rep Shahram Ahari sat down with a reporter and discussed

Zyprexa sales and marketing tactics—on camera. "We were instructed to downplay those side effects,"[5] said Ahari, referring to allegations that the schizophrenia medicine triggers weight gain, blood sugar changes, and diabetes in mentally ill patients.[6]

As of June 2007, "only" 20,000 YouTube visitors had viewed the unauthorized Zyprexa video.[7] The rogue video certainly cannot help the pharmaceutical giant as it battles ongoing Zyprexa-related legal claims in state and federal courts.

Companies Lose Control of Corporate Messages, Courtesy of Online Posts

In the days before social networking and video sites gave everyone a public platform, public relations people carefully controlled corporate messages and strategically managed exactly how and when information was released to the media, investors, regulators, customers, and other important audiences.

Now, thanks to social networking and video sites, employees have gained direct access to the public, and employers have lost their iron-fisted control over company messages. "Take a cruise through YouTube," writes the *Indianapolis Star*, "and you will find videos that mention companies such as Lilly, WellPoint, Best Buy, Vonage, AT&T, and McDonald's."[8]

To find out what your staff, former employees, and others are revealing about your organization online, join the 10 percent of companies that monitor social networking sites.[9]

> **e-Policy Rule 33:** Thanks to social networking and video sites, employees have gained direct access to the public, and employers have lost their iron-fisted control over company messages.

Social Networking and Video Sites Create Electronic Business Records

Like blogs, corporate websites, and other electronic business communication tools, social networking and video sites can create business records. As detailed in Chapter 2, all electronically stored information is subject to discovery in litigation. If employees use the organization's computer system to post comments on Facebook or upload videos to YouTube, that content may be subpoenaed, must be produced, and could be used as evidence in workplace lawsuits or regulatory audits.

> **e-Policy Rule 34:** If employees use the organization's computer system to post comments on Facebook or upload videos to YouTube, that content may be subpoenaed, must be produced, and could be used as evidence in workplace lawsuits or regulatory audits.

Remind Employees That a Policy Is a Policy

As part of your company's social networking and video site policy, notify employees that a policy is a policy. Whether using company-provided computer resources during business hours, surfing the Web at home via personal tools and accounts after hours, or accessing the Internet in hotel rooms or airports, *all* employees are obligated to adhere to *all* company employment policies at *all* times.

Impose Usage Rules to Safeguard Productivity

In the United States alone, a whopping 86.6 million people accessed online networking sites over the 31 days of December 2007, reports Nielsen Online.[10] Plus, according to Nielsen/NetRatings, "the interactive nature of social networking sites keeps visitors coming back."[11]

While there may be some benefit to authorized employees expanding their business networks on company-approved sites, like LinkedIn, for example, don't allow employees to waste valuable company time reading, writing, uploading, and viewing personal—or business-related —content on unauthorized social networking and video sites.

Establish rules to limit or ban employee access to unauthorized business and personal networking and video sites during working hours. Support your policy with technology tools designed to prohibit access to banned social networking and video site URLs. Of the 65 percent of companies that use software to block connections to off-limits websites, 50 percent are most concerned about employees' visiting social networking sites, according to American Management Association and ePolicy Institute research.[12]

Cell Phone Rules Can Help Manage Social Networking and Video Site Risks

As part of your organization's cell phone policy (see Chapter 19), incorporate rules to help govern the photos and videos that employees take, record, and upload to social networking and video sites.

Notify users that rules and policies apply, regardless of whether employees are using company-provided Smartphones at the office on company time or personal cell phones at home after business hours.

To help minimize social networking and video site risks, consider incorporating the following rules into your corporate cell phone policy:

- Limit cell phone, Smartphone camera, or video recorder use. Specify that employees are not to take, transmit, download, or upload any company-related photos or videos to social networking or video sites without first securing written permission from an authorized member of company management. In addition, you can require the written permission of the subject of the photo or video.

- Prohibit cell phone, Smartphone camera, or video recorder use to take, transmit, download, or upload prohibited photos and videos to outlawed social networking or video sites. Banned photos and videos should include:

  "funny," embarrassing, or unprofessional images of company employees, executives, customers, suppliers, or other third parties;

  company buildings (internal and external), offices, facilities, operations, products, services, confidential data, and internal documents; and

  company logos, signage, trademarks, business cards, letterhead, literature, or any other printed or electronic content that can be used to identify the company or employees.

Social Networking Cuts Careers Short

Use formal policy and employee training to notify users that any employee who criticizes or embarrasses the company, reveals company secrets, or otherwise breaks any employment rule or policy via a social networking or video site faces disciplinary action, up to and including termination.

In the United States, private employers operating in employment-at-will states have the right to fire employees for just about any reason, including violation of social networking policies, video site rules, and other employment policies, as long as the dismissal is not discriminatory or in retaliation for whistle-blowing or union organizing.[13]

To date, less than 1 percent of employers have fired workers for posting business-related content on social networking or video sites, according to the 2007 Electronic Monitoring & Surveillance Survey from American Management Association and ePolicy Institute.[14] With some 87 million Americans visiting social networking sites on a monthly basis,[15] it's safe to assume that the number of online networking and video site violations—and terminations—will grow.

The First Amendment Does Not Protect Social Networkers

Many U.S. employees mistakenly believe that the First Amendment grants them the right to say or post whatever they want on video sites, social networking profiles, and personal blogs. It doesn't. The First Amendment only restricts government control of speech; it says nothing about private employers.

That said, legal experts note that state or federal employees may be protected by the First Amendment.[16] In addition, some states have recently put laws in place to protect employees' after-hours behavior. Colorado and Minnesota, for example, have enacted laws to protect employees from discrimination when they engage in lawful activities away from the office and after business hours, according to employment lawyer George Lenard of the law firm Harris Dowell Fisher & Harris, as reported by the *New York Times*.[17]

Not all states offer employees such protections. Employers are advised to retain the services of an employment law expert to research the termination-related laws of every state in which your organization operates or employs workers.

REAL-LIFE VIDEO SITE DISASTER STORY: RACIST REMARKS CUT COP'S CAREER SHORT

Susan L. Purtee, a 15-year veteran of the Columbus, Ohio, police department triggered a citywide uproar when offensive personal videos she and her sister had posted on YouTube and their personal website went public.

In the videos, Purtee and her sister disparaged Jews, blacks, Cubans, and illegal immigrants. The mayor and other city leaders denounced the videos, and a formal investigation to determine whether Purtee had engaged in conduct unbecoming of an officer was launched.

Purtee did not appear in uniform or identify herself as a Columbus police officer in any of the videos, but the sisters' website does note that she works in law enforcement.

When asked about the videos, Purtee's sister told the *Columbus Dispatch*, "We've had a lot of fun with it. I don't see that we've ever harmed anybody."

City officials and the public disagreed, and the fallout from the officer's YouTube videos was extensive. The Anti-Defamation League labeled the videos anti-Semitic, racist, and hateful. Columbus's mayor expressed concern for the reputation of the police department and the city.

Equally troubling is the fact that "the videos provide strong fodder for defense attorneys with cases involving Purtee," according to attorney R. William Meeks. "Good lawyers labor to impeach the credibility of all witnesses against their clients, police included . . . An obvious area of impeachment is bias," Meeks said. As an example of how bias can torpedo a prosecution, Meeks pointed to Mark Fuhrman, the police officer whose history of making racist remarks came to light when he testified against O. J. Simpson in his murder case.[18]

RECAP & e-POLICY ACTION PLAN

1. Social networking and video sites increase the risk of confidentiality breaches and information leaks when employees and ex-employees disclose proprietary or private matters in words, pictures, and videos.

2. Unlike mainstream news sites that authenticate information and vet sources before posting content, social networking and video sites allow anyone to post anything—without regard to fact checking or potential fallout.

3. Thanks to social networking and video sites, employees have gained direct access to the public, and employers have lost their iron-fisted control over company messages.

4. Combine written policy with employee training and monitoring technology to help manage social networking and video site use, content, and risks.

PART SEVEN

Software Rules

CHAPTER 18

Software Risks, Rules, Policies and Best Practices

Would you walk into your local computer store and steal a package of software for business or personal use? Of course not. Yet many people who would never consider shoplifting from a retail store are guilty of "softlifting," or pirating, computer software.[1]

Worldwide, software piracy is so pervasive that 35 percent of the software installed on personal computers in 2006 was pirated, or illegally obtained. That amounts to more than $40 billion in global losses for the software industry, a 15 percent increase over the previous year, according to the 2007 BSA-IDC Global Software Piracy Study.[2]

Don't Let Software Pirates Sink Your Corporate Ship

Software piracy is the unauthorized duplication and use of licensed computer software. Software piracy poses a unique challenge to the software industry and employers. Unlike audio tapes and videotapes, which tend to lose quality with each duplication, computer software can be copied repeatedly with almost no impact on quality. For little or no cost, any PC user can produce thousands of copies of software that may have taken years of effort and millions of dollars to develop. In the United States alone, the software industry lost $7.3 billion as a result of piracy in 2006, an increase of $400 million over 2005, according to the 2007 BSA-IDC Global Software Piracy Study.[3]

Software piracy can take place at the office or in the home. Copyright laws apply equally, regardless of whether it is a $1,000 project management program that a department head has illegally copied and distributed to dozens of employees or a $100 computer game that is licensed to one person, then copied and shared with half a dozen friends and family members.

REAL-LIFE SOFTWARE PIRACY DISASTER STORY: UNLICENSED SOFTWARE COSTS COMPANY $3.5 MILLION

An international media firm, charged by the Business Software Alliance (BSA) with using unlicensed software, paid a whopping $3.5 million in 2007 to settle the piracy claim. In addition to the record-setting settlement, the offending company endured a police raid and the freezing of its assets as the BSA pursued the criminal complaint on behalf of software manufacturers Adobe, Autodesk, Avid, and Microsoft.[4]

Software Piracy Takes Many Forms

According to the Software & Information Industry Association (SIIA), software piracy takes a variety of forms and has developed a language of its own.

- *Softlifting:* If you purchase software with a single-user license, then load it on multiple computers or servers, you are guilty of softlifting. Individuals who copy and share software with friends and family members are softlifters. So are executives, managers, department heads, and employees who copy software for use by coworkers, independent contractors, clients, or other parties who are not licensed to use it.

- *Counterfeiting:* Individuals who illegally produce, distribute, and/or sell software that is made to look like the real thing are known as software counterfeiters. How can you tell the difference between legitimate and counterfeit software? As a rule, if a software deal looks too good to be true, it probably is.

- *Renting:* The unauthorized selling of software for temporary use is called *renting.* It also is illegal.

- *Original equipment manufacturer (OEM) unbundling:* Unscrupulous distributors sometimes sell software that has been unbundled, or separated, from the hardware with which it was intended to be sold. Never purchase software that does not come with complete documentation, including registration papers and a user manual. The paperwork is your proof that the deal is legitimate.

- *Uploading and downloading:* Software piracy extends to the Internet as well as programs copied onto disks and CDs. While it may be easy, it is illegal to upload or download copyrighted software from the Internet or bulletin boards without permission from the software copyright owner.

- *Hard disk loading:* It is illegal to install unauthorized copies of software onto the hard disks of personal computers. Dealers sometimes do this in order to create an incentive for consumers to purchase hardware.[5]

The Three Faces of Workplace Piracy

In business situations, software piracy typically takes three forms: violating a single user license, bringing software from home, and downloading licensed software from the Internet.

Single User License

Often an employer or employee will buy a piece of software with a single user license, then load it onto multiple computers throughout the office. Perhaps your organization hasn't adequately budgeted for the software needs of all employees, and a department head decides to copy programs in order to stretch dollars and complete assignments. Maybe your employees, eager for the flexibility of telecommuting, opt to download corporate software onto their home computers. Possibly a client, eager for all suppliers to use the same software, has provided your organization with one licensed copy and instructions to share it with everyone on the project team.

Whatever the reason, it is illegal and unethical to duplicate software that is licensed for single use. Employers who get caught with pirated software on their premises often pay a high price for what can be a very costly mistake. The fines for illegal software use run as high as $150,000 per title infringed. Multiply $150,000 times every employee in your office, and you could be looking at a staggering sum. Add the cost of buying replacement software for each employee's computer, and it's no surprise that a company sued for copyright infringement easily could face a six- to seven-figure bill. That's ironic, considering that some organizations mistakenly view software piracy as a means to stretch budgets.

> **e-Policy Rule 35:** It is illegal, unethical, and potentially very expensive to duplicate software that is licensed for single use. The high cost of software piracy really adds up when you calculate the expense of buying replacement software, the sting of negative publicity, and the havoc wreaked by virus-infected software.

Bringing Software from Home

Employees who bring software into the office from home also contribute to the piracy problem. Employees who think they are doing their colleagues and their company a favor by supplying duplicated software inadvertently may, in fact, be creating a legal problem that could cost everyone their jobs.

Internet Downloading

Downloading copyrighted software, clip art, fonts, and music from the Internet or bulletin boards also gets businesses into trouble. An employee who downloads software without securing permission from the copyright holder may save the organization time and money in the short run, but that short-term fix can prove very costly, in terms of lost productivity, fines, defense costs, and negative publicity should the software police pay a visit.

Softlifters Will Be Prosecuted

Think the software police are a joke? They're not. Software piracy is an expensive problem, both for the software manufacturers who lose money every time a title is copied illegally and for the employers who face civil or criminal consequences if caught with pirated programs in the workplace.

Fed up with business's illegal software use, the software industry and federal government have gotten tough with pirates. Software piracy is a federal offense. If suspected of using unlicensed software, you are likely to be visited by U.S. marshals and representatives of the SPA Anti-Piracy Division of the Software & Information Industry Association (SIIA) or the Business Software Alliance (BSA). Acting on a whistle-blower's tip, the SIIA and BSA can obtain a court order, raid your organization, audit your software usage, and assess heavy fines.

REAL-LIFE SOFTWARE PIRACY DISASTER STORIES: SIX-FIGURE SETTLEMENTS SINK PIRATES

Software piracy is a pervasive global problem. The following are a few recent cases in the United States alone: A Florida-based mortgage survey company settled a software copyright infringement case with the SIIA for $150,000 in 2007.[6] Three Midwestern financial services companies paid a combined $420,000 in 2008 to settle BSA claims of software piracy.[7] Three New York State–based companies paid $269,000 in 2008 to settle piracy claims filed by the BSA.[8]

The Software Police Rely on Whistle-Blowers' Tips

Both the SIIA and BSA operate on tips called in to their toll-free software piracy hotlines or sent electronically to their online hotlines. These hotlines, which generally field tips from disgruntled employees and vengeful ex-employees, have paid off for the software industry and corporate whistle-blowers alike.

The BSA and SIIA offer rewards of up to $1 million for verifiable reports of corporate piracy.[9] In 2006, SIIA received 523 piracy tips (two per business day), with more than half (58 percent) coming from IT staff and managers, the people most familiar with the organization's legal and illegal software use. Tipsters, on average, received just under $5,000 from SIIA in 2006.[10]

The High Cost of Software Piracy

If found guilty of using illegally copied software, your organization could face enormous fines. If sued for civil copyright infringement, the penalty is up to $150,000 per title infringed. If convicted of a criminal violation, the fine is up to $250,000, coupled with a maximum of five years in prison.[11]

Even cooperative companies are likely to end up with fines that cost the organization far more than it would have cost to buy new software in the first place.

The high cost of software piracy really starts to add up when you calculate the cost of buying replacement software, the sting of negative publicity, and the havoc wreaked by virus-infected pirated software.

> **e-Policy Rule 36:** If found guilty of using illegally copied software, your organization could face enormous fines. If sued for civil copyright infringement, the penalty is up to $150,000 per title infringed. If convicted of a criminal violation, the fine is up to $250,000 and up to five years imprisonment.

Workplace Piracy Is Fueled by Ignorance

The proliferation of software piracy may be due, in part, to ignorance. Employees and managers may not realize it is a crime to copy licensed software. Some employee-pirates actually may view themselves as corporate heroes, saving the organization dollars by copying software. Other employees may be unaware that one does not "own" software; one merely owns a license to use a software title. Regardless of the reason for duplicating licensed software, it is wrong legally and morally.

How to Avoid a Run-In with the Software Police

Employers who want to avoid a run-in with the software police should take a three-pronged approach to prevention: (1) educate employees and managers about software piracy, (2) establish and maintain a strict anti-piracy stance, and (3) incorporate a software usage policy into your organization's overall e-policy program.

The benefits of establishing a software usage policy include protecting your organization from piracy-related litigation, insulating your computers from defective software that could introduce viruses into your network, and reducing the overall costs of software usage.

> **e-Policy Rule 37:** Establish a strict software usage policy to protect your organization from litigation, insulate your computers from defective software that could carry viruses and other malicious intruders, and reduce overall software costs.

Software Usage Best Practices

While employees contribute significantly to the presence of illegal software in the workplace, employers typically are held legally responsible for software violations. The best advice for employers: Monitor and manage employees' software use before you face a time-consuming and costly lawsuit, stiff fines, or the loss of valuable data courtesy of virus-laden software. Here are some guidelines for employers who want to keep the workplace free from software piracy.[12]

Adopt an Antipiracy Stance

Make it clear to employees that your organization does not condone the illegal duplication of software and will not tolerate it. Violation of the organization's software usage policy could lead to disciplinary action or termination.

Review Copyright Law with Employees

From the moment of its creation, software automatically is protected by federal copyright law. Purchasing a license for a copy of software does not give you the right to make additional copies without permission of the copyright owner. The licensee is allowed to copy the software onto a single computer and make one backup copy for archival purposes. That's it.

The rules are simple. You must purchase a new software package for every computer on which a given program will run. No software, fonts, clip art, photos, videos, or music may be downloaded from the Internet without permission from the copyright holder. It also is illegal to rent, lease, or lend original copies of software without permission of the copyright owner.

> **e-Policy Rule 38:** Software is protected by federal copyright law. You must purchase new software for every computer on which a given program runs.

Audit Your Organization's Computers

Determine what software is available on each computer workstation and what licenses you own to support the software used. If you find illegal copies, destroy them and buy new software before the software police order you to do so. The time and money you invest in replacing illegal software will be a fraction of the productivity and financial loss you will experience if the SIIA or BSA catch you operating with pirated software.

Educate Managers and Department Heads

Managers should understand the organization's software costs, needs, and risks. Teach managers to treat software like any other business asset. Budget for it and take appropriate action against employee-pirates, as detailed in your software usage policy.

Teach Employees the Lingo of Pirates

To Internet insiders, "warez" means pirated or illegal software. In general, the standard in the Internet community is to create plural words that describe illegal activity by using the letter z instead of s. Notify employees that software or sites labeled "warez" usually contain illegal material and should be avoided and reported to the organization's information technology director.

Recognize the Hidden Costs of Software Piracy

Stolen software comes with no guarantees and no technical support. If you develop a problem or become infected with a computer virus, you are on your own. The solution to your problem could end up costing you more than licensed software would have cost in the first place. Make sure managers and employees understand that the few dollars they save by copying software today could wind up costing the company hundreds of thousands (possibly millions) of dollars tomorrow in fines and replacement costs.

Document Software Purchases

Attach copies of purchase orders to licenses. Register all software with the manufacturer. Appoint an employee or department to track and record the organization's software purchases and use.

Watch for Illegally Bundled Software

If a reseller offers a computer system that's bundled with numerous copies of popular software programs, check to see if all the software comes complete with full documentation, including license agreements, original disks, manuals, and registration cards. If not, run away from this "deal."

Understand Your License Agreements

Software usually includes specific license provisions that allow for the use of programs at work, home, or on your organization's computer network. If you are confused about what a license covers, call the software manufacturer and ask.

Remove Temptation

If employees' software needs exceed your organization's supply, fix the problem. Purchase needed software before employees, eager for a quick fix, start to copy programs.

Enforce Your Efforts

To be effective, your organization's antipiracy efforts must be communicated clearly and enforced consistently. Institute a program of continuing education for managers and employees. Conduct periodic audits. Make the retention of documentation mandatory. Put teeth in your self-policing program by consistently enforcing penalties for violators.

RECAP & e-POLICY ACTION PLAN

1. As an employer, you cannot afford to ignore software piracy or dismiss it as insignificant. Adopt a strict antipiracy stance and enforce it consistently.

2. Develop a comprehensive software piracy and policy training program for employees. Do not assume employees know anything about software piracy or the laws regarding copyright infringement.

Make it clear that softlifting is a serious crime that can trigger stiff penalties for the company and put employees' jobs at risk.

3. Make sure managers, supervisors, and department heads understand what software piracy is and why it is important for the organization to enforce a zero-tolerance posture regarding piracy. In particular, managers who traditionally have viewed software piracy as a victimless crime, and a relatively harmless way to stretch a departmental budget, need to be educated about the risks inherent in software piracy.

PART EIGHT

Cell Phone
and Texting Rules

CHAPTER 19

Cell Phone and Text Messaging Risks, Rules, Policies, and Best Practices

In business and personal life, the cell phone has become ubiquitous. In 2007, there were some 236 million business and residential cell phone users in the United States alone, up from 4.3 million in 1990, according to the Cellular Telecommunications & Internet Association.[1]

Cell phone technology actually has triggered a cultural shift in our society, with handheld phones making coin-operated pay phones and the iconic phone booth obsolete. Once a common—and in-demand—feature of airport terminals, street corners, and hotel lobbies, working pay phones in public booths are now almost impossible to find. As recently as 1998, there were 2.6 million pay phones in service across the United States. Today that number has dwindled to 1 million, motivating AT&T to announce it would vacate the coin-operated pay phone business by year-end 2008.[2]

It's no surprise that cell phone technology so swiftly brought the pay phone era to its end. The cell phone offers users the freedom to make or take a call, send text messages, and transmit photos and videos—features most callers simply never dreamed of just a few years ago.

Unfortunately, the cell phone, just like other electronic business communication tools, saddles employers with increased risks. Potentially costly cell phone–related disasters include driving-related insurance and legal claims, lost productivity, security breaches, data theft, business record gaffes, and etiquette breaches. Not to mention the fact that cell phone users can annoy and distract those around them.

> **e-Policy Rule 39:** Cell phones saddle employers with increased risks including driving-related insurance claims and lawsuits, lost productivity, security violations, data theft, business record gaffes, and etiquette breaches.

Recommended Best Practice: Hang Up when You Drive!

The cell phone is a multitasker's dream. The ability to conduct business by phone while driving has been a productivity-enhancing boon to many. For others, however, mobile phone convenience has cost lives and created legal nightmares.

American drivers logged about 1 billion minutes daily in cell phone calls in 2005, accounting for about 40 percent of all cell phone business.[3] When it comes to employees driving while talking or text messaging, employers must balance productivity (the ability to conduct business in transit) versus liability (employers may be held legally responsible when distracted employees cause traffic accidents while conducting business via cell phones).

Seventy-three percent of people use cell phones while driving, and another 20 percent admit to texting as they drive, according to Nationwide Insurance.[4] Unfortunately, motorists who use cell phones while driving are four times more likely to crash and injure themselves, according to the Insurance Institute for Highway Safety.[5] Eighty percent of crashes and 65 percent of near-crashes result from driver inattention within three seconds of the accident, reports the National Highway Traffic Safety Administration.[6] Drivers who talk on handheld or hands-free cell phones are just as impaired as drunken drivers, according to a University of Utah study.[7]

To help decrease driver distractions and increase traffic safety, some 40 countries restrict or ban cell phone use while driving.[8] The states of Washington, New York, New Jersey, Connecticut, California, and the District of Columbia are among the jurisdictions that have passed laws banning handheld cell phone use while driving. Text messaging while driving is illegal in states including Washington and New Jersey.[9] There's no doubt that other states will adopt similar legislation governing talking and texting while driving.

**REAL-LIFE CELL PHONE DISASTER STORIES:
EMPLOYERS LEGALLY RESPONSIBLE FOR
EMPLOYEES' CELL PHONE-RELATED ACCIDENTS**

According to the National Conference of State Legislatures, the precedent for cell phone–related employer liability dates back to 1999, when Smith Barney paid a $500,000 settlement to the family of a motorcyclist who was killed by a broker who was busy making sales calls on his personal cell phone at the time of the accident.

Smith Barney's half-million-dollar settlement was dwarfed by the state of Hawaii, which paid $1.5 million to a pedestrian who was hit by a teacher who was chatting on a cell phone while driving.

In Arkansas, a lumber company paid a whopping $16.2 million to a woman who was struck and disabled by an on-duty salesman who was talking on his cell phone while driving.[10]

e-Policy Rule 40: Employers may be held legally responsible for car crashes caused by distracted employees talking or texting while driving.

Employers May Be Legally Responsible for Crashes Caused by Employees Talking or Texting While Driving

Do you provide employees with company cars, operate a fleet of vehicles, employ professionals to drive trucks or operate heavy equipment, or require employees to drive their own cars during the ordinary course of business? If so, you'll want to establish rules prohibiting cell phone use and text messaging while driving. Fail to do so, and you'll face the possibility of distracted drivers causing potentially costly accidents.

e-Policy Rule 41: Ban all employee cell phone use (making calls, taking calls, listening to voice mail, or text messaging) while driving during business hours.

Under the legal principle of vicarious liability, an employer may be held legally responsible for the negligent acts (including car crashes) that employees commit in the course of business. While a clear and comprehensive cell phone policy that is supported by formal employee training may give your organization some defense from liability, it won't eliminate legal culpability 100 percent. The best advice is to ban all cell phone use (making calls, taking calls, listening to voice mail, or text messaging) while driving during business hours. Whether driving in your own car or a company-provided vehicle, or even using hands-free technology, cell phone use is banned. No exceptions.

Support Cell Phone Policy with Employee Education

To make your organization's cell phone policy stick, you must support it with employee education. Without formal training that spells out cell phone risks, company rules, and the penalties policy violators face, your policy is likely to meet resistance from employees who have grown accustomed to talking and texting while driving.

Outlaw Employee Cell Phone Use While Driving

Follow the lead of Johnson & Johnson and other companies that have established formal rules prohibiting employees from using cell phones while driving company-owned vehicles.[11] Keep your company and employees legal and reduce the risk of cell phone–related crashes and the resulting injuries, fatalities, insurance claims, and lawsuits. Instruct drivers to pull to the side of the road before engaging in either handheld or hands-free cell phone conversations. Better yet, impose a rule requiring that all phones (company-owned and personal) be turned off when employees are driving. Allow workers to make calls and check and respond to messages only after pulling off the road.

Put this rule in writing as part of your company's cell phone policy. Make it clear that the rule applies regardless of whether employees are driving their own cars or company-owned vehicles, whether they are using their own phones or company-provided cell phones, and whether they are using handheld or hands-free cell phones.

A rule is a rule, and all employees must abide by it while on company time, regardless of the vehicle or phone used. Insist that all employees sign and date an acknowledgment form, attesting that they have read the cell phone policy, understand it, and agree to comply with it, or accept the consequences, up to and including termination.

At the end of the day, a clearly written cell phone policy does not guarantee employers freedom from liability, but it might just save the life of an employee, innocent pedestrian, or passenger.

REAL-LIFE CELL PHONE DISASTER STORIES:
EMPLOYERS LIABLE WHEN
EMPLOYEE-DRIVERS CRASH

A Virginia jury awarded $2 million in damages to the family of a 15-year-old pedestrian who was hit and killed by an attorney who was driving erratically while using a handheld cell phone to conduct business. Bode & Grenier, the law firm representing the teen's family, sued both the driver and her employer on the grounds of vicarious liability and direct negligence.[12]

In another employment-related case, Atlanta-based construction company Beers Skanska Inc. paid $4.75 million to settle a lawsuit involving an employee who, while making business calls on a company-provided cell phone, caused a car crash that resulted in serious injuries.[13]

Text Messaging Policies and Best Practices

While text messaging, or texting, may be new to some business users, TXT MSG (in text-speak) actually is a long-established technology. According to the Mobile Data Association, text messaging dates back to 1992, when a British engineer used a computer to send the message "Merry Christmas" to a colleague's mobile handset.[14]

In the United States alone, texting nearly doubled in 2006, increasing to some 159 billion messages for the year, up from 81 billion the previous year, according to CTIA, the Wireless Association.[15] The word "texting" has become such a commonly used and recognized term that it was reported to be on the short list for inclusion in the 2008 edition of *Webster's New World College Dictionary.*[16]

Impose Rules to Manage Texting Risks

When it comes to texting risks, safety and legal liability are the two primary concerns of employers. Distracted drivers who cause traffic accidents while reading, writing, and replying to text messages risk lives and lawsuits. Texters who send offensive messages may open the organization up to claims of harassment, discrimination, or a hostile work environment.

**REAL-LIFE TEXTING DISASTER STORY:
DEFAMATORY MESSAGE STRIKES OUT**

In 2006, an irate mother filed suit against the St. Louis Cardinals baseball team for publishing a defamatory text message about her 17-year-old daughter on Busch Stadium's electronic message board, which posts text messages submitted by fans. During a class trip to a game against the Kansas City Royals, the Cardinals organization ran a message from one of the girl's classmates, proclaiming that "[Name] has an STD! Eww!"

According to the lawsuit, the message, which was seen by some 48,000 fans, so traumatized the victim that she stayed out of school for the balance of the semester. The lawsuit argued that the Cardinals "owed a duty of reasonable care to all fans in attendance," which was breached when the ball club posted the defamatory text message "to anyone who could read."[17]

4COL, Keep TXT MSG Professional and Businesslike

Because text messages are limited to 160 characters,[18] texters have created an abbreviation-based language that may prove confusing to the uninitiated, including parents (95 percent of whom say they don't understand text lingo[19]) and business people far removed from high school.

Similar to the abbreviations commonly used by some e-mail and IM users, text abbreviations have no place in business-related communications. Messages like "4COL, Keep TXT MSG Professional" ("For Crying Out Loud, Keep Text Messaging Professional") are bound to confuse uninitiated readers who don't know text-speak.

As part of your cell phone policy, incorporate a rule banning the use of text abbreviations in the course of written business communications. In addition to banning the use of abbreviated text-speak, be sure to give your employees specific and clear content rules and language guidelines for cell phone use and text messaging. Stress the fact that cell phones are to be used primarily for business reasons, and that all spoken conversations and text messages must be professional and businesslike. Use your cell phone policy to remind employees of your company's employment policies, which should outlaw gossip, rumors, defamatory comments, disparaging remarks, and other inappropriate commentary.

Inform employees that company-provided cell phones, pagers, and other electronic communication tools are intended for business use. Be clear. Be specific. Do not leave your content rules and language guidelines open to individual interpretation by employees. Spell out exactly what type of content and language is allowed, and what is banned. Remind employees that improper content puts the individual texter at risk of termination, public embarrassment, and possible criminal charges, as illustrated by the following real-life texting disaster story.

REAL-LIFE TEXTING DISASTER STORY: MAYOR'S POLITICAL CAREER SQUANDERED ON A KEYBOARD

When some 14,000 flirtatious and sexually charged text messages transmitted between Detroit Mayor Kwame M. Kilpatrick and his chief of staff, Christine Beatty, went public in 2008, the married mayor faced a political scandal that threatened his job and law license and a possible stint in prison.[20]

Transmitted on Beatty's city-owned pager, the amorous text messages indicate that the two had an intimate relationship. The messages also suggest that Kilpatrick and Beatty committed perjury by lying about the affair under oath during a 2007 lawsuit against the city. A felony perjury conviction carries a maximum prison sentence of 15 years.

Immediate fallout from the scandal included a call for the mayor's resignation from the city's 900-member municipal union and public embarrassment for Kilpatrick's wife and family as the tragic technosexual tale spread nationwide thanks to coverage in the *New York Times,* Associated Press, and other prominent media outlets.[21]

> While text transmitted via standard consumer-grade text messaging technology may disappear following delivery, messages sent via business-grade text messaging technology may be saved, stored, and used as evidence, just like e-mail.[22]
>
> Remind employees that company-provided cell phones, pagers, and texting tools are provided primarily for business purposes. Employees have absolutely no reasonable expectation of privacy when phoning or texting.

Incorporate Confidentiality Rules in Cell Phone and Text Messaging Policy

Be sure employees understand that an overheard cell phone conversation could put the company and its secrets at risk. Instruct employees to hold confidential and business-critical conversations in private.

Prohibit employees from disclosing or discussing passwords, account numbers, company financials, intellectual property, trade secrets, bids, proposals, or other confidential or proprietary information via cell phone in airport terminals, airplanes, trains, restaurants, bars, elevators, or any other location where they are likely to be overheard or read by others.

> **e-Policy Rule 42:** Address confidentiality rules as part of your cell phone and text messaging policy. Be sure employees understand that an overheard cell phone conversation or an indiscreet text message could put the company and its secrets at risk.

Enforce Cell Phone Camera and Video Rules

Cell phones with built-in cameras and video recorders can spell disaster for employers. In the hands of a malicious or disgruntled employee, a camera or video recorder may be too great a temptation to resist.

Merely 19 percent of employers use formal policy to control the capture and transmission of images via camera phone, according to American Management Association and ePolicy Institute research.[23]

Failure to impose written rules governing the use of cell phone camera and video capabilities is a potentially costly oversight.

Best practices call for the use of written policy to ban the use of cell phones to take, transmit, download, upload, print, or copy photos or videos that are not directly related to company business. Communicate the fact that prohibited photos and videos include, but are not limited to:

- "Funny," embarrassing, or unprofessional images

- Photos or videos of company buildings (internal and external), offices, or facilities

- Operations, products, services, confidential data, or internal documents

- Employees, executives, customers, suppliers, or any other third party without the express permission of the subject and company management.

> **e-Policy Rule 43:** Ban the use of cell phones to take, transmit, download, upload, print, or copy photos or videos that are not directly related to company business.

REAL-LIFE CELL PHONE DISASTER STORY: SNAPSHOT OF SEXUAL ABUSE

During a company meeting, a male employee used his cell phone camera to film up the skirt of a female colleague. The "cameraman" then downloaded the images to his company computer, recharged his phone, and continued filming his unsuspecting victim.

A coworker observed the violation but was wary of getting the cameraman fired or embroiling himself in an ugly situation. Instead, the witness anonymously consulted the *New York Times Magazine*'s ethics columnist for advice on how to handle the situation. The witness, who did eventually contact his employer's human resources department, told "The Ethicist" that the photographer was still employed by the company, and that the unsuspecting victim was still believed to be unaware that her privacy had been violated.[24]

This is a prime example of why employers should impose comprehensive cell phone rules, and then support those rules with formal employee training. A well-trained employee would not need to consult "The Ethicist" for advice. An informed employee would have recognized the cameraman's sleazy behavior as a violation of the company's cell phone policy (not to mention a breach of sexual harassment guidelines) and would promptly have alerted management to the violation. By hesitating, the witness gave the offender time to post the images online and then delete the evidence from his company computer.

Control Costs and Increase Productivity by Limiting Personal Cell Phone and Text Messaging Use

More than a quarter (27 percent) of employers have imposed policy governing personal cell phone use at work, according to American Management Association and ePolicy Institute research.[25] Decrease costs and increase productivity by setting clear limits on personal cell phone and texting use.

Cell phones have become such an integral part of daily life that it's easy for users to forget about the expenses associated with talking and texting—particularly if management is footing the bill. According to a Pew/Internet report on American cell phone use, 41 percent of cell phone owners make phone calls simply as a way to kill free time when traveling or waiting for someone. No wonder 36 percent of cell owners report that they are occasionally shocked by the size of their monthly bill.[26]

e-Policy Rule 44: Control costs, manage productivity, and mitigate risks by instituting written rules that make clear the fact that company-owned phones are to be used primarily for business use. Place limits on personal talking and texting, just as you restrict personal e-mail and Internet use.

REAL-LIFE CELL PHONE DISASTER STORY: CANDIDATE VETOES CELL PHONE MANNERS

When 2008 Republican presidential candidate Rudy Giuliani, in the middle of a formal address to the National Rifle Association, interrupted his own speech to take a cell phone call from his wife, he triggered a flurry of media coverage, a debate about political motives, and general concern that it is now acceptable to take a cell phone call anytime and anywhere.

The former mayor of New York City and one-time presidential hopeful is not alone. Twenty-four percent of cell phone users feel obligated to answer a cell phone call, even if it means interrupting a meeting or a meal.[27]

Best Practice: Apply Cell Phone and Text Messaging Policy to Help Reduce Workplace Liabilities and Increase Productivity

Use the following cell phone and text messaging dos and don'ts to help form the basis of your organization's own cell phone and text messaging policy.

Employee Dos

- Establish electronic content rules and language guidelines. Whether conducting a cell phone conversation or texting, employees must use a professional tone and businesslike language.

- Instruct employees to turn off their cell phones (whether company-provided or personal, handheld or hands-free) when driving any vehicle (whether company-owned or personal) during business hours. Insist that they pull off the road to make a call, take a call, send a text message, or check voice and text messages.

- Remind employees that a policy is a policy. Cell phone users and texters are expected to comply with all company rules and policies including sexual harassment and discrimination policies, ethics guidelines, code of conduct, confidentiality rules, content rules and language guidelines, cell phone and texting policy, computer policies, and any additional policies that your company has.

- Inform employees that they are expected to adhere to the company's rules regarding personal use of cell phones and other electronic business communication tools during business hours. Regardless of whether employees are using their own cell phone or a company-provided phone, they are required to adhere to the company's personal use rules governing when, where, why, with whom, and for how long they may engage in personal, nonbusiness-related talking and texting.

- Direct employees to report violations of the company's cell phone and texting rules and policy to the human resources manager. Remind them that failure to report a coworker's cell phone or texting violation may result in disciplinary action against the witness.

- Inform employees that any violation of the company's cell phone and texting policy may result in disciplinary action, up to and including termination.

Employee Don'ts

Be sure to specify that the following behavior has no place in your business environment.

- Make it clear that employees are not to discuss company business in any public setting in which they could be overheard. Inform them that not every location is right for a cell phone conversation, and encourage them to find a secluded spot (hotel room, car, private office, etc.) in which to conduct company business via their cell phones.

- Prohibit mentioning passwords, user names, account numbers, financial data, customers, prospects, or other confidential or proprietary company or personal information if there is any chance that their cell phone conversation could be overheard. An indiscreet one-sided conversation may be all a malicious party needs in order to gain access to valuable business or personal data.

- Educate employees not to assume their cell phone conversation is "safe" just because they don't mention the company by name. If they wear or carry an item that features the company logo, their name, or the organization's business address, a third party may put two and two together and identify the company.

- While talking or texting on a cell phone, prohibit employees from using language that is obscene, vulgar, abusive, harassing, profane, discriminatory, sexually suggestive, intimidating, misleading, defamatory, or otherwise offensive, objectionable, inappropriate, or illegal. Explain that jokes, disparaging remarks, and inappropriate comments related to ethnicity, race, color, religion, sex, age, disabilities, physique, sexual orientation, or sexual preference are prohibited.

- Prohibit using a cell phone camera or video recorder to take, transmit, download, upload, print, or copy photos or videos that are not directly related to company business. Prohibited photos and videos can include, but are not limited to, "funny" or embarrassing images (of anyone or anything), as well as photos or videos of company buildings (internal and external), offices, facilities, operations, products, services, confidential data, and internal documents.

- Prohibit using a cell phone camera or video recorder to take, transmit, download, upload, print, or copy photos or videos of coworkers, executives, customers, suppliers, or any other third party without getting the express permission of your subject and company management.

- Discourage employees from distracting officemates by engaging in unnecessary cell phone chatter.

- Prohibit driving a car or operating a vehicle (company-owned or personal) while talking or texting on a handheld or hands-free cell phone (company-provided or personal).

Cell Phone and Texting Etiquette

To help create a more civil work environment and keep customers happy, promote cell phone and texting etiquette by incorporating the following suggestions into your e-Policy.

- Require your employees to turn off their cell phones during business-related meetings, seminars, conferences, luncheons, dinners, receptions, brainstorming sessions, and any other situation in which a ringing phone or tapping fingers are likely to disrupt proceedings or interrupt a speaker's or participant's train of thought. If they fail to do so, they may find themselves among the 8 percent of cell phone users who admit that they have drawn criticism or angry stares from others when using cell phones in public, according to a Pew/Internet survey.[28]

- Instruct employees not to assume that texting is any less annoying or distracting than talking. If a pressing business matter requires them to check or transmit text messages during a meeting or other business gathering, have them leave the room—briefly—to do so.

- Encourage employees to keep their voices down. Eighty-two percent of Americans and 86 percent of cell phone users report that they are occasionally irritated by annoying cell phone users who conduct loud conversations in public.[29]

- Persuade your employees not to become like nearly a quarter of adult cell phone users (24 percent) who feel obligated to answer calls, even when they interrupt business meetings or meals, according to a Pew Survey.[30] Help them find a balance between their need to check voice mail and incoming text messages, and their obligation to adhere to the organization's cell phone and text messaging etiquette rules.

RECAP & e-POLICY ACTION PLAN

1. Cell phones saddle employers with increased risks including driving-related insurance claims and lawsuits, lost productivity, security breaches, and etiquette violations.

2. Under the legal principle of vicarious liability, employers may be held legally responsible for crashes caused by distracted employees taking or texting while driving.

3. Ban all cell phone use (making calls, taking calls, listening to voice mail, texting) while driving during business hours.

4. Address confidentiality rules as part of your organization's cell phone and texting policy. An overheard conversation or indiscreet message could put the company and its secrets at risk.

5. Ban the use of cell phones to take, transmit, download, upload, print, or copy photos or videos that are not directly related to company business.

6. Apply cell phone and texting policy and etiquette rules to help reduce workplace liabilities and increase productivity.

PART NINE

Monitoring and Compliance Rules

Minimize Risks—and Maximize Compliance— with Training, Discipline, and Monitoring

CHAPTER 20

Employee Education Policies and Best Practices

Although there is no such thing as entirely risk-free electronic business communication, employers who want to ensure that employees' electronic business communication is as clean and compliant as possible are urged to adopt the 3-E approach to electronic risk management:

1. Establish written rules and formal policies addressing all electronic business communication tools and technologies—old, new, and emerging.

2. Educate all employees about electronic risks, rules, regulations, and responsibilities.

3. Enforce written rules and policies with a combination of disciplinary action and management technology tools including policy-based monitoring, filtering, blocking, and archiving tools.

Employers Drop the Ball when It Comes to e-Policy Education

Fewer than half of all employers (42 percent) surveyed by American Management Association and ePolicy Institute in 2006 formally educate employees about e-mail risks, policy, and usage. Only 21 percent of organizations define "electronic business records" for users, and merely 2 percent of bosses educate employee-bloggers about often-misunderstood First Amendment rights and privacy expectations.[1]

Failure to inform employees about electronic risks, rules, and responsibilities is a potentially costly oversight. Based on the legal principle known as vicarious liability, an employer may be held legally responsible for employee misconduct—intentional or accidental. That said, the courts and regulators appreciate, and tend to respond favorably to, policy and training that is consistently applied.

> **e-Policy Rule 45:** Combine electronic rules with continuing education, and you may find your employees more compliant and the courts and regulators more accepting of the fact that you have made every effort to keep your organization free of inappropriate electronic conduct and content.

Demonstrate Your Commitment to Best Practices with Comprehensive, Continuing Education

You may one day need to prove to a court that your organization is indeed fully committed to a formal, comprehensive electronic risk management program that includes written policy, employee education, and enforcement through a combination of disciplinary action and technology tools.

To that end, make e-policy training mandatory for all employees in every office. Conduct employee and executive training either live onsite, through live webinars or archived training modules online, or via videotape. Conclude formal training programs with a certification quiz designed to demonstrate employees' participation in training and their understanding of electronic risks and rules. Consider suspending the computer privileges of any employee who fails the mandatory certification test.

Maintain Records of Training Program Materials and Participants

Save, store, and, in the event of a lawsuit, be prepared to produce training-related materials including:

- *Written electronic usage and content rules and policies.* If you are adhering to best practices, your organization is formally reviewing and updating all electronic policies every 12 months. Be sure to date and number every new edition of each policy, so you can demonstrate what rules and procedures were implemented when. Remember, when it comes to successful electronic risk management, it simply is not good enough to draft a policy, put it on a shelf, and forget about it. To be effective, rules, policies, and procedures must evolve as new electronic tools and technologies emerge.

> **e-Policy Rule 46:** Best practices call for e-Policies to be formally reviewed and updated every 12 months.

- *e-policy-related training literature and materials.* Whether you conduct policy training in person on-site, or via video, webinar, or archived online training modules, you'll want to maintain a complete file of the following: all instructor manuals and scripts, participant workbooks, PowerPoint presentations and scripts, handout materials, certification quizzes, and any other printed or electronic materials related to your e-policy training program.

- *Employee acknowledgment forms.* Require every employee who attends e-policy training to sign and date an attendance form, acknowledging that the employee has attended training, understands all electronic rules and policies, and agrees to comply with the organization's written rules and policies or accept the consequences, up to and including termination.

- *Video tapes and/or audio tapes of training sessions.* If you record live training or offer video/audio training as an alternative to on-site seminars, be sure to keep copies of the tapes. If you repeat the same training program in multiple offices, you are probably safe retaining just one representative tape, but check with your legal counsel to be certain.

- *Archived webinars.* If you offer employee education in the form of online webinars, be sure to retain and archive all electronic programs.

- *All other records related to the organization's e-policy training program.*

Fifteen Tips for Effective Employee Education

To be an effective part of your organization's electronic risk management program, continuing education must work in concert with your organization's written rules and policies. The most effective training is comprehensive and ongoing. Depending on your organization's electronic risks, rules, regulations, resources, policies, and procedures, incorporate the following tips and topics into your organization's e-policy training program:

1. *Identify a champion to lead the e-policy charge.* Show employees you mean business by having a senior company official (the more senior the better) and a compliance officer or lawyer introduce the organization's e-policy program to employees. Clearly explain the following:

   • Why the organization is implementing a formal electronic risk management program, complete with electronic rules and e-Policies.

   • What roles individual employees play in e-policy compliance including adhering to written rules and policies.

   • What penalties e-policy violators face. In 2007, a combined 58 percent of employers fired employees for e-mail and Web violations, according to American Management Association and ePolicy Institute research.[2] Use your formal training program to inform employees that failure to comply with the organization's electronic business communication policies and procedures may result in disciplinary action, up to and including termination.

2. *Review e-mail and other electronic risks and liabilities.* Address the risks (such as lawsuits, regulatory investigations, security breaches, confidentiality violations, lost productivity, negative publicity, and employee terminations) facing the organization and individual employees.

3. *Remind users that the easiest way to control risk is to control written content.* Explain that the organization's technology tools exist primarily for business purposes. Review the type of content and language that employees are permitted and not permitted to use when engaged in electronic business communication at the office or at home.

4. *Establish netiquette rules.* Employers are required to maintain a civil business environment, free from harassment, discrimination,

hostility, and other forms of abusive or inappropriate behavior and language. As part of your comprehensive policy program, be sure to establish netiquette, or online etiquette, rules.

5. ***Stress the fact that a policy is a policy.*** Inform employees that a policy is a policy, regardless of the technology or tool used to communicate. Make sure employees understand that all company rules and policies—including ethics rules, code of conduct, confidentiality rules, harassment and discrimination policies—apply to all electronic communications whether at the office, on the road, or at home.

REAL-LIFE E-MAIL DISASTER STORY: INAPPROPRIATE E-MAIL VIOLATES COMPANY ETHICS RULES

Boeing's former president and CEO, Harry Stonecipher, lost his job, damaged his reputation, generated unwanted international news coverage, and created a public relations nightmare for Boeing when e-mail records revealed that he had been having a consensual extramarital affair with a female Boeing executive—and using the company's computer system to transmit "graphic" electronic love notes. Stonecipher was forced to resign, in part because his indiscretion violated the company's code of conduct, undercutting Stonecipher's credibility as the company's chief ethics enforcer and placing Boeing in a "potentially embarrassing and damaging situation."[3]

---

6. ***Explain copyright law.*** Define "copyright" for employees who may not understand the principle of copyright protection. Review copyright law, copyright infringement, and the penalties facing the organization and individuals for using copyright-protected material without permission of the copyright holder.

7. ***Cover trade secrets and confidential information.*** Don't assume that all employees know what type of material the organization regards as confidential or otherwise valuable. Define the terms "trade secret," "confidential," "proprietary," and "intellectual property." Explain how confidential material that belongs to the organization, business partners, suppliers, customers, prospects, and other third parties is to be handled. Discuss the organization's legal and financial risks should trade secrets be revealed or company

financials be disclosed. Explain the risks that individual employees face (disciplinary action, termination, lawsuits) for revealing confidential company information.

8. ***Discuss First Amendment and privacy expectations and realities.*** When it comes to freedom of speech, privacy, and ownership, many employees are misguided—dangerously so. Let employees know that they have no reasonable expectation of privacy when using the company computer system. Explain that the First Amendment only restricts government control of speech; it says nothing about private employers.

    If you are a private employer operating in an employment-at-will state, explain what that means in terms of employees' job security. Be certain that employees understand that management can—and will—fire employees who write, transmit, download, upload, post, copy, or print content that violates any of the organization's written rules and policies whether at the office using the organization's computer system or at home on the employee's own time and equipment.

9. ***Explain monitoring policies and procedures.*** The federal Electronic Communications Privacy Act (ECPA) makes clear the fact that an employer-provided computer system is the property of the employer. While the ECPA gives employers the right to monitor all e-mail transmissions and Internet activity that take place on the organization's system, only two states (Delaware and Connecticut) require employers to inform employees that they are being monitored. Nonetheless, it is a good idea for all employers to let employees know that the company is monitoring and to explain exactly how monitoring is accomplished (whether you use technology tools to automate the process or employ responsible people to manually review e-mail transmissions and Web surfing). Be sure employees understand that they have absolutely no reasonable expectation of privacy when using the organization's computer system.

10. ***Define "electronic business records" and explain ESI policy and procedures.*** Forty-three percent of workers are so confused by the concept of electronic business records that they can't distinguish business-critical e-mail that must be retained from insignificant messages that may be deleted.[4] Much of that confusion stems from a lack of education. Don't leave electronic business record management to chance. Use formal training to explain:

- Exactly what a business record is.

- Why it is essential for the organization to retain e-mail and other ESI.

- What the individual employee's role is (if any) in the record retention and deletion process.

- How, in the event of a lawsuit, an employee's inappropriate or personal content could potentially harm the organization professionally and embarrass the user personally.

11. ***Address regulatory rules.*** Are your regulated employees among the 43 percent who either don't adhere to regulatory rules governing e-mail retention—or simply don't know if they are compliant?[5] The SEC, FINRA, and other regulators take e-mail and IM compliance seriously—and they expect management to enforce regulatory rules, or accept the consequences including six- and seven-figure monetary fines.

    If you employ regulated employees, assign your compliance officer or legal counsel the task of getting up to speed with regulators' e-mail, IM, and other electronic usage, content, and retention guidelines. Once you know what the regulators' rules are, share that information with all regulated employees as part of your formal e-policy training program.

12. ***Define "personal use."*** If you allow personal e-mail, Internet, or cell phone use, explain to employees exactly what type of personal use is acceptable and unacceptable. Let your staff know when personal e-mail or other electronic communication is allowed, for how long, with whom, and under what circumstances. Remember, clear guidelines are always easier to understand and adhere to. If "some" personal use is allowed, employees and managers will have to individually interpret where the line is drawn, and you may not be comfortable with their conclusions.

13. ***Provide every employee with a signed copy of each e-policy.*** Put a master set of electronic rules, policies, and procedures in the organization's comprehensive employee handbook. Make electronic copies available via the company's e-mail or intranet system strictly as a follow-up to formal on-site, online, or video training. Do not rely solely on e-mail or the intranet to educate employees.

14. ***Train until you are certain that every employee understands each electronic rule and policy, and is clear on what constitutes***

appropriate and inappropriate use of the organization's computer and electronic business communication systems.

15. ***Reinforce training among executives and employees.*** Send policy reminders via IM, e-mail, and text message. Hold periodic refresher training to update employees on new electronic risks, rules, and policy changes. Make annual policy training mandatory for everyone. Post policy updates on the company's intranet site. In short, do whatever it takes to raise employees' electronic awareness and keep them focused on their individual roles in making the company's electronic risk management initiative a success.

Does that sound like a lot of material to cover in the course of training? The topics to address in an effective continuing education program are as comprehensive as the risks you face every time an employee accesses your computer system.

RECAP & e-POLICY ACTION PLAN

1. The courts and regulators appreciate consistent rules and policies that are supported by comprehensive employee training.

2. A combination of written electronic rules and policies, coupled with employee education and technology tools, may motivate compliance and help prevent workplace lawsuits and other electronic risks.

3. Approach e-policy training as an ongoing, continuing education program, not a one-time-only event.

4. Conclude training by requiring all employees to sign and date an acknowledgment form confirming that they have undergone e-policy training; understand the organization's electronic rules, policies, and procedures; and agree to comply with the organization's electronic rules and policies or accept disciplinary action up to and including their termination.

5. You may one day need to prove in court that your organization is fully committed to a formal, comprehensive electronic risk management program that includes written policy, training, and enforcement. Save, store, and (if subpoenaed) be prepared to produce all literature, materials, and records related to the organization's electronic business communication training program.

CHAPTER 21

Disciplinary Rules, Policies, and Best Practices

When it comes to the enforcement of electronic rules and policies, strict disciplinary procedures can pay big dividends. Make an example of one e-policy violator today, and you may avoid firing an entire department tomorrow. In addition, your ability to walk into court and demonstrate a consistent pattern of policy enforcement may help bolster your defense should your organization one day become embroiled in litigation.

> **e-Policy Rule 47:** Private employers in employment-at-will states (which most states are) have the right to fire employees for just about any reason—including inappropriate computer use—as long as federal discrimination guidelines aren't violated.

Not all bosses fire users for e-mail and Internet violations. Some warn or reprimand offenders, others suspend computer privileges, and still others impose monetary fines. But the number of employers who have terminated employees for e-mail and Internet misuse grew significantly between 2001 and 2007. E-mail-related dismissals alone doubled during the six-year period, according to American Management Association and ePolicy Institute research.

E-MAIL AND WEB MISUSE TRIGGERS EMPLOYEE TERMINATIONS

Employers Who Have:	2001	2007
Fired employees for e-mail violations	14%	28%
Fired employees for Internet violations	26%	30%[1]

WHAT CONSTITUTES A TERMINATION-WORTHY E-MAIL OFFENSE?

The 28 percent of employers who fired workers in 2007 for e-mail abuse cited a variety of termination-worthy offenses:

Violation of any company policy (ethics, harassment/discrimination, e-mail, etc.)	64%
Inappropriate/offensive language/content	62%
Excessive personal use of the company system	26%
Breach of confidentiality rules	22%
Other	12%[2]

WHAT CONSTITUTES A TERMINATION-WORTHY INTERNET VIOLATION?

The 30 percent of employers who fired workers in 2007 for Internet misuse cited a variety of termination-worthy offenses:

Viewing/downloading/uploading pornographic or otherwise offensive/inappropriate content	84%
Violation of any company policy (ethics, harassment/discrimination, Internet, etc.)	48%
Excessive personal use of the company system	34%
Other	8%[3]

RECAP & e-POLICY ACTION PLAN

1. The courts and regulators appreciate formal rules and policies that are supported by comprehensive employee training and consistent enforcement in the form of disciplinary action and monitoring.

2. A disciplinary policy that calls for the termination of e-mail and Internet violators may help motivate employee compliance and prevent workplace lawsuits and other electronic risks.

3. Wrap up e-policy training by requiring employees to sign and date an acknowledgment form confirming that they have undergone e-policy training; understand electronic risks, rules, policies, and procedures; and agree to comply with the organization's electronic rules and policies or accept disciplinary action, up to and including their termination.

CHAPTER 22

Monitoring Rules and Tools

The federal Electronic Communications Privacy Act (ECPA) gives U.S. employers the legal right to monitor all employee computer activity and transmissions. The ECPA makes clear the fact that the organization's computer system is the property of the employer, and employees have absolutely no reasonable expectation of privacy when using company computer systems, tools, and technologies.

Courts in the United States have consistently ruled that employees should assume their computer activity is being watched—even if they have not been formally notified of monitoring. The courts generally support the position that informed employees neither would nor should assume that their e-mail transmissions are their own. Even in cases in which employers have told workers that incoming and outgoing e-mail is *not being monitored*, the courts have ruled that employees still should not expect privacy when using a company system.[1]

Internet and E-Mail Monitoring Helps Keep Online Employees In Line

Electronic monitoring is the easiest, most effective way to track e-mail and Internet use and misuse whether accidental or intentional. Best practices call for all employers—regardless of company size, industry, regulatory situation, or status as a public or private entity—to take advantage of the law and monitor all online activities and transmissions.

That said, if you are a U.S.-based employer with employees and operations abroad, you may not be able to apply your domestic monitoring policy to employees who are stationed outside of the United States. In the United Kingdom, for example, a premium is placed on employee privacy.

English law allows organizations to monitor Web surfing and e-mail transmissions, but employers are legally required to alert employees to monitoring and to use the least intrusive surveillance methods possible.[2]

Before implementing domestic monitoring rules and tools abroad, seek the advice of a lawyer who is familiar with the laws and regulations governing employee privacy and monitoring in each country in which you have a presence.

> **e-Policy Rule 48:** Electronic monitoring is the easiest, most effective way to track e-mail and Internet use and misuse. Take advantage of your legal right to monitor—and manage—employees' internal and external online activity and transmissions.

Electronic Monitoring and Surveillance Practices, 2001–2007

American Management Association and the ePolicy Institute have been tracking employers' electronic monitoring and surveillance practices since 2001. Over the years, U.S.-based employers have grown increasingly committed to tracking employee Web use.

HOW DOES YOUR COMPANY COMPARE WITH OTHER EMPLOYERS?		
Employers who:	2001	2007
Monitor website connections	62%	66%
Store and review employees' computer files	36%	43%
Block connections to inappropriate websites	38%	65%
Monitor the blogosphere for company-related posts	NA	12%
Monitor social networking sites for company-related content (videos, photos, text)	NA	10%[3]

Enforce Internet Rules with URL Blocking Tools

Employers have grown significantly less tolerant of employees who engage in nonwork-related Web surfing during business hours. Between 2001 and 2007, the number of employers who use URL blocking tools to prevent employees from accessing inappropriate, time-wasting, or otherwise off-limit websites has increased across the board, according to American Management Association and ePolicy Institute research.

If you have any doubt about your employees' willingness to comply with Internet policy, do not hesitate to combine URL blocking tools with monitoring technology to help solve your people problem.

WHAT TYPE OF WEB SURFING WORRIES EMPLOYERS MOST?

The number of employers who use technology to block employee access to websites rose 27 percent between 2001 and 2007, with 65 percent of employers using URL blocking technology in 2007 versus 38 percent in 2001.

When it comes to Web surfing, what are employers most concerned about?

Sites Blocked:	2001	2007
"Adult" sites (sexual, romantic, pornographic)	77%	96%
Game sites	26%	61%
Social networking sites	NA	50%
Entertainment sites	18%	40%
Shopping and auction sites	13%	27%
Sports sites	15%	21%
External blogs	NA	18%
Other sites	12%	23%[4]

> **e-Policy Rule 49:** Reduce the likelihood of inappropriate e-mail and Web use triggering lawsuits and other disasters by combining written content and usage rules, employee education, discipline, and policy-based content monitoring, filtering, and blocking tools.

Best Practices Call for the Monitoring of External and Internal E-Mail

Thanks to the revised FRCP, e-mail now plays an increasingly significant evidentiary role in litigation and regulatory investigations. In 2006, nearly a quarter of employers (24 percent) had employee e-mail subpoenaed by courts or regulators. Another 15 percent of companies found themselves in courtrooms, defending lawsuits that were triggered specifically by employees' smoking gun e-mail.[5]

Employers cannot afford to allow employees to engage in unmonitored and unfiltered e-mail conversations—outgoing, incoming, or internal. Reduce the likelihood of inappropriate, nonbusiness-related e-mail triggering a potentially costly and protracted workplace lawsuit by combining written content and usage rules with employee education supported by disciplinary action and policy-based content monitoring and filtering tools.

E-MAIL MONITORING: HOW DO YOU COMPARE WITH OTHER EMPLOYERS?

Employers Who:	2007
Monitor e-mail	43%

Of the 43% of bosses who monitor e-mail, the majority are concerned primarily with external (incoming and outgoing) transmissions.

Monitor external e-mail (incoming and outgoing)	96%
Monitor internal e-mail (among in-house employees)	58%[6]

Internal E-Mail Is Just as Dangerous as External E-Mail—Monitor Both

The fact that 42 percent of employers who monitor e-mail don't track internal transmissions among coworkers is a potentially costly oversight. As detailed in Chapter 7, some employees tend to play it fast and loose with language and content when using internal e-mail to communicate with coworkers about business and personal matters. In internal e-mail, users will sometimes express controversial opinions, discuss confidential company matters, and gossip about colleagues. Employees also have been known to transmit off-color jokes, pornographic images, and adults-only videos to work buddies via in-house e-mail.

Whether transmitted internally or externally, offensive content is offensive content. Many e-mail-related lawsuits and class-action claims have been filed by employees who are offended by the pervasive downloading, uploading, and e-mailing of pornographic, racist, sexist, and otherwise inappropriate and hostile content within the confines of the company.

Failure to manage and monitor internal e-mail is a bad business practice. Protect your organization and your employees by installing monitoring and filtering technology tools that are designed to capture, review, and as necessary block the transmission of all e-mail messages and attachments whether internal or external, incoming or outgoing.

WHO READS AND REVIEWS EMPLOYEE E-MAIL?

Of the 43 percent of U.S. companies that monitored e-mail in 2007, 73 percent relied on technology to automate the surveillance process. At 40 percent of companies, individuals from various departments were assigned the task of manually eyeballing coworkers' e-mail transmissions.

Employers Who	2007
Use technology to automatically monitor e-mail	73%
Assign individuals to manually monitor and read e-mail	40%

Which Departments Are Assigned to Manually Read and Review Employee E-Mail?

IT	73%
HR	34%
Legal	18%
Compliance	17%
Other	17%
Outside third party	4%[7]

Protect Outbound Information with Policy-Based Content Filtering Tools

In addition to monitoring employees' internal and external e-mail content, best practices call for the use of policy-based content filtering technology. Content filtering tools that are based on your policy allow management to track and block content as it leaves or enters the system, in the following ways:

- Using an automated search tool, employers can seek out and block the transmission of target words and phrases that you do not want transmitted to competitors, reporters, or other third parties. These target words and phrases can include the names of executives, patients, customers, or trade secrets.

- Filtering technology can capture and block obscene, harassing, discriminatory, or otherwise offensive or objectionable content from entering or leaving your system.

- Monitoring and filtering technology also can be used to spot and stop particularly large attachments that warrant a review by management since they may contain customer lists, credit card data, or other valuable or proprietary information.

Use Technology to Keep Your Site and System Safe and Intruder-Free

In light of regulatory rules and FRCP requirements governing the preservation and production of legally valid e-mail and other electronically stored information, it is vital that employers install security technology including firewalls, antispam software, and antivirus tools. This will stop malicious intruders and thieves from invading your computer system and altering, stealing, or otherwise tampering with financial records, protected health information, intellectual property, e-mail, and other ESI.

In addition to protecting your network, be sure to take advantage of technology tools that are designed to keep unauthorized persons from entering buildings, offices, and computer rooms.

HOW EMPLOYERS CONTROL PHYSICAL ACCESS TO BUILDINGS AND COMPUTER ROOMS	
Employers Who Use	2007
Smart card technology	52.0%
Videotape for security reasons	48.0%
Fingerprint scans	2.0%
Assisted global positioning or GPS to monitor employee IDs or smart cards	1.0%
Facial recognition	0.4%
Iris scans	0.4%[8]

Keep Monitoring, Filtering, Blocking, and Security Tools Current

Just as electronic business communication tools are ever-evolving, so too are the technologies that are designed to keep your site and system safe and intruder-free. Assign your chief information officer or IT director the task of regularly reviewing and updating your organization's monitoring, filtering, blocking, data/network security, and physical access/building security tools.

Think of this technology as investments in risk management and litigation prevention. The cost of upgrading monitoring and security tools is minimal compared to the six to seven figures you could spend defending or settling a lawsuit or regulatory audit.

> **e-Policy Rule 50:** Think of monitoring, filtering, and security technology as investments in risk management and litigation prevention.

Use Formal, On-site Training to Alert Employees to Monitoring

While the ECPA gives U.S. employers the legal right to monitor e-mail and Internet activity, there is no federal law requiring management to notify employees that computer use and content are being tracked.

Only two states, Delaware and Connecticut, require employers to alert workers to computer monitoring. Nonetheless, the majority of employers (83 percent) report that they do in fact inform employees that computer use, including time spent at the computer, matter or content viewed, and keystrokes entered, is monitored. Another 84 percent of bosses notify workers that the company reviews computer files. An additional 71 percent of managers let users know that their e-mail transmissions are tracked,[9] according to the 2007 Electronic Monitoring & Surveillance Survey from American Management Association and the ePolicy Institute.

Unfortunately, organizations don't always employ the most effective means to alert employees of monitoring.

HOW EMPLOYERS ALERT EMPLOYEES OF ELECTRONIC MONITORING	
Employers Who	2007
Relied on the company's employee handbook	70%
Relied on e-mail notices	40%
Used written notices	35%
Relied on intranet postings	32%
Informed employees as part of a formal, on-site e-policy training program	27%[10]

As indicated in the table, only 27 percent of employers adhered to best practices and informed employees about monitoring as part of a formal, on-site e-policy training program. You cannot expect an uninformed workforce to comply with policy. And you cannot trust employees on their own to access the company intranet system or retrieve a copy of the employee handbook in order to educate themselves. Best practices call for formal employee training. On-site training is the best approach, granting employees the opportunity to ask questions and gain a thorough understanding of electronic rules, policies, and procedures. If you have a geographically dispersed workforce, you may want to consider online training in the form of live webinars or archived training modules as an alternative to live on-site training.

RECAP & e-POLICY ACTION PLAN

1. The federal Electronic Communications Privacy Act (ECPA) gives U.S. employers the legal right to monitor all employee computer activity and transmissions.

2. Users have absolutely no reasonable expectation of privacy when using company computer systems, tools, and technologies.

3. The courts and regulators appreciate consistent rules and policies that are supported by comprehensive employee training and up-to-date monitoring and security technology.

4. A combination of policy, training, and technology tools may help motivate employee compliance with policies and prevent lawsuits and other electronic risks.

5. If you have any doubt about your employees' willingness to comply with Internet policy, do not hesitate to combine URL blocking tools with monitoring technology to help solve your people problem.

PART TEN

User Rules

CHAPTER 23

How to Communicate Online Without Getting Fired

Ten Tips for Employees Who Want to Protect Their Privacy—and Keep Their Jobs

Tip 1: Know That Big Brother Is Reading over Your Electronic Shoulder

There simply is no privacy in cyberspace. Employers, law enforcement agencies, courts, regulators, the media, and the public are likely to access your online transmissions, posts, and history one day—if they haven't done so already.

When it comes to workplace computer monitoring, U.S. employers are primarily concerned about inappropriate Web surfing, with 66 percent of bosses watching workers' Internet connections, and another 45 percent tracking content, keystrokes, and time spent at the keyboard.

An additional 43 percent of U.S. employers monitor employee e-mail, either taking advantage of technology to accomplish the job automatically (73 percent) or assigning an individual to manually read and review workers' messages (40 percent).

Employee use of new and emerging technologies is under scrutiny at work, too, according to the 2007 Electronic Monitoring and Surveillance Survey from American Management Association and ePolicy Institute. Twelve percent of bosses regularly monitor the blogosphere, and another 10 percent keep an eye on social networking sites to determine what type of content employees, ex-employees, competitors, customers, critics, fans, and others are posting about the company, its people, products, and services.[1]

Your Boss Isn't the Only One Who's Monitoring Your Electronic Transmissions

Every time you send an e-mail message, your intended recipient's employer and the employers of any unintended readers to whom your message is forwarded or copied gains access to your e-mail. Consequently, your business and personal e-mail could be archived (possibly forever) and (in the event of a lawsuit, regulatory investigation, or Freedom of Information Act request) turned over to courts, regulators, and reporters, along with the company's own business record e-mail and other electronically stored information.

If you engage in instant messaging, and your company or your IM buddy's organization is among the 13 percent of businesses that retain instant messenger chat,[2] then those brief, real-time conversations also are subject to review by unintended readers.

As discussed throughout this book, e-mail and other ESI create the electronic equivalent of DNA evidence. Twenty-four percent of employers have had e-mail subpoenaed by courts, and another 15 percent have gone to court to battle lawsuits triggered by employee e-mail.[3] If you use the company e-mail system to transmit personal messages, there's a good chance that your private (potentially embarrassing and career-altering) e-mail has been saved and stored right along with business-critical e-mail.

Should a lawsuit or other investigation hit, expect to see your personal e-mail messages, IM chat, and history of Web surfing subpoenaed and made available to judges, lawyers, forensic investigators, jurors, expert witnesses, the media, and the public. To prevent potential embarrassment, save your personal correspondence and surfing for your home computer.

Government employees face additional exposure thanks to state and federal Freedom of Information statutes that give the media and taxpayers ready access to government employees' e-mail, IM, text messages, and other forms of electronic business communication.

The PATRIOT Act authorizes law enforcement agencies to seize corporate e-mail, and your employer is under no obligation to inform you that your electronic correspondence has been turned over to federal, state, or local authorities.

As detailed in Chapter 4, SOX, GLBA, HIPAA, SEC, FINRA, FDA, EPA, and IRS are just a few of the government and industry regulations and regulators that subpoena and audit workplace e-mail to ensure compliance with content and retention rules.

Copied, forwarded, and improperly addressed e-mail regularly lands in the electronic inboxes of competitors, the media, and other unintended internal and external readers.

> **e-Policy Rule 51:** Assume you are being monitored at the office and at home, too. Always think before you write, send, or surf!

Tip 2: Expect No Privacy When Using the Company Computer System

In the United States, the ECPA makes it clear that a company-provided computer system is the property of the employer. Employees, therefore, have absolutely no reasonable expectation of privacy when using the system to transmit e-mail, surf the Web, or engage in any other form of electronic communication.

Courts in the United States have consistently ruled that employees should assume that their workplace computer activity is being watched— even if they have not been formally notified of monitoring. While most states don't legally require employers to notify staff that their online activity is being monitored, the court system generally supports the position that informed employees neither would nor should assume that their e-mail transmissions are their own. Even in cases in which employers have told workers that incoming and outgoing e-mail is *not* being monitored, the courts have ruled that employees still should not expect privacy when using a company-provided e-mail system.[4]

Private employers in employment-at-will states (which most states are) have the right to fire employees for just about any reason— including accidental and intentional e-mail violations and inappropriate Internet use. So, if you are thinking about filing an invasion of privacy lawsuit to protest computer monitoring or a wrongful termination claim in response to your e-mail or Internet-related termination, think again. It's unlikely you will have much luck making your case in court.

Tip 3: Writing or Posting Online About Your Job, Boss, or Coworkers May Get You Fired

Whether working on company equipment during business hours or on personal technology tools at home after work, posting text, photos, or videos about your company, its people, products, and services can be an express route to the unemployment line—regardless of whether those postings are negative or positive.

Whether blogging on the company's business blog, social networking on Facebook, sharing videos on YouTube, or operating your own personal website, never write about or otherwise reference your employer or job without formal authorization from management.

That means no:

- mentions of your company, boss, or colleagues

- references to your job title or work assignments

- photos of yourself or other staff in company uniforms

- videos of company facilities, products, or people

- posting of your business card, corporate e-mail address, or company letterhead

- use of company trademarks, logos, or other visual identifiers

- links to company-operated websites or blogs.

Violate this e-policy rule today, and you may find yourself out of work tomorrow.

Tip 4: Anonymous Posts Do Not Guarantee Protection from Detection

Let's face it, anonymity creates an atmosphere in which some people might be tempted to post content that may be irresponsible, offensive, harassing, defamatory, or otherwise inappropriate. At the end of the day, however, there is no guarantee that anonymous blogging or other nameless postings will protect closeted writers from detection.

**REAL-LIFE BLOGGING DISASTER STORIES:
EMPLOYEES MAY FIND THEMSELVES TERMINATED
FOR ANONYMOUS BLOGGING**

St. Louis Post-Dispatch reporter Daniel Finney learned this lesson the hard way when his computer hard drive was seized and he was suspended from his job after posting "lengthy passages about his job as a *Post-Dispatch* features writer" on his personal blog—under the pseudonym Roland H. Thompson.

In his anonymous personal blog, "Roland H. Thompson" took "frequent, thinly veiled potshots against his employer and co-workers."[5]

In another case of anonymous blogging, a male blogger who had successfully operated a popular blog for 18 months under a female pseudonym actually outed himself. For a year and a half, Assistant U.S. Attorney David Lat used his dishy blog, Underneath Their Robes, to gossip about federal judges under the guise of a female lawyer named Article III Groupie. Lat finally ended his anonymity in a story in *The New Yorker*. He told the magazine that he was revealing his true identity because the successful blog left him feeling "frustrated that I was putting a lot of time into this and was unable to get any credit for it."[6]

According to the *New Jersey Law Journal*, Lat did receive "credit" from his employer once his identity was revealed. In accordance with his superior, Lat deactivated Underneath Their Robes shortly after *The New Yorker* hit newsstands. The blog, which violated policy requiring assistant U.S. attorneys to get approval before talking with the media, may have ongoing fallout. As Lat told *The New Yorker*, "I only hope the judges I appear in front of don't read it."[7]

Finally, consider the case of Heather Armstrong, the blogger who is credited with coining the term "dooced," which means to lose your job for blogging. According to the *New York Times,* Armstrong used her blog Dooce.com to complain "colorfully about everything from her boss to obnoxious coworkers." While she kept the name of her employer a secret, never revealing the name of the software company that employed her, one reader did not share her sense of discretion. That reader not only figured out where Armstrong worked, but also followed up with an e-mail to Armstrong's employer, detailing the nature of the blogger's rants. Armstrong was fired immediately.[8]

On a legal note, the courts have not responded consistently to organizations that have attempted to force Internet service providers to disclose the identities of anonymous bloggers who have posted allegedly defamatory statements.[9] Until the courts formally weigh in on this issue, it is in your best interest to steer clear of pseudonyms, whether you are posting content for business or personal reasons.

Tip 5: Familiarize Yourself with Your Employer's Rules and Policies First; Log On Second

Don't communicate online until you have read (and fully understand) all of your organization's employment and e-policies, including e-mail, Internet, IM, blog, cell phone, text messaging, and social networking rules. Familiarize yourself with the company's electronic communication guidelines, code of conduct, confidentiality rules, sexual harassment and discrimination guidelines, and any other rules and policies your employer may impose. Watch your language and adhere to all company employment policies—unless you want to lose your job over an e-mail gaffe or thoughtless text message.

> **e-Policy Rule 52:** Remember, a policy is a policy, regardless of the communication tool used to transmit information. Violation of any employment policy, whether committed via e-mail, the Internet, a video site, or any other electronic communication tool, can get you fired.

Tip 6: Realize That the First Amendment Does Not Protect Bloggers or Social Networkers

Do you believe that, under the First Amendment, you have a right to free speech, which grants you the right to say whatever you want on a personal blog, social networking site, or video sharing site?

Many U.S. bloggers and social networkers mistakenly believe that the First Amendment protects their jobs. It doesn't. The First Amendment only restricts government control of speech; it says nothing about private employers.

Until recently, government employees had some First Amendment protections not available to private sector employees.[10] No longer. The United States Supreme Court recently ruled that government entities are free to fire employees if their comments—online posts included—are harmful to the mission and function of the workplace.[11]

Tip 7: Don't Be Lulled into a False Sense of Security by Personal E-Mail Accounts or Public IM Tools

Depending on the type of technology your employer uses, it is possible for the IT department to track e-mail messages that are sent via personal e-mail accounts like Gmail, Hotmail, or AOL. Scanning technology also enables employers to search the company system for the presence of unauthorized IM downloads from the Web (Yahoo! Messenger and AOL AIM, for example).

E-mail messages and IM chat that is transmitted via personal e-mail accounts and Web-based IM tools travel outside the organization's firewall and across the public Internet, where they can be intercepted and snatched by data thieves, business competitors, foreign governments, and other malicious third parties. Consequently, the use of private e-mail accounts and IM tools may trigger a security breach—and the loss of your job.

Unless your company's written e-policy specifically allows the use of private e-mail accounts and IM software at work, be sure to stick solely with company-provided resources.

Tip 8: The Easiest Way to Control Your Risk of Termination Is to Control Your Written Content

In other words, watch your language. Monitoring and filtering technology typically works hand in hand with written policy to seek out e-mail transmissions and links to websites that violate the company's language and content rules.

That means no obscene, pornographic, sexual, harassing, discriminatory, defamatory, menacing, or threatening language. Don't transmit gossip, rumors, jokes, disparaging, or defamatory remarks. Don't violate confidentiality rules or expose trade secrets. If you are surfing the Web, steer clear of any sites—pornography, gambling, auctions, sports, news, games—that your employer has ruled off-limits.

> **e-Policy Rule 53:** If you don't want your online activity singled out for review and potential disciplinary action, then simply adhere to all of your employer's electronic rules and policies.

Tip 9: Understand That You Can Be Fired for Any Reason—Including Writing and Surfing, Talking and Texting

Do you work in an employment-at-will state? If you do, watch it! Private employers operating in employment-at-will states (which include most of them) may fire employees for just about any reason, as long as it is not discriminatory or in retaliation for whistle-blowing or union organizing.[12]

Laws prevent employers from terminating employees on the basis of race, ethnicity, sex, age, religion, disability, and sexual orientation in some places. But when it comes to online communication, even keeping your personal blog or social networking page clean of work-related material won't necessarily protect you from termination.

As Attorney Daniel M. Klein of Atlanta-based Buckley & Klein told the *New York Times*: "It doesn't matter if you blog about skydiving or pornography. If your employer feels the blog makes you a poor representative of their corporate values, the executives have the freedom to disassociate themselves from you."[13]

That said, according to the National Workrights Institute, five states—California, New York, Colorado, Montana, and North Dakota—have enacted laws limiting the circumstances under which an employer can fire an employee for an off-duty activity that is not related to the job. Those five states make it tougher for the boss to fire an employee who leads a private life the boss disapproves of.[14]

In addition, employee-bloggers in states with anti-SLAPP (Strategic Litigation Against Public Participation) statutes may have some recourse against employers who are found to have "improperly quashed their employees' First Amendment rights" in connection with blog-related activities.[15]

The National Labor Relations Act offers employees some protections if they are writing about wages or working conditions. And workers who are employed by the government or belong to unions may have some protections not available to at-will employees. Although, as noted in Tip 6, a recent Supreme Court ruling empowers local, state, and federal governments to fire employees for comments that harm an agency or its mission.[16]

Tip 10: Don't Use Your E-Mail Inbox as an Ad Hoc Filing System

If—in spite of these warnings—you still insist on using your employer's e-mail system for personal reasons, be sure to empty your inbox of all nonbusiness-related mail at the end of each day. Either forward personal mail to your home account or simply delete it from your mailbox.

While it's true that e-mail never disappears completely, there's no point making it any easier than necessary for your company's chief information officer or an external computer forensic investigator to locate and read your private, nonbusiness-related electronic correspondence in the event of an employment review, civil lawsuit, criminal investigation, regulatory audit, or Freedom of Information Act request.

Bonus Tip: Be Aware That Employers Are Prescreening Job Applicants' Blogs, Social Networking Profiles, and Video Posts, Too

The Society for Human Resource Management reported as early as 2005 that some employers are taking time to review prospective employees' personal blogs before hiring them.[17] With 70 million Facebook members alone, it's no surprise that interviewers are now scrutinizing job candidates' social networking profiles and video site postings—for an unfiltered look at the real person behind the résumé.[18]

In the course of job interviews, one Missouri school superintendent, for example, asks potential teachers if they have a Facebook or MySpace page. If the candidate says yes, then the superintendent suggests taking an immediate look at the would-be teacher's profile, according to the Missouri State Teachers Association, as reported by the *Washington Post*.[19]

That example should serve as a wake-up call to all current job candidates—and any employee who may one day want (or need) to make a job change. Do you really want to give a prospective employer one more reason to reject you? If you're in the job market, consider deactivating your personal blog, discontinuing your social networking page, or editing your posts to focus solely on content that is certain to appeal to prospective employers by highlighting your expertise, experience, or eagerness to fulfill your career goal.

RECAP & e-POLICY ACTION PLAN

1. Writing or posting content about your job, boss, or coworkers may get you fired.

2. The First Amendment does not protect bloggers or social networkers who work for private employers.

3. Employment-at-will means you can be fired for any reason—including inappropriate or offensive use of e-mail, the Internet, camera phones, or other electronic business communication tools.

4. Know the law. Some union workers, for example, may have protections not available to at-will employees.

5. Beware: Some employers screen job applicants' personal blogs and social networking profiles.

6. There simply is no privacy in cyberspace. Employers, law enforcement agencies, the courts, regulators, the media, and the public may one day access your online transmissions, posts, and history—if they haven't done so already.

CHAPTER 24

Q&A: Answers to Employees' Most Commonly Asked e-Policy and Privacy Questions

Establishing or updating a corporate e-policy program provides employers with the ideal opportunity to educate employees about electronic risks, rights, and rules. Yet, only 42 percent of employers conduct the e-policy training, according to the 2006 Workplace E-Mail, Instant Messaging & Blog Survey from American Management Association and ePolicy Institute.[1] Consequently, many users are not only ill informed, but also they are likely to make career-shattering errors when it comes to electronic policy, privacy, monitoring, compliance, and other important issues.

The following list of frequently asked questions and answers is offered to help clarify employees' understanding of workplace risks and thereby shape more appropriate electronic behavior both at the office and at home. In addition, employers are encouraged to incorporate a similar Q&A into their organizations' own formal e-policy training programs.

Q. Isn't it illegal for my employer to read my e-mail?

A. No, it is not illegal. In the United States, the ECPA makes clear the fact that an employer-provided computer system is the property of the employer. As such, the company has every right to monitor all the e-mail that is transmitted via the company's system whether business-related or personal, internal or external. The employee, in turn, has absolutely no reasonable expectation of privacy when using the company computer system to transmit e-mail or engage in other online communication or activity.

Your boss may be among the 43 percent of employers who monitor employee e-mail.[2] In addition, your recipient's employer and the employers of anyone to whom your messages are forwarded or copied are likely to review and possibly retain your e-mail, too.

Best advice: Use the company's e-mail system primarily for business reasons and in accordance with your organization's written e-mail policy. Save any personal, private, or potentially embarrassing messages for transmission from home via your own computer, on your own time, using your own personal e-mail account.

Q. **Is it true that my boss can fire me for personal blog content that I post at home, on my own time, on my own nonbusiness-related blog, via my own computer?**

A. Yes. If you work for a private employer in an employment-at-will state, then your boss can fire you for just about any reason, as long as the dismissal is not discriminatory or in retaliation for whistle-blowing or union organizing.[3]

Laws prevent employers from terminating employees on the basis of race, ethnicity, sex, age, religion, disability, and sexual orientation in some jurisdictions. But when it comes to blogging, even keeping your personal blog clean of work-related material won't necessarily protect you from termination. As one attorney notes, "If your employer feels the blog makes you a poor representative of their corporate values, the executives have the freedom to disassociate themselves from you."[4]

Employees have been fired, or "dooced," for:

- blogging about their employers' people, products, and services

- posting photos of themselves dressed in company uniforms while off duty

- posting embarrassing photos about the goings-on inside companies

- notifying the blogosphere to what a jerk a particular manager is or what a joke a company's policies and procedures are

At the end of the day, blogging (negatively or positively) about your job or your boss is likely to get you fired—regardless of whether you blog at home or at the office, with your own equipment or the company's, anonymously or under your own name.

Q. **My brother lost his job when monitoring software revealed that he was spending too much time surfing the Web for personal reasons. Was his dismissal legal? Can my brother sue his former employer for invasion of privacy or wrongful termination?**

A. Yes, an employer has the legal right to monitor Internet use and terminate employees for Internet abuse. No, it is unlikely that your brother could successfully sue his former boss on the grounds of invasion of privacy or wrongful termination related to Web use and monitoring.

The ECPA gives U.S. employers the legal right to monitor all employee computer activity and transmissions. The ECPA makes clear the fact that the organization's computer system is the property of the employer. As such, employees have absolutely no reasonable expectation of privacy when using company-owned computer systems, tools, and technologies.

Courts in the United States have consistently ruled that employees should assume that their computer activity is being watched—even if they have not been formally notified of monitoring. The courts generally support the position that informed employees neither would nor should assume that their e-mail transmissions are their own. Even in cases in which employers have told workers that incoming and outgoing e-mail is not being monitored, the courts have ruled that employees still should not expect privacy when using a company system.[5]

At the end of the day, anyone who is employed by a private company in an employment-at-will state can be fired for just about any reason—including violation of the

company's Internet policy or any other employment policy.
Employees are advised to review all company computer rules
and other employment policies before engaging in any form of
electronic communication—at the office during business
hours, at home on their free time, or on the road for professional or personal reasons.

Q. **Doesn't the First Amendment protect my job by guaran-
teeing my right to express my opinions online?**

A. Not if you are employed by a private company. Many
privately employed U.S. workers mistakenly believe that the
First Amendment protects their jobs by granting them the
right to say whatever they want via personal blogs, websites,
social networking sites, and video sites. It doesn't. The First
Amendment only restricts government control of speech; it
says nothing about private employers.

Even government employees have lost some of the First
Amendment protections previously available to them. Thanks
to a recent U.S. Supreme Court ruling, government entities
now are free to fire employees for posting comments harmful
to an agency's mission and function.[6]

Q. **Exactly how does e-mail monitoring work? Is my boss
personally reading all my e-mail messages, business and
personal?**

A. Probably not. Of the 43 percent of organizations that
monitor employee e-mail, most (73 percent) use software or
other technology tools to automatically monitor e-mail. Only
40 percent of businesses assign an individual to manually read
workers' e-mail. When e-mail is manually read and reviewed
by an individual, the task typically falls not to the big boss but
to members of the following departments: IT (73 percent),
human resources (34 percent), legal (18 percent), compliance
(17 percent), other (17 percent), and outside third party (4
percent).[7]

If you want to know how your organization handles e-mail
monitoring, and who (if anyone) is manually reading
employees' messages, start by taking a look at the company's
e-mail policy. If the information is not provided in the written
policy, your next stop would be to the chief information officer

or human resources director. At most companies, they will have answers to monitoring questions and concerns.

 How does e-mail monitoring technology work?

A. Best practices call for the use of content monitoring and filtering technology that is based on your company's e-mail policy. These tools allow management to track and block content as it leaves, enters, or is transmitted within the system. Using an automated search tool, employers can seek out and block the transmission of target words and phrases—including, for example, the names of executives, trade secrets, customers, or patients, along with language that is obscene, harassing, discriminatory, or otherwise offensive or objectionable.

Monitoring and filtering technology also can be used to spot and stop particularly large attachments, which may contain customer lists, credit card data, or other valuable or proprietary information—and always warrant a review by management.

 What happens if a coworker uses the company e-mail system to send me a pornographic photo or an off-color joke that violates my employer's e-mail policy? Can I lose my job because of someone else's action?

A. You cannot control other employees' actions, but you can control your own. If you receive an offensive, inappropriate, or otherwise noncompliant e-mail message from a coworker, do not forward, copy, file, or reply to the message. Do not download, file, or print any message attachments. Doing so will position you as a policy violator, right along with the original sender.

Depending on your organization's e-mail policy, you might be instructed to delete the offending message immediately, forward it to a designated member of management for review, or leave it in your inbox for later review by IT, HR, or legal.

Do not fall prey to temptation. Even though other employees may be violating the company's e-mail policy, you must adhere to electronic business communication rules and all other employment policies—100 percent—or risk termination.

I use e-mail to stay in touch with my kids during the workday. They check in with me after school via e-mail, and they know to use e-mail in an emergency if they cannot reach me by phone. Do I have to tell my kids to stop e-mailing me?

A. Probably not. Most employers recognize that some personal e-mail use is warranted. While an e-policy may clearly state that the company's e-mail system is reserved for business use, the policy probably allows for brief communication between work and home. And most employers allow workers to use e-mail to communicate in the case of personal emergencies.

The type of personal communication that is typically prohibited includes any correspondence that pulls you away from your job for extended periods of time or otherwise puts company resources (computer and human) at risk. Generally prohibited is the posting of purely personal, nonfamily, and nonemergency messages that are designed, for example, to advertise a garage sale, solicit a charitable donation, or campaign for a political candidate.

That said, of the 28 percent of bosses who fired employees for e-mail violations in 2007, more than a quarter (26 percent) cited excessive personal use of the company system as the reason for dismissal, according to the 2007 Electronic Monitoring & Surveillance Survey from American Management Association and the ePolicy Institute.[8]

To reduce the likelihood of e-mail-related termination, be sure to review your company's personal use rules regarding how much personal e-mail use you are allowed to engage in, when, why, with whom, under what circumstances, for how long, and during what periods of the work day. Then be sure to comply with those personal use rules 100 percent—no exceptions.

Q. Why can't I bring my own personal software from home into the office? If I paid for it, and it will help me do my job, what's the problem?

A. When you purchase software, you aren't actually buying the software itself. You are purchasing a license to load the software onto one computer. It is illegal to load software that has a single user license onto multiple computers. The term for this is softloading.

In addition to being ethically wrong, softloading puts the company at risk on a number of levels. You could carry a virus into the office via your software. If illegally duplicated software malfunctions, you will not be able to access technical support through the manufacturer's help line. And, if the software police come calling and find illegal software on your workstation computer (or other employees' desktop or laptop computers), then it is the company, not the individual employee, who will be held liable.

 I know of two supervisors who are visiting adults-only websites during business hours. I've seen pornographic images on their computer screens as I've passed by their offices. What should I do? I know they are violating the company's Internet policy, but I'm afraid I'll lose my job if I turn them in.

A. Well-written electronic rules and policies should apply to all employees—managers and supervisors as well as staff. If you know of any employee (executive or support staff, full time or part time) who is violating the company's electronic rules and policies, then you should alert the human resources director. The information you provide should be held in strict confidence and checked out thoroughly. If a violation is unearthed, it is management's responsibility to take appropriate action.

It is in the company's best interest to treat all policy violators equally, regardless of an employee's title, years of experience, or popularity. Should the company become embroiled in Internet-related litigation, management will want to demonstrate that they have adhered to best practices and consistently applied written policy backed by disciplinary action and technology tools. Disciplinary rules that are applied inconsistently may suggest to the court that the company is not truly committed to policy compliance.

Will I lose my job if a malicious hacker attacks the company's network and shuts us down for a period of time?

A. Ideally, your company has taken every precaution to avoid the type of denial of service attack that would shut the computer system down for an extended period. If the organization is adhering to best practices, then management has conducted an internal risk assessment and put into place an electronic risk management policy, assessed and shored up computer security capabilities and procedures, developed comprehensive e-mail and Internet policies, and devoted time and energy to employee education.

There is no way to predict when or how electronic disaster may strike, or what impact it might have on the company and its employees. However, the development and implementation of a strategic electronic risk management program, based on best practices and incorporating policy, training, and technology, can go a long way toward minimizing—and in some cases eliminating—potentially costly risks.

Q. **I've heard the term "social engineering" associated with hackers, but I'm unclear what it means or how it applies to me. Please explain.**

A. When hackers prey on the naiveté of employees or the carelessness of employers in order to gain information and access to a computer system, that is social engineering. Don't make it easy for hackers to access the company's computer system. Don't share your password with anyone. Don't post or keep lists of passwords in unsecured locations. Turn off your computer if you are going to be away from your desk for more than an hour. Unless you've been authorized to do so, do not divulge information about the company's computer system to any outsider, in person, on the phone, through e-mail, or online via a chat room, website, social networking site, or any other means.

Q. **No one expects e-mail messages to be well-written and error-free. With e-mail, a typo is just a typo. No big deal! So why should I adhere to all the rules spelled out in the company's electronic writing style policy?**

A. Every message you write, whether electronic or on paper, is a reflection of the company's credibility and your professionalism. Your e-mail correspondence is expected to be just as polished and professional as your written letters and proposals. Check every e-mail message for accuracy, brevity, and clarity. Run each document through spell check. And adhere to the company's formal electronic writing style guidelines.

> **e-Policy Rule 54:** Every message you write, whether electronic or on paper, is a reflection of the company's credibility and your professionalism. Your e-mail correspondence is expected to be just as polished and professional as your written letters and proposals.

Q. **My company provides me with a cell phone for business use. Am I allowed to use it for personal reasons, too?**

A. That depends on your company's personal use rules. Twenty-seven percent of employers have put policy in place to govern personal cell phone use at work, according to American Management Association and ePolicy Institute research.[9] Before using your company-provided cell phone for nonbusiness-related talking and texting, be sure to review your employer's written personal use rules and policy. If you can't locate a formal personal use policy, then ask your company's human resources director to review the rules with you.

Q. **Can my boss monitor my text messages?**

A. Maybe. Text transmitted via standard consumer-grade text messaging technology may disappear following delivery, but messages sent via business-grade text messaging technology may be saved, stored, and used as evidence, just like e-mail.[10]

As a general rule, bear in mind the fact that company-provided cell phones, pagers, and texting tools are provided primarily for business purposes. You have absolutely no reasonable expectation of privacy when talking or texting via a company-provided cell phone, Smartphone, or other electronic business communication tool.

Best advice: Know the rules before communicating electronically. Use business tools for business communication, and save personal communication for your own home-based equipment and accounts.

Q. **A coworker was fired because of a video she posted on YouTube. What right does my boss have to monitor a public video site or manage what employees do on their own time and in their own homes?**

A. Ten percent of employers in 2007 reported monitoring social networking sites for company-related content including videos.[11] Any employee who criticizes or embarrasses the company, reveals company secrets, or otherwise breaks an employment rule or policy—whether via a video site, social networking page, blog, or personal website—faces disciplinary action, up to and including termination.

In the United States, private employers operating in employment-at-will states have the right to fire employees for just about any reason, including violation of the company's video site rules, social networking policies, and other employment policies. To date, fewer than 1 percent of employers have fired workers for posting business-related content on video or social networking sites, according to the 2007 Electronic Monitoring & Surveillance Survey from American Management Association and ePolicy Institute.[12] However, with some 87 million Americans visiting social networking sites every month,[13] it's safe to assume that the number of online video and networking site violations—and terminations—will grow.

RECAP & e-POLICY ACTION PLAN

1. With less than half of all employers conducting formal e-policy training, many workplace users are ill informed and confused when it comes to electronic policy, privacy, monitoring, compliance, and other important issues.

2. Employees are advised to familiarize themselves with electronic rules—and comply 100 percent with company policies—or face potential disciplinary action, termination, or other personal risks.

3. Employers can help minimize electronic risks—and maximize compliance—by incorporating formal training into strategic electronic business communication programs. Educate employees and executives about electronic business communication risks, rules, policies, and procedures. Best practices call for formal on-site training, giving employees the opportunity to ask questions and receive informed answers in order to clear up any confusion surrounding electronic risks, rules, and resources.

PART ELEVEN

Electronic Writing Rules

e-Policy 101: How to Draft Effective e-Policies for Your Organization

When drafting and formatting your organization's formal e-Policies, focus on accessibility and readability. You want to create written policy documents that are easy for users and managers to read, understand, and comply with. A company policy that is poorly written, or is simply too cumbersome to work through, serves no purpose.

> **e-Policy Rule 55:** When drafting and formatting e-Policies, focus on accessibility and readability. The goal is to create written policy documents that are easy for users to read, understand, and comply with.

The following are 10 tips to help ensure that your company's written e-mail policy and other electronic business communication rules maximize readability, comprehension, and compliance.

Keep Written Policies Brief

Unless you want your employees' eyes to glaze over, don't produce one massive policy document covering the use of all electronic business communication tools and technologies (e-mail, instant messenger, Web, intranet, blogging, social networking, software, cell phones, text messaging, etc.).

Increase the odds of having employees read, remember, and adhere to written rules and policies by writing and distributing separate, brief policy documents governing the use of each individual electronic business communication tool. In other words, draft separate policies for e-mail, IM, the Internet, and all other tools and technologies—old, new, and emerging.

Keep each written e-policy short, simple, and straight to the point. Period.

> **e-Policy Rule 56:** Increase the odds of having employees read, remember, and adhere to written rules and policies by writing and distributing separate, slim policy documents governing the use of each individual electronic business communication tool.

Write Policies in Plain English

To help minimize risks and maximize employee compliance, be sure to write clear policies in plain English. No legal gobbledygook. No confusing technical terms. No acronyms or abbreviations that may not be understood by all employees.

State rules, policies, and procedures in a clear manner that is not open to interpretation by individual employees. For example, don't use vague rules like this one: "Employees are allowed a limited amount of appropriate, personal, nonbusiness-related instant messaging." This kind of writing leaves it up to the individual user to determine what constitutes "limited," "appropriate," and "personal."

Instead, be as specific as possible: "Employees may use IM to communicate with spouses, children, domestic partners, and other family members. Employees' personal use of IM is limited to lunch breaks and authorized work breaks only. Employees may not use IM during otherwise productive business hours. Employees who need to hold personal communications with persons other than spouses, children, domestic partners, and other family members via IM (the company's IM system or the employee's personal IM client) must first obtain permission from management. Employees are prohibited from using IM to operate a business, conduct an external job search, solicit money for personal gain, campaign for political causes or candidates, or promote or solicit funds for a religious or other personal cause. Employees are prohibited from using IM to play online games, visit chat rooms, or engage in illegal activity including but not limited to gambling and drug dealing."

Enhance Readability by Incorporating Plenty of White Space

Use white space, or blank space, to enhance readability and add visual impact. While the use of white space will result in slightly longer policy documents, the trade-off is worth it.

A ten-page, double-spaced document that is accessible and easy to read is considerably less intimidating than a two-page, single-spaced policy that is crammed full, margin-to-margin and header-to-footer, with dense information written in a tight, tiny typeface.

To maximize white space and enhance visual appeal:

- Double space the lines in your document.

- Leave margins of at least an inch on both sides. Learning goes up when notes are written down on paper. Make it easy for employees to jot down important lessons as they work through your company's formal e-policy training program.

- Incorporate an extra line or two before and after particularly important sections to make the copy stand out.

Make Typeface Work for You, Not Against You

Use a standard, businesslike typeface such as Times New Roman, Courier, or Arial. Go no smaller than an 11-point or 12-point font size for the body copy.

Rely on Boldface Headlines and Subheads

Emphasize important copy points while using as few words as possible. Headlines and subheads can help employees navigate the e-policy document, locating information and working their way through the rules quickly and easily. Stick with standard typefaces, but use a larger font size, perhaps 14-point, and bold type to make headlines and subheads stand out.

Communicate Important Information in Small, Bite-Size Chunks

Use bulleted or numbered lists to maximize readability. If you prefer to write in paragraph form, incorporate numbered lists into your paragraphs. For example: "The success of the company's software usage policy depends largely on employee support. To that end, we ask you to adhere to three rules: (1) comply fully with the company's software policy; (2) check with the chief information officer if you have any questions about legal versus illegal software use; and (3) report any software policy violations or suspected violations to the human resources director. Your report and identity will be held in strict confidence."

Include a Table of Contents in Each Policy

Doing so will help make it easy for employees to locate information quickly as questions arise and concerns develop.

Incorporate a Glossary of Electronic Business Communication, Legal, and Technology Terms

To help eliminate confusion and enhance awareness, provide users with a glossary of commonly used electronic business communication, legal, and technology terms. Be sure to include your organization's definition of "electronic business record." From a legal, regulatory, and management perspective, "electronic business record" may be the most important term you can define and share with employees.

Include Contact Information (Names, E-Mail Addresses, Phone Numbers) for e-Policy Team Members

Let employees know who to contact when questions arise regarding electronic business communication risks, rules, policies, and procedures.

Employ an Effective e-Policy Distribution System

It's not enough simply to write policy, you also must ensure that every employee receives a copy of each electronic business communication policy.

You cannot expect an uninformed workforce to comply with policy. And you cannot trust employees on their own to access the company's intranet system or retrieve a copy of the employee handbook in order to educate themselves about e-mail and Internet risks, rules, policies, and procedures.

Best practices call for formal employee training. On-site training is the best approach, granting employees the opportunity to ask questions and gain a thorough understanding of electronic risks and policies. If you have a geographically dispersed workforce, you may want to consider online training in the form of webinars or archived training modules as an alternative to live on-site training.

RECAP & e-POLICY ACTION PLAN

1. When drafting and formatting your organization's formal e-Policies, focus on accessibility and readability. Your goal is to create written policy documents that are easy for users and managers to read, understand, and comply with.

2. At the end of the day, a company policy that is poorly written or is simply too cumbersome to work through is no better than no policy at all.

3. Implement an effective policy distribution system to ensure that all employees have read, understand, and agree to comply with all the organization's e-Policies.

CHAPTER 26

Establishing Electronic Writing Style Policies for Employees

To ensure the production of e-mail messages and other electronic documents that reflect the organization's overall professionalism and credibility, streamline electronic communications for employees. To do this, consider establishing a company-wide electronic writing style policy.

> **e-Policy Rule 57:** To ensure the production of e-mail messages and other electronic documents that reflect the organization's overall professionalism and credibility, streamline electronic communications for employees. To do this, consider establishing a company-wide electronic writing style policy.

The following are a few recommended rules and best practices to incorporate into your organization's electronic style sheet.

Context

E-mail is contextual, with each individual message and reply relating to one another and contributing to the meaning of the entire e-mail chain. Valuable information is gathered as messages travel from writer to reader to writer once again. Thus, when a message is taken out of context and read in isolation, it is easy for the meaning to be misunderstood, misconstrued, or lost entirely. To help limit the likelihood of e-mail-related mishaps and misinterpretations, be sure to incorporate the following rules into your organization's electronic writing style policy.

• *Salutations:* Every e-mail message should begin with a salutation, and your list of electronic writing rules should start with salutations, too. Instruct employees to begin each message (both original messages and comments that may be added as part of a long series of replies) with a salutation such as "Dear Bridget:" or "Bridget," for example. The combination of an opening salutation plus a closing signature (see point 3) will help establish the e-mail's contextual chain. The result: Electronic communication improves, and you may find your e-mail business records are more readily accepted as complete, authentic, and legally valid in litigation situations.

• *Titles:* While you are thinking about salutations, your organization may want to establish a rule to govern the way in which external readers are addressed. Should employees address customers, clients, and other nonemployees formally ("Mr.," "Ms.," "Dr.," "Professor," etc.), or are first names allowed? If "Mr." and "Ms." are required, at what point in the business relationship may employees make the switch to the reader's first name? This is the type of relatively minor but potentially thorny issue that can slow down the writing process for employees who just cannot decide how to address an e-mail recipient.

• *Signatures:* The inclusion of a signature at the end of every e-mail message serves two purposes: (1) the writer's signature helps establish all-important context by signaling the end of the message and identifying the sender; and (2) a comprehensive signature file saves your reader valuable time by providing comprehensive contact information including the sender's name, title, company, street address, phone and fax numbers, e-mail address/hyperlink, Web address/hyperlink, blog address/hyperlink, etc. If the reader wants to contact the writer in any way other than return e-mail, all the necessary contact information is at hand. As part of your organization's electronic writing style policy, consider establishing a standard signature block that all employees must use in formal business-related messages. For example:

Nancy Flynn
Executive Director
The ePolicy Institute
2300 Walhaven Ct.
Columbus, OH 43220

614-451-3200 (phone)
614-451-8726 (fax)
nancy@epolicyinstitute.com
www.epolicyinstitute.com

Let employees know that in informal correspondence or an ongoing back-and-forth series of messages between the same two people, a less formal sign-off is appropriate. On those occasions, use your name (first name only or first and last depending on your relationship with the reader), preceded by one of three approved sign-offs (*Best, Sincerely, Cordially*) For example:

Best,
Nancy Flynn

Rules governing salutations, formal signature blocks, and casual sign-offs serve several equally important purposes: (1) Formal rules help speed the writing process for indecisive or inexperienced writers; (2) clear guidelines reduce the possibility of employees' wrapping up business correspondence with quirky signatures or inappropriate sign-offs; (3) otherwise cold electronic messages are warmed up thanks to salutations and sign-offs; (4) signatures give readers a clear stop sign—there's no need to scroll the screen to determine whether or not the writer has concluded his or her message; (5) readers save time and aggravation that might otherwise be spent searching the Web, phone book, or other sources for the writer's contact information; and (6) thanks to the opening salutation and closing signature, the contextual string of the e-mail conversation is established, leaving no doubt who said what.

Capitalization

Is there consistency within your organization when it comes to capitalization? How do your employees handle the capitalizing of job titles, departments, job functions, etc.? Does management, for example, prefer the phrases "the company" and "the organization" to be capitalized? Use your electronic writing style policy to let employees know what words are to be capitalized, under what circumstances.

Names

Do employees consistently refer to your organization by the same name? If not, is there any chance of creating confusion among readers? Consider adopting a policy whereby, on the first reference, the company name is spelled out in full (The ePolicy Institute™), then on every additional reference, a company-approved shortened version of the name may be used (ePolicy Institute). This type of naming policy prevents employees from using a considerably less formal and potentially confusing name, "ePolicy," while saving them the aggravation of writing out the company name in full throughout an e-mail message or IM chat.

Technical Terms and Professional Jargon

High-tech industries and certain professions (medical and legal, for example) tend to have a language of their own. Industry insiders often use technical terms and professional jargon freely, assuming that all readers share their education and experience and will have no trouble understanding the meaning of their words.

The language of insiders is best restricted to the company intranet, internal blogs, enterprise IM, and other in-house electronic communication tools. A jargon-laden message that is forwarded to a nontechnical recipient or lands on the screen of an external reader could create confusion and lessen the reader's acceptance of future messages from the writer in question.

Spellings

Does your organization or industry regularly use words that have optional spellings (theatre or theater, catalogue or catalog, disc or disk, etc.)? Simplify life for your employees by incorporating a corporate vocabulary list, complete with preferred spellings, into your organization's electronic writing style policy.

Working Around Oddities

While we all know that proper nouns and sentences should always begin with a capital letter, company names (ePolicy Institute, for example) sometimes begin with lowercase letters. If that's the case for your organization or client companies, be sure to address this issue in your electronic writing style policy.

For example, instruct employees to rewrite any sentence in which a lowercase company name appears as the first word. Consider the sentence, "ePolicy Institute, dedicated to helping employers limit e-mail and Internet-related risks through effective electronic business communication policies and training programs, offers on-site seminars and online webinars to clients worldwide." This sentence easily can be reworked as, "Dedicated to helping employers limit e-mail and Internet-related risks through effective electronic business communication policies and training programs, ePolicy Institute offers on-site seminars and online webinars to clients worldwide."

Avoid Humor and Other Communication Pitfalls

The introduction of your company's electronic writing style policy offers a great opportunity to remind employees of electronic content and language rules, netiquette guidelines, and other employment policies.

Start by reminding employees that jokes have no place in work-related e-mail. Save the humorous anecdotes for golf outings, lunch meetings, and other in-person gatherings. Because e-mail is an impersonal medium offering none of the benefits of inflection, facial expression, or body language, electronic humor is risky business. Electronic jokes are likely to fall flat or be misconstrued by the reader. At best, an attempt at humor could irritate or agitate the recipient, spelling disaster for a business relationship. An employee's "joke" could trigger a hostile work environment claim, resulting in costly and protracted litigation.

Communicating with International Readers

One of the beauties of e-mail is that it enables writers to communicate quickly and easily with colleagues and customers around the globe. If your employees will be communicating electronically with readers in other countries, be sure to establish communication guidelines and language conventions to simplify the writer's job and enhance the reader's understanding. The following are a few tips:

• Remember that international electronic communication poses unique language, cultural, and time challenges. Think about your international reader's communication needs before writing and sending your message.

• English may be the international language of commerce, but that does not mean that every reader, intended and hidden, will have a trouble-free experience with messages that are written in English. Determine who your reader is and what your reader's language needs are before you start writing. If necessary, have your message translated.

• International correspondence calls for more detailed and specific information than domestic e-mail. For example, a message that reads, "The teleconference to review employment policies will begin at 6:00 p.m. on 6/5/09," could have disastrous results. Americans would read that date as June 5, 2009. Europeans would interpret it as May 6, 2009. And Japanese readers, using a year, month, day order, would face more confusion.

Because Europeans use a 24-hour military clock, be sure to write international e-mail according to that format. "The employment policy teleconference will begin at 6:00 p.m. on 6/5/09" becomes "The employment policy teleconference will begin at 18:00 on 5 June, 2009."

Similarly, when sending domestic e-mail to geographically dispersed business associates throughout the United States, be sure to indicate the time zone (Eastern, Central, Mountain, Pacific) when scheduling meetings or discussing time-sensitive deadlines.

• Measurements can prove equally challenging when sending e-mail abroad. To eliminate confusion, give the metric measurement, followed by its American equivalent in parentheses. For example, "The staff training facility is located 10 kilometers (6.2 miles) from company headquarters."

• Do not assume that all speakers of a given language are culturally similar. English-speaking Americans differ culturally from English-speaking Americans who either live in other parts of the country or have different ethnic backgrounds. Spanish-speaking Mexicans differ culturally from Spaniards, and French-speaking Canadians differ culturally from the French.

• Even if you are sending an e-mail to an employee at one of your own organization's overseas offices, avoid using technical language, jargon, acronyms, abbreviations, or humor. Given language and cultural differences, there is too much opportunity for misunderstanding and confusion.

• Be specific and avoid vague language. If you send a hold-the-date message to announce the fact that the company's annual meeting will be held on 25 November, 2010 at a Midwest location, U.S. readers will understand what you are referring to geographically, but international readers are likely to be in the dark (or at a minimum confused) about the location of the Midwest in relation to well-known U.S. cities like New York or Los Angeles.

• Also be mindful of terms that change in meaning depending on the country in which they are used. A U.S.-based *organization* would become an *organisation* if it moved to the United Kingdom. In the United States, a boot is a type of shoe. In the United Kingdom, on the other hand, a boot is the trunk of a car. Word choice plays a significant role in the clarity of communication and the overall effectiveness of e-mail.

The Language of Electronic Abbreviations

Instruct employees to use only legitimate and recognizable abbreviations, not their own personal shorthand. Don't overuse abbreviations. Too many abbreviations can make a sentence difficult to read, annoying and confusing the reader in the process. On-screen writing is tough enough to read without trying to decipher the writer's shorthand. When using an uncommon abbreviation, be sure to clarify it on the first reference by spelling out the word or phrase and citing the abbreviation in parentheses. For example, "Since 2001, American Management Association (AMA) and The ePolicy Institute have conducted an annual survey of workplace e-mail and Internet policies and procedures." The abbreviation may then be used alone throughout the rest of the document.

Electronic Acronyms Create New Challenges

The need to keep text messages and IM chat brief has spawned an electronic vocabulary of acronyms. While some electronic acronyms (FYI and FAQ, for example) would be familiar to nearly all readers, others may prove challenging to many business users, particularly older employees who are unaccustomed to the language of texting and instant messaging. Instruct employees not to use acronyms if there is any doubt the reader will understand their meaning.

Smileys Dumb Down Communication

Unlike one-on-one meetings and telephone conversations, e-mail is a communications tool that is totally devoid of inflection, facial expression, and body language. To help readers interpret the e-mail writer's attitude and tone, smileys, or emoticons, have been created as visual shorthand. Smileys, created with standard keyboard characters, are used by some electronic writers to substitute for facial expression and body language. The smiley generally follows the punctuation mark at the end of the sentence. :)

The equivalent of e-mail slang, smileys have no place in business writing. Readers who are unfamiliar with smileys won't understand their meaning. And readers who do understand them will likely interpret their use as an indication that the writer is not a professional. Employees should rely on the strength of their writing, rather than smileys, exclamation points, and uppercase letters, to communicate electronic messages effectively.

E-Mail Formatting Guidelines

As part of your comprehensive electronic writing style policy, you'll want to establish formatting guidelines to help employees enhance the effectiveness of e-mail messages. No matter how important a message may be, when it comes to formatting e-mail, readability is the name of the game. If a message is not legible, the recipient may not have the patience to work through it. Tips for making e-mail as readable as possible follow.

- *Select the right typeface.* E-mail that is composed of unusual type or exceptionally large or small characters is just plain hard to read. Electronic business correspondence calls for a polished, professional look. Accomplish that by using a standard typeface such as Times New Roman, Courier, or Arial. Enhance reader comfort by sticking with 11-point or 12-point font sizes. A good typeface policy for business e-mail is not too small, not too large, and not too fancy.

- *Resist the urge to use capital or lowercase letters.* In an effort to draw attention to on-screen messages, many e-mail correspondents write entirely in the uppercase. Bad idea. A message that is written in all uppercase letters is more difficult to read than one written in standard style. In addition, when you write entirely in the uppercase, your reader may think you are "shouting" and take offense. The human eye is used to reading a mix of uppercase and lowercase letters. It may be quicker to write in all uppercase or lowercase, but the result will be a document that is difficult to read, and which may turn off readers.

- ***Create visual emphasis.*** You will save writing time and ease the reader's job as well by emphasizing important points with lists of numbers or bullet substitutes. As an alternative to numbered lists, you can construct lists within paragraphs. This approach saves space while maximizing readability. Example: "Manage electronic business communication risk through the implementation of the "3-Es": (1) Establish written policy; (2) Educate the workforce; and (3) Enforce policy with a combination of disciplinary action and technology tools.

- ***Limit most e-mail to one screen page.*** Generally, an e-mail message should be contained on one screen, and only a small portion of the screen at that. When you start to think your e-mail message has gone on too long, or if you need to support your message with letterhead, charts, graphics, or written backup, then it is time to consider attaching a separate document to your message.

Use Conversational, Business-Appropriate Language

Use your organization's electronic writing style policy to remind employees of the organization's content rules. Whether communicating via e-mail or IM or posting content on the company's business blog or website, electronic writers should use business-appropriate language and strike a tone that is conversational, yet professional. Instruct employees to adhere to the ABCs of effective electronic business writing: accuracy, brevity, and clarity.

Take time also to review the organization's retention policy and archiving procedures, and remind employees that inappropriate content that is committed to writing today may someday return to haunt the user and harm the company in the event of a lawsuit, regulatory audit, Freedom of Information Act request, or other call for the production and review of e-mail and other electronically stored information.

Special Circumstances

Before rolling out your electronic writing style policy to employees, be sure to review all of your organization's risks, rules, tools, and technologies. For example, if you incorporate VaporStream Confidential Messaging as a means to conduct recordless, private electronic conversations (Chapter 7), then you will need to provide employees with VaporStream-specific writing rules. Unlike e-mail—which is a contextual medium in which a string of messages and replies can be created, maintained for the course of the conversation, and archived forever—VaporStream doesn't create a message trail. Once VaporStream messages are read, they are gone forever, leaving no trail of messages and replies for later reference. Consequently, among other VaporStream-specific writing guidelines, users must write "stand-alone" messages that leave readers with no question about authorship or meaning.

Grammar for Grown-Up Electronic Writers

Help speed the writing process and boost the self-confidence of writers by incorporating a grammar, punctuation, and mechanics refresher in your electronic writing style policy. As part of your effort to create accurate, brief, and clear electronic communication, provide employees with dictionaries, writing style manuals, and grammar and punctuation guidelines. Remind employees also to take advantage of spell-check, grammar-check, and other automatic tools that are built into the organization's e-mail system.

Educate Electronic Writers

To ensure effective electronic business communication—and real understanding of and compliance with the organization's electronic writing style policy—introduce your company's new writing rules in the course of a formal, on-site or online training program for all electronic writers. Consider retaining the ePolicy Institute or another experienced writing skills trainer to teach employees how to write effective e-mail.

RECAP & e-POLICY ACTION PLAN

1. Enforce electronic content rules by imposing an electronic writing style policy. Put your rules in writing to make it easy for employees to follow the organization's approved electronic writing guidelines.

2. Focus your electronic writing style policy on the tenets of accuracy, brevity, and clarity—the ABCs of electronic business writing.

3. Address content rules and language issues in your electronic writing style policy. One of the easiest, most effective ways to control electronic risk is to control written content. Train employees to monitor their electronic content, adopting professional language and a conversational tone for business communications.

4. E-mail is intended as a quick means of communication. Help speed the writing process and boost the self-confidence of employee-writers by incorporating a grammar, punctuation, and mechanics refresher in your electronic writing policy. As part of your effort to create accurate, brief, and clear electronic communication, provide employees with dictionaries, writing style manuals, and grammar and punctuation guidelines. Remind employees also to take advantage of spell-check, grammar-check, and other automatic tools that are built into the organization's e-mail system.

5. Bring a professional writing coach on board to introduce employees to your new electronic writing style policy, while providing a refresher course on business writing basics and effective electronic writing skills.

Fifty-Seven e-Policy Rules to Help Keep Your Organization in Business . . . *and Out of Court*

e-Policy Rule 1: Through the implementation of a comprehensive e-policy program that combines written rules with employee education supported by discipline and technology tools, organizations can effectively minimize electronic risks and maximize compliance.

e-Policy Rule 2: You cannot afford to ignore new and emerging technology. If you fail to provide the hot, must-have technologies of the day, chances are your tech-savvy employees will bring them in through the back door. Left undetected and unmanaged, that's a recipe for disaster!

e-Policy Rule 3: Electronically stored information (ESI) creates the electronic equivalent of DNA evidence. ESI can—and will—be subpoenaed and used as evidence for or against your organization should it one day become embroiled in a workplace lawsuit.

e-Policy Rule 4: Clearly written and effectively communicated e-Policies can help employers demonstrate to courts and regulators that the organization has made every effort to manage electronic use and content.

e-Policy Rule 5: Your ability to formally define, effectively retain, successfully archive, and quickly produce electronic business records is one of the most important jobs your organization can undertake.

e-Policy Rule 6: There is no one-size-fits-all definition of a business record. Every organization must develop its own definition on a companywide or department-by-department basis.

e-Policy Rule 7: E-mail and other electronically stored information is subject to discovery and may be used as evidence in litigation.

e-Policy Rule 8: The retention of e-mail business records is fundamentally a legal issue. Legal must take the lead in determining precisely which e-mail messages and other data will be preserved, exactly how and where data will be stored, and specifically when—if ever—electronically stored information will be deleted.

e-Policy Rule 9: Failure to manage e-mail and other electronically stored information can have a costly and otherwise devastating impact on your organization's bottom line, reputation, and future.

e-Policy Rule 10: Don't take chances with e-mail evidence. Combine formal retention rules and litigation hold policies with reliable archiving technology to ensure that electronically stored information is properly preserved and promptly produced.

e-Policy Rule 11: A destructive retention policy that calls for the purging of e-mail on regular intervals may render you the only party in the courtroom who is unable to produce copies of your own e-mail. That's a position you never want to be in!

e-Policy Rule 12: Consult with legal counsel to ensure that your organization is compliant with the e-mail-related regulations of the industries, states, and countries in which you operate.

e-Policy Rule 13: To ensure regulatory compliance and safeguard protected data, implement an e-mail management program that addresses content, security, retention, and archiving.

e-Policy Rule 14: The effective management of e-mail business records is an essential business task. Your ability (or inability) to preserve, protect, and produce electronic evidence can make (or break) your case, your company, and your career in the event of a workplace lawsuit or regulatory investigation.

e-Policy Rule 15: Safeguard your organization's e-mail records and ensure their forensic compliance with automatic archiving technology that guarantees your organization's ability to produce *precisely* the e-mail messages and attachments you need, *exactly* when you need them, *specifically* to courts' and regulators' specifications.

e-Policy Rule 16: Notify employees that they have no reasonable expectation of privacy when it comes to computer use—regardless of whether they are using the organization's resources and systems or their own personal accounts and tools.

e-Policy Rule 17: Institute personal use rules in conjunction with your organization's privacy policy. Let employees know exactly how much personal e-mail and Internet use they are allowed to engage in, when, why, with whom, and under what circumstances.

e-Policy Rule 18: Personal e-mail accounts and IM tools transmit messages across the public Web, outside the organization's secure firewall. Reduce risks by enforcing a strict ban on all personal e-mail accounts and any web-based IM tools that are not supported by IM gateway/management software.

e-Policy Rule 19: Left unmanaged, e-mail and IM can result in the rapid-fire transmission of proprietary and protected content that can pose a threat to the organization, its people, products, reputation, and future.

e-Policy Rule 20: E-mail leaves behind an electronic footprint that *never disappears completely.* Messages and attachments live on forever—in your system, the networks of intended recipients, and the systems of everyone else who, intentionally or accidentally, receives copies of your transmissions.

e-Policy Rule 21: Business is not required to communicate via e-mail. Unless the law or regulators demand a record of your discussion or transaction, private recordless communication—conducted in person, on the phone, or via electronic confidential messaging—is legal and may be the most appropriate form of business communication.

e-Policy Rule 22: If your company touches credit cards, Social Security numbers, protected health information, financial data, or other sensitive and private consumer information, then you must adopt policies and procedures to ensure compliance with data breach notification laws.

e-Policy Rule 23: To help control e-mail risk, stop and think before you write and send.

e-Policy Rule 24: Incorporate netiquette, or electronic etiquette, rules into the organization's e-policy program to help maximize civil business behavior.

e-Policy Rule 25: IM is nothing more than turbocharged e-mail. Like e-mail, it is written correspondence that creates an electronic business record.

e-Policy Rule 26: Assume that your employees are already using instant messaging—without your knowledge, authorization, rules, or policies.

e-Policy Rule 27: Video snacking opens the organization up to bandwidth waste, security breaches, and lost productivity. Apply written policy, monitoring technology, and URL blocks to manage video snacking risks.

e-Policy Rule 28: Use written Internet policy to notify employees that the company's Internet system is a business tool that is intended primarily for authorized commerce, communication, research, and other business-related purposes.

e-Policy Rule 29: Use written Internet policy to notify employees that they are prohibited from using company computer resources to create, view, print, copy, download, upload, transmit, file, or forward content that is offensive, objectionable, or otherwise in violation of *any* company rule or policy.

e-Policy Rule 30: The blog is an electronic communications powerhouse that could have more impact on business communications and corporate reputations than e-mail, instant messaging, and traditional marketing-oriented websites combined.

e-Policy Rule 31: The casual, conversational, anything-goes nature of the blog makes it appealing to blog writers and readers—and potentially dangerous to business.

e-Policy Rule 32: Unlike mainstream news sites that authenticate information and vet sources before posting content, social networking and video sites allow anyone to post anything—without regard to fact checking or potential fallout.

e-Policy Rule 33: Thanks to social networking and video sites, employees have gained direct access to the public, and employers have lost their iron-fisted control over company messages.

e-Policy Rule 34: If employees use the organization's computer system to post comments on Facebook or upload videos to YouTube, that content may be subpoenaed, must be produced, and could be used as evidence in workplace lawsuits or regulatory audits.

e-Policy Rule 35: It is illegal, unethical, and potentially very expensive to duplicate software that is licensed for single use. The high cost of software piracy really adds up when you calculate the expense of buying replacement software, the sting of negative publicity, and the havoc wreaked by virus-infected software.

e-Policy Rule 36: If found guilty of using illegally copied software, your organization could face enormous fines. If sued for civil copyright infringement, the penalty is up to $150,000 per title infringed. If convicted of a criminal violation, the fine is up to $250,000 and up to five years imprisonment.

e-Policy Rule 37: Establish a strict software usage policy to protect your organization from litigation, insulate your computers from defective software that could carry viruses and other malicious intruders, and reduce overall software costs.

e-Policy Rule 38: Software is protected by federal copyright law. You must purchase new software for every computer on which a given program runs.

e-Policy Rule 39: Cell phones saddle employers with increased risks including driving-related insurance claims and lawsuits, lost productivity, security violations, data theft, business record gaffes, and etiquette breaches.

e-Policy Rule 40: Employers may be held legally responsible for car crashes caused by distracted employees talking or texting while driving.

e-Policy Rule 41: Ban all employee cell phone use (making calls, taking calls, listening to voicemail, or text messaging) while driving during business hours.

e-Policy Rule 42: Address confidentiality rules as part of your cell phone and text messaging policy. Be sure employees understand that an overheard cell phone conversation or an indiscreet text message could put the company and its secrets at risk.

e-Policy Rule 43: Ban the use of cell phones to take, transmit, download, upload, print, or copy photos or videos that are not directly related to company business.

e-Policy Rule 44: Control costs, manage productivity, and mitigate risks by instituting written rules that make clear the fact that company-owned phones are to be used primarily for business use. Place limits on personal talking and texting, just as you restrict personal e-mail and Internet use.

e-Policy Rule 45: Combine electronic rules with continuing education, and you may find your employees more compliant and the courts and regulators more accepting of the fact that you have made every effort to keep your organization free of inappropriate electronic conduct and content.

e-Policy Rule 46: Best practices call for e-Policies to be formally reviewed and updated every 12 months.

e-Policy Rule 47: Private employers in employment-at-will states (which most states are) have the right to fire employees for just about any reason—including inappropriate computer use—as long as federal discrimination guidelines aren't violated.

e-Policy Rule 48: Electronic monitoring is the easiest, most effective way to track e-mail and Internet use and misuse. Take advantage of your legal right to monitor—and manage—employees' internal and external online activity and transmissions.

e-Policy Rule 49: Reduce the likelihood of inappropriate e-mail and Web use triggering lawsuits and other disasters by combining written content and usage rules, employee education, discipline, and policy-based content monitoring, filtering, and blocking tools.

e-Policy Rule 50: Think of monitoring, filtering, and security technology as investments in risk management and litigation prevention.

e-Policy Rule 51: Assume you are being monitored at the office and at home, too. Always think before you write, send, or surf!

e-Policy Rule 52: Remember, a policy is a policy, regardless of the communication tool used to transmit information. Violation of any employment policy, whether committed via e-mail, the Internet, a video site, or any other electronic communication tool, can get you fired.

e-Policy Rule 53: If you don't want your online activity singled out for review and potential disciplinary action, then simply adhere to all of your employer's electronic rules and policies.

e-Policy Rule 54: Every message you write, whether electronic or on paper, is a reflection of the company's credibility and your profession-alism. Your e-mail correspondence is expected to be just as polished and professional as your written letters and proposals.

e-Policy Rule 55: When drafting and formatting e-Policies, focus on accessibility and readability. The goal is to create written policy documents that are easy for users to read, understand, and comply with.

e-Policy Rule 56: Increase the odds of having employees read, remember, and adhere to written rules and policies by writing and distributing separate, slim policy documents governing the use of each individual electronic business communication tool.

e-Policy Rule 57: To ensure the production of e-mail messages and other electronic documents that reflect the organization's overall professionalism and credibility, streamline electronic communications for employees. To do this, consider establishing a company-wide electronic writing style policy.

e-Policy Dos and Don'ts

Best Practices to Help Minimize Risks and Maximize Compliance

Do

• Establish comprehensive, written rules and policies that address employee use of e-mail, the Internet, and all other electronic business communication tools—old, new, and emerging. Assign experienced legal counsel a lead role in the company's e-policy program. Among other business-critical tasks, have your legal expert:

> Create a formal definition of "business record" for your company;

> Review all electronic rules and policies to ensure that all applicable laws and regulations are addressed;

> Determine record life cycles and retention policies;

> Establish and enforce litigation hold policies; and

> Oversee the preservation and production of e-mail records and other electronically stored information in the event of a workplace lawsuit or regulatory investigation.

• Establish an e-policy team to oversee the development and implementation of the organization's e-risk management program. The ideal corporate e-policy team would include a lawyer who is experienced with electronic business communication risks and requirements, along with the organization's chief compliance officer, records manager, IT director, human resources manager, and training manager.

- Be proactive. Today's investment in policy, training, and technology is nothing compared to the six- to seven-figure legal defense and settlement costs that are often associated with e-mail-related litigation.

- Remember that e-mail and other electronically stored information create the electronic equivalent of DNA evidence, which can sink careers and savage companies. Impose formal rules and written policies to manage content, use, and risk.

- Bear in mind the fact that business is not required to communicate via e-mail. Unless the law or regulators demand a record of your discussion or transaction, private recordless communication is legal and may be the most appropriate form of business communication. Employers who are eager to keep secrets safe and eyes-only conversations under wraps are advised to take advantage of the law and limit e-mail use to situations in which a business record is required. When your legal counsel or compliance officer agrees that the need for secrecy outweighs the need for a permanent business record, then take advantage of your right to communicate in a confidential, recordless fashion via telephone, a face-to-face meeting, or VaporStream Confidential Messaging (see Chapter 7).

- Educate employees and executives about electronic business communication risks, rules, policies, and procedures. Best practices call for formal on-site training, giving employees the opportunity to ask questions and clear up any confusion surrounding electronic risks, rules, and resources.

- If on-site training is not an option for your company, then implement online training, complete with a certification quiz to demonstrate employees' comprehension of the organization's electronic risks and rules.

- Communicate the fact that the organization's computer system and electronic business communication tools and technologies—including but not limited to e-mail, instant messenger, Internet, blogs, cell phones, and text messaging—are to be used primarily for business communication. But don't stop there. Provide clear guidance on what is, and is not, considered appropriate business use and content.

- Bear in mind that some personal use of your organization's computer system may be warranted. American workers today put in more on-the-job hours than at any other time in history. For employees who leave the house before dawn and don't return until well past dark, e-mail messages, IM chat, and text messaging via company-provided cell phones may be the most efficient and effective ways to stay in touch with family members.

For the sake of employee morale and retention, savvy employers generally are willing to accommodate their employees' need to check in electronically with children, spouses, domestic partners, schools, and babysitters among others. Do not leave your personal use policy open to individual interpretation. Let your employees know exactly where you stand on this issue, and precisely how much personal use, with whom, under what circumstances, and during what periods of the day is acceptable.

• Incorporate an overview of your organization's discrimination and sexual harassment policies within your electronic policies. Because of the relaxed, informal nature of some electronic business communication tools, employees may put in writing comments they never would say aloud. Make sure employees understand that, regardless of how it is transmitted, an inappropriate comment is an inappropriate comment. All it takes is one offensive message or posting to land you on the wrong side of an expensive, protracted lawsuit.

• Remind employees that a policy is a policy, regardless of whether employees are at the office, at home, on the road, in a customer's office, or at any other location. Employees are expected to adhere to all company policies (including but not limited to ethics guidelines, code of conduct, harassment and discrimination policies, confidentiality rules, computer policies, and telecommunications rules) at all times.

Regardless of whether employees are using company-provided technology tools during business hours or their own personal computers or cell phones on their own time in their own homes, employees are required to comply with all company policies 100 percent of the time.

• Review your written electronic rules and policies with all employees. New hires and long-time employees, managers and supervisors, full-time professionals and part-time staff, telecommuters and temporary employees, independent contractors and freelancers— everyone should be informed of all of your electronic business communication rules, as well as all other employment policies.

• Require all employees to sign and date a copy of every company policy to confirm they have read and understand each rule and policy, and they agree to comply with every policy, or they are willing to accept the consequences.

• Incorporate your written electronic business communication rules and policies into your organization's employee handbook and new-hire orientation materials—but not to the exclusion of formal on-site or online training. You cannot expect employees to access rules and policies on their own, outside of a formal training environment. And you should not expect an untrained workforce to recognize electronic risks, understand electronic rules, or comply with electronic business communication policies.

•   Address ownership issues and privacy expectations. Let employees know that the company computer system belongs to the organization, not the individual user. Explain that the ECPA gives U.S. employers the legal right to monitor all employee e-mail transmissions and Internet activity. If management monitors employees' computer use, say so. Be sure to let employees know why you are monitoring, what you are looking for, and exactly how monitoring works—automatically via technology or manually via human review.

•   Explain that employees have absolutely no reasonable expectation of privacy when using the company's computer system. Make sure employees understand that their electronic transmissions and postings can, and will, be reviewed at any time without notice or permission of the employee. If there is any chance you may want to monitor employees' home computers, personal blogs, social networking sites, or other personal electronic tools and technologies, make that clear as well.

•   Remind government employees that the federal Freedom of Information Act and similar state statutes give the media and taxpayers ready access to e-mail messages and other electronically stored information.

•   Notify employees that management may grant local, state, and federal law enforcement agencies access to an employee's e-mail transmissions and Internet activity—without informing the user.

•   Establish netiquette, or electronic etiquette, policies for all electronic business communication tools, including but not limited to e-mail, IM, blogs, social networking and video sites, cell phones, text messaging, and camera phones. Apply netiquette guidelines equally to managers and staff to help reduce risks and ensure civil business behavior.

•   Define "business record" on a company-wide or department-by-department basis. There is no one-size-fits-all definition of business record. Every company is obligated to establish its own formal definition of electronic business records—and then to educate all employees about business record risks, rules, policies, and procedures. Be sure to notify employees of their individual roles, if any, in the retention and disposition of business-critical e-mail and other electronic business records.

• Ensure that e-mail messages and attachments can be promptly produced in a legally compliant fashion in accordance with legal, regulatory, and business management requirements. Take advantage of the comprehensive and automatic features of real-time archiving technology like ArcMail's archiving solution, Defender, to guarantee immediate access to archived data; automatic capture and storage of internal and external e-mail in one central location; and protection against malicious intruders intent on altering, deleting, or stealing your files (see Chapter 5).

• Establish content and physical security rules as part of your overall electronic risk management program. Put into place procedures and tools designed to protect your system, secrets, and customer or patient data from malicious intruders, internal saboteurs, and data thieves.

• Apply technology tools to help manage people problems. Take advantage of technology to automate necessary tasks including the monitoring and filtering of e-mail, IM, and Internet use and content; retaining and archiving e-mail and IM business records; purging insignificant, personal, and other nonrecord e-mail from the system; and blocking access to banned websites, external blogs, and unauthorized social networking sites.

• Take advantage of technology to automatically track external blogs and social networking sites to see what type of content outside parties are posting about your company, its people, products, services, and secrets. Be prepared to respond swiftly if monitoring reveals that executives have been defamed by bloggers or trade secrets have been exposed on video sites.

• Review and update e-Policies annually. To be effective, electronic rules and policies must address all current and emerging risks, regulations, laws, and technologies. An e-risk management program that includes an annual policy review will help establish the fact that your organization has applied best practices and made every effort to keep employees legally compliant, should you one day find yourself battling a workplace lawsuit.

• Enforce policies with consistent disciplinary action. Use your formal training program to let employees know what type of penalties—up to and including termination—await policy violators. When it comes to discipline, be fair and consistent. Apply established penalties for all e-policy violations, regardless of the offending party's rank, title, years of service, or popularity. When it comes to policy compliance, a penalty is a penalty.

• Make all managers and supervisors aware of the important roles they play when it comes to monitoring and managing employees' electronic behavior.

Don't

• Assign one individual sole responsibility for single-handedly establishing and enforcing your organization's electronic rules and policies. If human and financial resources allow, form an e-policy team that includes your in-house legal counsel, compliance officer, chief information officer or IT director, human resources director, training manager, and records manager. Smaller organizations may want to draw upon the expertise of outside e-policy, records management, and legal consultants.

• Rely solely on e-mail, the company's intranet system, or an employee handbook (printed or electronic) to communicate electronic business communication rules and policies to employees. Distribute written e-Policies to employees as part of formal on-site training. Require each employee to read, sign, and date a hard copy of each policy. Following initial formal training, feel free to use e-mail messages, along with the company's intranet system, to remind employees of the company's rules, policies, and commitment to enforcement.

• Expect employees to train themselves. Educate employees about the what's, why's, and how's of your organization's electronic business communication rules and policies. Make employees aware of their risks, rights, and responsibilities—and the repercussions they will face if they accidentally or intentionally violate any of your policies.

• Create separate policies for the executive ranks. Establish corporate rules and policies, and insist that all officers, executives, managers, supervisors, professionals, and staff adhere to them—equally and consistently.

A supervisor who turns a blind eye to an employee's online gambling addiction, a manager who winks at department-wide software piracy, a board member who sends risqué jokes to senior executives, a smitten boss who texts love notes to a subordinate—all put the organization at risk.

- Forget your international associates. If you do business, employ workers, or operate facilities abroad, then have your legal counsel investigate the laws and regulations governing online privacy and monitoring for each country in which you have a presence.

- Ignore new and emerging technology. Even if your organization does not currently use IM, operate a blog, or provide employees with BlackBerry Smartphones, you cannot afford to ignore new and emerging technology. If you fail to provide the hot, must-have technologies of the day, chances are your tech-savvy employees (particularly younger employees whose social lives revolve around IMing, texting, and social networking) will bring them in through the back door and load them onto your system without management approval or IT oversight.

- Allow employees to dismiss the organization's electronic rules and policies as insignificant or unenforceable. Make sure employees understand that their computer activity will be monitored. Stress the fact that e-policy violators will face disciplinary action that may include termination. Let employees know you mean business by enforcing your e-Policies consistently.

Sample Electronic Business Communication Policies

The following fill-in-the-blank e-policy samples are offered to help employers develop effective e-mail, IM, confidential messaging, Internet, intranet, blog, social networking and video site, cell phone and text messaging, and software policies. Under the guidance of competent legal counsel, feel free to edit and adapt these sample policies as appropriate for your industry, organization, and employees.

These fill-in-the-blank sample policies are intended strictly as examples. Sample policies are offered with the understanding that neither the author nor the publisher of this book are engaged in rendering legal counsel, regulatory advice, or other professional services.

If legal, regulatory, technology, or other expert assistance is required, the services of competent professionals should be sought.

E-Mail Policy

The Company provides employees with electronic communications tools, including an e-mail system.

This written e-mail policy governs employees' use of the Company's e-mail system at the Company's headquarters and district offices, as well as at remote locations including but not limited to employees' homes, client offices, supplier offices, hotels, and airports.

The Company's e-mail rules and policies apply to employees' use of desktop computers, laptops, Blackberry Smartphones, cell phones, and other handheld devices, whether provided by the Company or owned by the employee or a third party.

The Company's e-mail rules and policies apply to full-time employees, part-time employees, independent contractors, interns, consultants, agents, and third parties including but not limited to suppliers and clients.

Any employee who violates the Company's e-mail rules and policies is subject to disciplinary action, up to and including termination.

1. E-Mail Exists for Business Purposes. The Company's e-mail system is provided primarily for business purposes. Employees may use the Company's e-mail system for personal use in accordance with this policy.

2. Authorized Personal Use of E-Mail. Employees may use the Company's e-mail system to communicate with spouses, children, domestic partners, and other family members. Employees' personal use of the Company's e-mail system is limited to lunch breaks and work breaks only. Employees may not use the Company's e-mail system during otherwise productive business hours.

Employees who need to hold personal communications with persons other than spouses, children, domestic partners, and other family members via the Company's e-mail system must obtain permission from management.

Employees are prohibited from using the e-mail system to operate a business, conduct an external job search, solicit money for personal gain, campaign for political causes or candidates, or promote or solicit funds for a religious or other personal cause.

Employees are prohibited from using the e-mail system to play online games, visit chat rooms, shop online, or engage in illegal activity including but not limited to gambling and drug dealing.

3. Personal E-Mail Tools and Accounts Banned. Employees are prohibited from using personal Web-based (Gmail, AOL, etc.) e-mail accounts for business or personal communications.

4. Employees Have No Reasonable Expectation of Privacy. The e-mail system is the property of the Company. All passwords, user IDs, and messages created and transmitted are the property of the Company. The Company reserves the right to monitor all e-mail transmissions conducted via the Company's computer system. Employees have no reasonable expectation of privacy when it comes to business and personal use of the Company's e-mail system.

The federal Electronic Communications Privacy Act gives management the legal right to access and disclose all employee e-mail transmissions. All employee e-mail messages (incoming, outgoing, and internal) will be monitored. The Company reserves the right to monitor, inspect, copy, review, and store at any time and without notice any and all usage of the Company's e-mail system, and any and all files, information, software, and other content created, sent, received, downloaded, uploaded, accessed, or stored in connection with employee usage. The Company reserves the right to disclose e-mail text and images to regulators, the courts, law enforcement, and other third parties without the employee's consent.

5. Prohibited Use of the Company's E-Mail System: Offensive Content and Harassing/Discriminatory Activities Are Banned. Company employees have the right to work in an environment that is free from hostility of any kind.

Employees are prohibited from using the Company's e-mail system to engage in activities or transmit content that is harassing, discriminatory, menacing, threatening, obscene, defamatory, or in any way objectionable or offensive.

Employees are prohibited from using the Company's e-mail system to:

- Send, receive, solicit, print, copy, or reply to text or images that disparage others based on their race, religion, color, sex, sexual orientation, national origin, veteran status, disability, ancestry, or age.

- Send, receive, solicit, print, copy, or reply to jokes (text or images) based on sex, sexual orientation, race, age, religion, national origin, veteran status, ancestry, or disability.

- Send, receive, solicit, print, copy, or reply to messages that are disparaging or defamatory.

- Spread gossip, rumors, and innuendos about employees, clients, suppliers, or other outside parties.

- Send, receive, solicit, print, copy, or reply to sexually oriented messages or images.

- Send, receive, solicit, print, copy, or reply to messages or images that contain foul, obscene, off-color, or adult-oriented language.

- Send, receive, solicit, print, copy, or reply to messages or images that are intended to alarm others, embarrass the Company, negatively impact employee productivity, or harm employee morale.

6. Confidential, Proprietary, and Personal Information Must Be Protected. Unless authorized to do so, employees are prohibited from using the e-mail system to transmit confidential information to outside parties. Employees may not access, send, receive, solicit, print, copy, or reply to confidential or proprietary information about the Company, employees, clients, suppliers, and other business associates.

Confidential information includes but is not limited to client lists, credit card numbers, Social Security numbers, employee performance reviews, salary details, trade secrets, passwords, and information that could embarrass the Company and/or employees were it to be made public.

Employees also are prohibited from using the e-mail system to transmit copyright-protected information without permission of the copyright holder.

7. Handling Unsolicited E-Mail that Violates Company Policy. The Company's e-mail policy prohibits employees from sending inappropriate or offensive material. Employees also are prohibited from receiving material that violates the Company's e-mail policy.

In the event that an employee receives e-mail messages that violate policy, the employee is to take the following steps:

(a)   If You Know the Sender: If an employee receives e-mail that violates Company policy, and the employee knows the sender, then the employee must immediately instruct the sender to stop sending this type of material.

(b)   If You Don't Know the Sender: If an employee receives e-mail that violates Company policy, and the employee does not know the sender, the employee should not respond or reply to the message. Instead, the employee should immediately notify the IT manager, who will attempt to block receipt of this type of material in the future.

Employees who follow these procedures will not be deemed to have violated policy. Employees who fail to follow these rules and continue to receive banned material may be deemed to be policy violators and may be disciplined or terminated for violating the Company's e-mail policy.

8. Passwords. E-mail passwords are the property of the Company. Employees are required to provide the CIO with current passwords and user IDs. Only authorized personnel are permitted to use passwords or user IDs to access another employee's e-mail without consent. Misuse of passwords/user IDs, the sharing of passwords/user IDs with nonemployees, and/or the unauthorized use of another employee's password/user ID will result in disciplinary action, up to and including termination.

9. Writing Style and Netiquette. E-mail messages should be treated as formal business documents, written in accordance with the Company's Electronic Writing Style Policy. Style, spelling, grammar, and punctuation should be appropriate and accurate. The rules of netiquette, as detailed in the Company's Netiquette Policy, must be adhered to.

10. E-Mail Blasts. Employees are prohibited from sending organization-wide e-mail messages to all employees without approval from the compliance or IT department. Employees are prohibited from sending e-mail blasts (mass mailings) to external parties without approval from the compliance or IT department. Only the chief information officer and/or systems administrator may generate public e-mail distribution lists (e-mail blasts). Employees are prohibited from requesting e-mail replies to organization-wide e-mail or external e-mail blasts without permission from the compliance or IT department.

Violations. These guidelines are intended to provide Company employees with general examples of acceptable and unacceptable use of the Company's e-mail system. A violation of this policy may result in disciplinary action up to and including termination.

Acknowledgment. If you have questions about the above e-mail policy, address them to the chief information officer before signing the following agreement.

I have read the Company's E-Mail Policy, and agree to abide by it. I understand that a violation of any of the above rules, policies, and procedures may result in disciplinary action, up to and including my termination.

_____   _____
Employee Name (Printed)   Employee Signature

_____
Date

Source: © 2009 Nancy Flynn, Executive Director, ePolicy Institute, www.epolicyinstitute.com. For informational purposes only. No reliance should be placed on this without the advice of legal counsel. Individual electronic business communication policies should be developed with assistance from competent legal counsel.

IM Policy

The Company provides employees with electronic communications tools, including an instant messaging (IM) system.

This written IM policy governs employees' use of the Company's own IM system, as well as employees' use of personal IM software. This IM policy applies to IM use at the Company's headquarters and district offices, as well as at remote locations including but not limited to employees' homes, client offices, supplier offices, hotels, and airports.

The Company's IM rules and policies apply to employees' use of desktop computers, laptops, and handheld devices, whether provided by the Company and/or owned by the employee or a third party.

The Company's IM rules and policies apply to full-time employees, part-time employees, independent contractors, interns, consultants, agents, and third parties including but not limited to suppliers and clients.

Any employee who violates the Company's IM rules and policies is subject to disciplinary action, up to and including termination.

1. IM Tools Exist for Business Purposes. The Company allows IM access primarily for business purposes. Employees may use the Company's IM system, as well as personal IM clients, for personal use in accordance with this policy.

2. Authorized Personal Use of IM. Employees may use IM to communicate with spouses, children, domestic partners, and other family members. Employees' personal use of IM is limited to lunch breaks and work breaks only. Employees may not use IM during otherwise productive business hours.

Employees who need to hold personal communications with persons other than spouses, children, domestic partners, and other family members via IM (the Company's IM system or the employee's personal IM client) must first obtain permission from management.

Employees are prohibited from using IM to operate a business, conduct an external job search, solicit money for personal gain, campaign for political causes or candidates, or promote or solicit funds for a religious or other personal cause.

Employees are prohibited from using IM to play online games, visit chat rooms, or engage in illegal activity including but not limited to gambling and drug dealing.

3. Employees Have No Reasonable Expectation of Privacy. Instant messages created and transmitted on Company computers are the property of the Company, regardless of whether the employee uses the Company's IM system or the employee's personal IM client. All messages created and transmitted are the property of the Company. The Company reserves the right to monitor all IM transmitted via the Company's computer system. Employees have no reasonable expectation of privacy when it comes to business and personal use of the Company's IM system and/or messages transmitted via employees' personal IM clients. Employees' IM transmissions will be monitored.

The Company reserves the right to monitor, inspect, copy, review, and store at any time and without notice any and all usage of IM, and any and all files, information, software, and other content created, sent, received, downloaded, uploaded, accessed, or stored in connection with employee usage.

The Company reserves the right to disclose IM text and images to regulators, the courts, law enforcement, and other third parties without the employee's consent.

4. Prohibited Use of IM: Offensive Content and Harassing/Discriminatory Activities Are Banned. Company employees have the right to work in an environment that is free from hostility of any kind.

Employees are prohibited from using IM to engage in activities or transmit content that is harassing, discriminatory, menacing, threatening, obscene, defamatory, or in any way objectionable or offensive.

Employees are prohibited from using IM to:

- Send, receive, solicit, print, copy, or reply to text or images that disparage others based on their race, religion, color, sex, sexual orientation, national origin, veteran status, disability, ancestry, or age.

- Send, receive, solicit, print, copy, or reply to jokes (text or images) based on sex, sexual orientation, race, age, religion, national origin, veteran status, ancestry, or disability.

- Send, receive, solicit, print, copy, or reply to messages that are disparaging or defamatory.

- Spread gossip, rumors, and innuendos about employees, clients, suppliers, or other outside parties.

- Send, receive, solicit, print, copy, or reply to sexually oriented messages or images.

- Send, receive, solicit, print, copy, or reply to messages or images that contain foul, obscene, off-color, or adult-oriented language.

- Send, receive, solicit, print, copy, or reply to messages or images that are intended to alarm others, embarrass the Company, negatively impact employee productivity, or harm employee morale.

5. Confidential, Proprietary, and Personal Information Must Be Protected. Unless authorized to do so, employees are prohibited from using IM to transmit confidential information to outside parties. Employees may not access, send, receive, solicit, print, copy, or reply to confidential or proprietary information about the Company, employees, clients, suppliers, and other business associates.

Confidential information includes but is not limited to client lists, credit card numbers, Social Security numbers, employee performance reviews, salary details, trade secrets, passwords, and information that could embarrass the Company and/or employees were it to be made public.

Employees also are prohibited from using IM to transmit copyright-protected information without permission of the copyright holder.

6. Do Not Use IM to Communicate with Lawyers. In order to preserve the attorney-client privilege for communications between lawyers and clients, never use IM to seek legal advice or pose a legal question. Instead, make a phone call or schedule an in-person meeting.

7. Send IM Messages Only to Those Who Need to Read Them. Send IM only to readers with a legitimate need for your information. Do not engage in excessive, unnecessary chat that is not directly related to business, and that distracts from legitimate job-related tasks.

8. Public Statements About the Company. With the exception of authorized marketing and customer service activities, employees are prohibited from using IM to distribute or publicize any advertisement, promotional literature, press release, or other information that could be interpreted as a general public statement, position, or product/service endorsement by the Company, without the authorization of the public relations or marketing director.

9. User IDs. User IDs are the property of the Company. The Company reserves the right to prohibit the use of inappropriate and/or offensive user names.

Employees should share their user names with others strictly on a need-to-know basis.

Employees are prohibited from printing IM user IDs on business cards and/or other literature that is widely and generally distributed.

Employees may not misrepresent, obscure, suppress, or replace their own (or another person's) identity in any IM message or other electronic communication.

10. IM Business Record Retention. IM messages create business records, and are subject to the Company's written and consistently applied rules for purging, retaining, and archiving electronically stored information.

11. Violations. These guidelines are intended to provide Company employees with general examples of acceptable and unacceptable use of the Company's IM system. A violation of this policy may result in disciplinary action up to and including termination.

Acknowledgment. If you have questions about the above IM policy, address them to the chief information officer before signing the following agreement.

I have read the Company's IM Policy, and agree to abide by it. I understand that a violation of any of the above rules, policies, and procedures may result in disciplinary action, up to and including my termination.

_____   _____

User Name   User Signature

_____

Date

Recorded E-Mail Policy and VaporStream Confidential Messaging

The Company provides employees with electronic communication tools, including an e-mail system for the transmission of business records and Vapor-Stream Confidential Messaging for recordless conversations that do not require the retention of permanent records.

This Recorded E-Mail and VaporStream Confidential Messaging Policy, which governs employee use of the Company's e-mail system and Vapor-Stream Confidential Messaging, applies to e-mail and VaporStream use at the Company's headquarters and district offices, as well as at remote locations, including but not limited to employees' homes, airports, hotels, and client and supplier offices.

The Company's e-mail and VaporStream rules and policies apply to full-time employees, part-time employees, independent contractors, interns, consultants, suppliers, clients, and other third parties. Any employee who violates the Company's e-mail and/or VaporStream rules and policies is subject to disciplinary action, up to and including termination.

1. E-Mail Exists for Business Record Purposes. The Company provides e-mail access primarily for the transmission of business record messages (e-mail messages and attachments with ongoing legal, compliance, business, or operational purpose, or historical value to the Company). Employees may not use the Company's e-mail system to transmit nonrecord messages (see Business Use of VaporStream). If you have any doubt whether or not a message is a business record, ask yourself if you would retain the message if it had been sent in paper form. If the answer is yes, then the message is probably a record, and you should transmit it via the e-mail system and retain it according to the Company's record retention policy.

In addition, employees may not use the Company e-mail system for personal use (see Personal Use of VaporStream). Employees are prohibited from using personal e-mail software (Yahoo!, Hotmail, etc.) for business or personal communication at the office.

Employees are prohibited from using e-mail to operate a business, conduct an external job search, solicit money for personal gain, campaign for political causes or candidates, or promote or solicit funds for a religious or other personal cause.

2. Business Use of VaporStream. Confidential and recordless messages (those with no ongoing legal, compliance, business, or operational purpose, or historical value to the Company) should be communicated and transmitted via VaporStream Confidential Messaging, rather than the Company's e-mail system.

Non-business-record messages include, but are not limited to, administrative notices (an invitation to the company picnic or a departmental meeting notice, for example).

Confidential messages include, but are not limited to, conversations related to private, proprietary, secret, or otherwise confidential business or personal matters.

Confidential and non-business-record messages do not need to be retained as Company records for legal or regulatory purposes. Confidential and recordless messages are kept temporarily (by VaporStream) until they are read. Using the Company e-mail system to transmit confidential and nonrecord messages wastes valuable Company computer resources and employee time. If you have any doubt whether or not a message is a business record, ask yourself if you would retain the message if it had been sent in paper form. If the answer is yes, then the message is probably a record, and you should transmit it via the e-mail system and retain it according to the Company's record retention policy and schedule.

3. Personal Use of VaporStream. Employees may use VaporStream to communicate with spouses, children, domestic partners, family members, teachers, physicians, and child care providers. However, employees' personal use of VaporStream is limited to lunch breaks and work breaks only. Employees may not use VaporStream for personal communication during otherwise productive business hours.

Employees are prohibited from using VaporStream to operate a business, conduct an external job search, solicit money for personal gain, campaign for political causes or candidates, or promote or solicit funds for a religious or other personal cause.

4. Privacy. The Company's computer and e-mail systems are the property of the Company. The Company has the legal right to monitor usage of employee e-mail transmissions and other computer-related activity or transmissions on the Company system. Employees have no reasonable expectation of privacy when using the Company's computer system.

VaporStream Confidential Messaging operates outside of the company's system and offers writers and readers a high level of privacy and confidentiality. Use VaporStream Confidential Messaging to keep company secrets safe and private conversations under wraps. Use the Company's e-mail system only when a permanent business record is required for legal, regulatory, or business reasons.

5. Offensive Content and Harassing or Discriminatory Activities Are Banned. Employees are prohibited from using electronic communication tools to engage in activities or transmit content that is harassing, discriminatory, menacing, threatening, obscene, defamatory, or in any way objectionable or offensive. Employees are prohibited from using electronic communication tools to:

- Send, receive, solicit, or reply to text or images that disparage others based on their race, religion, color, sex, sexual orientation, national origin, veteran status, disability, ancestry, or age.

- Send, receive, solicit, or reply to jokes (text or images) based on sex, sexual orientation, race, age, religion, national origin, veteran status, ancestry, or disability.

- Send, receive, solicit, or reply to messages that are disparaging or defamatory.

- Spread gossip, rumors, and innuendos about employees, clients, suppliers, or other outside parties.

- Send, receive, solicit, or reply to sexually oriented messages or images.

- Send, receive, solicit, or reply to messages or images that contain foul, obscene, off-color, or adult-oriented language.

- Send, receive, solicit, or reply to messages or images that are intended to alarm others, embarrass the Company, negatively impact employee productivity, or harm employee morale.

6. Confidential, Proprietary, and Personal Information Must Be Protected. Unless authorized to do so, employees are prohibited from using the Company's e-mail system to transmit confidential information to outside parties. Employees may not access, send, receive, solicit, print, copy, or reply to confidential or proprietary information about the Company, employees, clients, suppliers, and other business associates.

Confidential information includes but is not limited to client lists, credit card numbers, employee performance reviews, salary details, Social Security numbers, trade secrets, passwords, and information that could embarrass the Company and employees were it to be made public.

Trained and certified VaporStream users who have successfully completed the Company's formal VaporStream Confidential Messaging training program are authorized to transmit approved confidential data and engage in approved sensitive/private conversations via VaporStream Confidential Messaging.

If you have questions about the authorized and approved use of Vapor-Stream, contact the Company's compliance officer.

7. Business Record Retention. E-mail messages can create written business records, also known as electronically stored information (ESI), and are subject to the Company's written and consistently applied rules, policies, and procedures for retaining, deleting, and archiving business records. See the Company's electronic business record retention policy for more information.

8. Violations. These guidelines are intended to provide Company employees with general examples of acceptable and unacceptable use of the Company's e-mail system and VaporStream Confidential Messaging. A violation of this policy may result in disciplinary action up to and including termination.

Acknowledgment. If you have questions about the above policies and procedures, address them to the compliance officer before signing the following agreement.

I have read the Company's Recorded E-Mail and VaporStream Confidential Messaging Policy and agree to abide by it. I understand that a violation of any of the above policies and procedures may result in disciplinary action, up to and including my termination.

_____   _____
User Name   User Signature

_____
Date

Internet/Intranet Policy

(Organization) provides employees with a network connection and Internet/
intranet access. This policy governs all use of (Organization's) network and
Internet/intranet access at headquarters, remote offices, hotels, airports,
employees' homes, and any other location.

The (Organization) network and Internet/intranet access are intended for
business use only. Employees may access the Internet for personal use only
during nonworking hours, and strictly in compliance with the terms of this
policy.

All information created, transmitted, acquired, downloaded, or uploaded
via the organization's network and Internet or intranet is the property of (Organization). Employees should have no expectation of privacy regarding this
information. The organization reserves the right to access, read, review,
monitor, and copy all messages, content, and files on its computer system at
any time and without notice. When deemed necessary, the organization may
disclose text or images to law enforcement agencies or other third parties
without the employee's consent.

No employee may use a password unless it has been disclosed in writing
to (Organization's) chief information officer.

Alternate Internet Service Provider connections to (Organization's)
internal network are not permitted unless expressly authorized by the organization and properly protected by a firewall or other appropriate security
device(s).

Files downloaded from the Internet may not be viewed or opened until
scanned with virus detection software. Employees are reminded that information obtained from the Internet is not always reliable and should be verified for
accuracy before it is used.

Prohibited Activities. Employees are prohibited from using (Organization's)
network or Internet/intranet access for the following activities:

1. Downloading software without the prior written approval of (Organization's) chief information officer. (See [Organization's] Software Usage
   Policy.)

2. Disseminating or printing copyrighted materials, including articles and
   software, in violation of copyright laws.

3. Sending, receiving, printing, or otherwise disseminating (Organization's) proprietary data, trade secrets, or other confidential information in violation of organization policy or written agreements.

4. Operating a business, usurping business opportunities, soliciting money for personal gain, or searching for jobs outside (Organization).

5. Making offensive or harassing statements and/or disparaging others based on race, color, religion, national origin, veteran status, ancestry, disability, age, sex, or sexual orientation.

6. Viewing, downloading, uploading, sending, or soliciting sexually oriented messages or images.

7. Visiting sites featuring pornography, terrorism, espionage, theft, or drugs.

8. Gambling or engaging in any other criminal activity in violation of local, state, or federal law.

9. Engaging in unethical activities or content.

10. Participating in activities, viewing, or writing content that could damage (Organization's) professional reputation.

Compliance and Violations.

1. Managers are responsible for ensuring employee compliance with this policy.

2. Employees who learn of policy violations should notify (Organization's) chief information officer or human resources director.

3. Employees who violate this policy or use (Organization's) network, Internet, or intranet access for improper purposes will be subject to discipline, up to and including termination.

Acknowledgment. If you have questions about the above Internet/Intranet Policy, address them to the Chief Information Officer before signing the following agreement.

I have read the Company's Internet/Intranet Policy, and agree to abide by it. I understand that a violation of any of the above rules, policies, and procedures may result in disciplinary action, up to and including my termination.

_____   _____
User Name   User Signature

_____
Date

Blog Policy

The Company provides employees with external blog access, primarily for business purposes. Employees using the company's external blog are responsible for behaving professionally, ethically, and responsibly in the blogosphere. To that end, the Company has established the following blog policy.

Employees are required to adhere to the Company's blog policy when at the office (or elsewhere) using the Company's business blog system for business or personal reasons. Employees also are expected to comply with the Company's blog policy when at home (or elsewhere) using a personal blog for business or personal reasons.

Violations of the Company's blog policy, whether they occur on the Company's blog or the employee's own personal blog or a third party's blog, will result in disciplinary action, up to and including termination.

1. Employee-bloggers are required to write under their own names, whether using a company-hosted business blog or a personal blog. Pseudonyms and anonymous postings are prohibited.

2. Employee-bloggers are required to identify themselves, by name and title, as employees of the Company, when using a company-hosted business blog.

3. Employee-bloggers must incorporate the following legal disclaimer into their business and personal blogs: "The opinions expressed on this blog are my own personal opinions. They do not reflect the opinions of my employer, (Company)."

4. Employee-bloggers are prohibited from attacking, defaming, harassing, discriminating against, menacing, threatening, or otherwise exhibiting inappropriate or offensive behavior or attitudes toward coworkers, supervisors, executives, customers, vendors, shareholders, the media, other bloggers, or other third parties, whether using a company-hosted business blog or a personal blog.

5. Employee-bloggers are prohibited from disclosing confidential, sensitive, proprietary, top secret, or private information about the Company,

employees, executives, customers, partners, suppliers, or other third parties, whether using a company-hosted business blog or a personal blog.

6. Employee-bloggers are prohibited from disclosing financial information about the Company without permission from the investor relations department, whether using a company-hosted business blog or a personal blog. This includes revenues, profits, forecasts, and other financial information.

7. Employee-bloggers may discuss the Company's competitors, but must do so in a respectful, professional manner, whether using a company-hosted business blog or a personal blog.

8. Employee-bloggers must adhere to the Company's written content and language guidelines, whether using a company-hosted business blog or a personal blog. Prohibited content includes, but is not limited to, obscene, profane, adult-oriented, pornographic, harassing, discriminatory, menacing, threatening, and otherwise offensive text, art, photos, videos, graphics, cartoons, and other content.

9. Employee-bloggers are prohibited from posting copyright-protected material without the express, written permission of the copyright owner, whether using a company-hosted business blog or a personal blog.

10. Employee-bloggers may not post content or conduct activities that fail to conform with local, state, and federal laws, whether using a company-hosted business blog or a personal blog.

11. Employee-bloggers must comply with all of the Company's written rules and policies, including but not limited to the Company's blog policy, sexual harassment and discrimination policy, ethics guidelines, code of conduct, electronic communications policy, whether using a company-hosted business blog or a personal blog.

12. Violation of the Company's blog policy (or any other Company policy) will result in disciplinary action, up to and including termination, whether using a company-hosted business blog or a personal blog.

Acknowledgment and Signature. If you have questions about the above blog policy, address them to the human resources director before signing the following agreement.

I have read the Company's Blog Policy, and agree to abide by it. I understand that a violation of any of the above rules, policies, and procedures may result in disciplinary action, up to and including my termination.

_____   _____
Employee Name (Printed)   Employee Signature

_____
Date

© 2009, Nancy Flynn, Executive Director, ePolicy Institute, www.epolicyinstitute .com. For informational purposes only. No reliance should be placed on this without the advice of legal counsel. Individual electronic business communication policies should be developed with assistance from competent legal counsel.

Social Networking and Video Site Policy

The Company prohibits employees from accessing external social networking sites and external video sites via company computer resources (including but not limited to desktops, laptops, BlackBerry Smartphones, handheld and hands-free cell phones, and the Internet system) during business hours (including but not limited to time engaged in business-related activities at Company headquarters and branch offices or on the road/at remote locations including vehicles, airplanes, airports, trains, hotels, restaurants, clients' offices, prospects' offices, suppliers' offices, and employees' homes).

The Company recognizes, however, that some employees may, for personal reasons, access, view, operate, and post, download, or upload content to external social networking sites and video sites on their own time via their own computer equipment and personal Internet accounts.

When operating, accessing, viewing, downloading, uploading, or posting content (including but not limited to text, photos, videos, and art of any kind) to external social networking or video sites, employees are responsible for behaving professionally, ethically, responsibly, and in accordance with all of the Company's employment rules and policies. To that end, the Company has established the following social networking and video site policy, which all employees are obligated to comply with at all times—during business hours on Company time and computer resources and after working hours on employees' own time and personal computer tools and Internet accounts.

Violations of the Company's social networking and video site policy, whether they occur at work during business hours using Company computer resources or on the employees' own time and own computer equipment and technology tools, will result in disciplinary action, up to and including termination.

- Social networking and video site users are required to write/post content under their own names. Pseudonyms and anonymous postings are prohibited, whether using a personal social networking site, public video site, or a Company-hosted social networking or video site.

- Employees are prohibited from mentioning the Company or identifying themselves as employees of the Company via text, photos, art, Company logos, Company uniforms, Company letterhead, Company products, Company trademarks, or any other image, copy, or content, when using a personal social networking site or public video site.

- Employees must incorporate the following legal disclaimer into their personal social networking pages and public video site posts: "The opinions expressed on this social networking profile (video site) are my own personal opinions. They do not reflect the opinions of my employer."

- Employees are prohibited from attacking, defaming, harassing, discriminating against, menacing, threatening, or otherwise exhibiting inappropriate or offensive behavior, attitudes, opinions, or commentary toward or about coworkers, supervisors, executives, customers, vendors, shareholders, the media, or other third parties, when using a personal social networking site or public video site.

- Employees are prohibited from disclosing confidential, sensitive, proprietary, top secret, or private information about the Company, its products, services, trade secrets, financials, plans, research and development, employees, executives, customers, partners, suppliers, or other third parties, when using a personal social networking site or public video site.

- Employees are prohibited from using a Company-provided or personal cell phone or Smartphone camera or video recorder to take, transmit, download, or upload to social networking or video sites any photos or videos of coworkers, executives, customers, suppliers, and any other third party without first securing the written permission of your subject and an authorized member of management.

- Employees are prohibited from using a Company-provided or personal cell phone or Smartphone camera or video recorder to take, transmit, download, or upload any business- or company-related photos or videos to social networking or video sites without first securing written permission from an authorized member of company management. Banned photos and videos include, but are not limited to, the following: (1) "Funny," embarrassing, or unprofessional images of company employees, executives, customers, suppliers, or other third parties. In other words—do not take, transmit, download, or upload "funny," embarrassing, or unprofessional photos or videos of anyone; (2) Company buildings (internal and external), offices, facilities, operations, research, products, services, confidential data, and internal documents; (3) Company uniforms, logos, signage, trademarks, business cards, letterhead, literature, or any other printed or electronic content that can be used to identify the Company or employees.

- Employees are prohibited from disclosing financial information about the Company without permission from the investor relations department. This includes revenues, profits, forecasts, and other financial information, when using a personal social networking site or public video site.

- Employees must adhere to the Company's written content and language guidelines. Prohibited content includes, but is not limited to, obscene, profane, adult-oriented, pornographic, harassing, discriminatory, menacing, threatening, and otherwise offensive text, art, photos, videos, graphics, cartoons, or other images and content, when using a personal social networking site or public video site.

- Employees are prohibited from posting copyright-protected material without the express written permission of the copyright owner, when using a personal social networking site or public video site.

- Employees may not post content or conduct activities that fail to conform with local, state, and federal laws when using a personal social networking site or public video site, or a Company-hosted social networking or video site.

- Employees must comply with all of the Company's written employment rules and policies, including but not limited to the Company's social networking and video site policy, sexual harassment and discrimination policy, ethics guidelines, code of conduct, confidentiality rules, and netiquette policy, when using a personal social networking site or public video site.

- Violation of Company's social networking and video site policy (or any other Company policy) will result in disciplinary action, up to and including termination.

Acknowledgment and Signature. If you have questions about the above social networking and video site policy, address them to the human resources director before signing the following agreement.

I have read the Company's Social Networking and Video Site Policy, and agree to abide by it. I understand that a violation of any of the above rules, policies, and procedures may result in disciplinary action, up to and including my termination.

_____   _____
Employee Name (Printed)   Employee Signature

_____
Date

© 2009, Nancy Flynn, Executive Director, ePolicy Institute, www.epolicyinstitute .com. For informational purposes only. No reliance should be placed on this without the advice of legal counsel. Individual electronic business communication policies should be developed with assistance from competent legal counsel.

Cell Phone and Text Messaging Policy

The Company provides employees with electronic business communications tools, including cell phones with text messaging capabilities.

This written policy governs employees' use of Company-provided cell phones and the organization's text messaging (texting) system, as well as employees' use of personal cell phones and personal texting tools. This cell phone and text messaging policy applies to cell phone and text messaging use at the Company's headquarters and district offices, as well as at remote locations including but not limited to Company-provided vehicles, employee-owned or leased vehicles, rental cars, employees' homes, clients' offices, suppliers' offices, hotels, trains, airports, and airplanes.

The Company's cell phone and text messaging policy applies to employees' use of cell phones, Smartphones, BlackBerries, and other mobile handheld and hands-free phones, whether provided by the Company and/or owned by the employee or a third party.

The Company's cell phone and text messaging policy applies to full-time employees, part-time employees, independent contractors, interns, consultants, agents, and third parties including but not limited to suppliers.

Any employee who violates the Company's cell phone and text messaging policy is subject to disciplinary action, up to and including termination.

1. Cell Phones and Texting Technology Exists for Business Purposes. The Company provides cell phones with texting capabilities for business purposes. During business hours, employees may use Company-provided cell phones and the Company's texting system, as well as personal tools and accounts, for personal use strictly in accordance with this policy.

2. Authorized Personal Use of Cell Phones and Texting. Employees may use Company-provided cell phones and texting to communicate with spouses, children, domestic partners, teachers, babysitters, physicians, and emergency personnel including police, fire, and 911 dispatchers. Employees' personal use of cell phones to talk or text is limited to lunch breaks, work breaks, and Company-recognized emergencies only. Employees may not use Company-provided or personal cell phones to talk or text during otherwise productive business hours.

Employees who need to hold personal communications with persons other than spouses, children, domestic partners, teachers, babysitters, physicians, and emergency personnel via personal or Company-provided cell phone must first obtain verbal permission from an authorized member of management.

Employees are prohibited from using Company-provided cell phones (talking or texting) to operate a business, conduct an external job search, solicit money for personal gain, campaign for political causes or candidates, promote or solicit funds for a religious or other personal cause, or violate any Company employment policy.

Employees are prohibited from using Company-provided cell phones to play online games, visit chat rooms, or engage in any illegal activity including but not limited to gambling and drug dealing.

3. Business Record Retention. Text messages transmitted via the Company's system create business records, and are subject to the Company's written and consistently applied rules for retaining and archiving electronically stored information.

4. Employees Have No Reasonable Expectation of Privacy. Text messages created and transmitted on the Company's system via Company-provided cell phones are the property of the Company. The Company reserves the right to monitor all text transmitted via the Company's system. Employees have no reasonable expectation of privacy when it comes to business and personal use of the Company's cell phone/texting system.

The Company reserves the right to retain, monitor, inspect, copy, review, and store at any time and without notice any and all usage of the Company's cell phone/texting system, and any and all files, information, software, and other content created, sent, received, downloaded, uploaded, accessed, or stored in connection with employee usage.

The Company reserves the right to disclose text messages to regulators, the courts, law enforcement, and other third parties without the employee's consent.

5. Cell Phone and Text Messaging Rules. Company employees have the right to work in an environment that is free from hostility of any kind. When using Company-provided or personal cell phones, employees are required to adhere to the following cell phone and texting rules:

- Obey the Company's electronic content rules and language guidelines. Whether conducting a cell phone conversation or texting, you must use a professional tone and businesslike language. You are prohibited from using language that is obscene, vulgar, abusive, harassing, profane, discriminatory, sexually suggestive, intimidating, misleading, defamatory, or otherwise offensive, objectionable, inappropriate, or illegal. Jokes, disparaging remarks, and inappropriate comments related to ethnicity, race, color, religion, sex, age, disabilities, physique, sexual orientation, or sexual preference are prohibited.

- Turn off cell phones (Company-provided or personal, handheld or hands-free) when driving any vehicle (Company-owned or personal) during business hours. Pull off the road to make a call, take a call, send a text message, or check voice and text messages.

- Remember that a policy is a policy. Cell phone users and texters are expected to comply with all Company rules and policies including sexual harassment and discrimination policies, ethics guidelines, code of conduct, confidentiality rules, content rules and language guidelines, cell phone and texting policy, and computer policies among others.

- Adhere to the Company's rules regarding personal use of cell phones and other electronic business communication tools during business hours. Regardless of whether you are using your own cell phone or a Company-provided phone, employees are required to adhere to the Company's personal use rules governing when, where, why, with whom, and for how long you may engage in personal, nonbusiness-related talking and texting.

- Never discuss Company business in any public setting in which you could be overheard. Not every location is right for a cell phone conversation. Find a secluded spot (hotel room, car, private office, etc.) in which to conduct Company business via your cell phone.

- Do not mention passwords, user names, account numbers, financial data, customers, prospects, or other confidential or proprietary Company or personal information if there is any chance that your cell phone conversation could be overheard. An indiscreet one-sided conversation may be all a malicious party needs in order to gain access to valuable business or personal data.

- Never assume your cell phone conversation is "safe" just because you don't mention the Company by name. If you wear or carry an item that features the Company logo, your name, or the organization's business address, a third party may put two and two together and identify the Company by overhearing your indiscreet conversation.

- Do not use cell phone cameras or video recorders to take, transmit, download, upload, print, or copy photos or videos that are not directly related to Company business and have not been approved by an authorized member of Company management. Prohibited photos and videos include, but are not limited to, "funny," embarrassing, or unprofessional images (of anyone or anything), as well as photos or videos of Company buildings (internal and external), offices, facilities, operations, products, services, confidential data, and internal documents.

- Never use a cell phone camera or video recorder to take, transmit, download, upload, print, or copy photos or videos of coworkers, executives, customers, suppliers, or any other third party without getting the express permission of your subject and Company management.

- Do not distract officemates by engaging in unnecessary cell phone chatter.

- Turn off your cell phone during business-related meetings, seminars, conferences, luncheons, dinners, receptions, brainstorming sessions, and any other situation in which a ringing phone or tapping fingers are likely to disrupt proceedings or interrupt a speaker's or participant's train of thought.

6. Violations. These guidelines are intended to provide Company employees with general examples of acceptable and unacceptable use of the Company's cell phone and text messaging tools and system.

- Employees are obligated to report violations of the Company's cell phone and texting rules and policy to the human resources manager. Failure to report a coworker's cell phone or texting violation may result in disciplinary action against the witness.

- Employees should remember that any violation of the Company's cell phone and texting rules and policy may result in disciplinary action, up to and including termination.

Acknowledgment. If you have questions about the above cell phone and text messaging policy, address them to the chief information officer before signing the following agreement.

I have read the Company's Cell Phone and Text Messaging Policy, and agree to abide by it. I understand that a violation of any of the above rules, policies, and procedures may result in disciplinary action, up to and including my termination.

_____   _____

User Name   User Signature

_____

Date

Software Usage Policy

Software piracy is both a crime and a violation of the Company's software usage policy.

Employees are to use software strictly in accordance with its license agreement. Unless otherwise provided in the license, the duplication of copyrighted software (except for backup and archival purposes by the software manager or designated department head) is a violation of copyright law. In addition to violating copyright law, unauthorized duplication of software is contrary to the Company's standards of employee conduct.

To ensure compliance with software license agreements and the organization's software usage policy, employees are required to follow these procedures:

1. Employees must use software in accordance with license agreements and Company's software usage policy. Employees acknowledge they do not own software or its related documentation. Unless expressly authorized by the software publisher, employees may not make additional copies of software, except for archival purposes.

2. The Company prohibits the use of unauthorized software or fonts. Employees illegally reproducing software may be subject to civil and criminal penalties including fines and imprisonment. Employees and managers should not condone the illegal copying of software under any circumstances. Employees who make, use, or otherwise acquire unauthorized software will face disciplinary action, up to and including termination.

3. Employees are prohibited from giving software or fonts to clients, customers, vendors, and other outsiders. Under no circumstances will the Company use software that has been brought into the organization from an unauthorized source, including, but not limited to, the Internet, home, friends, and colleagues.

4. Employees who suspect or become aware of software misuse are required to notify the chief information officer, human resources director, or department manager.

5. All software used on organization-owned computers will be purchased through authorized Company procedures.

Acknowledgment. If you have questions about the above software usage policy, address them to the chief information officer before signing the following agreement.

I have read the Company's software usage policy, and agree to abide by it. I understand that a violation of any of the above rules, policies, and procedures may result in disciplinary action, up to and including my termination.

_____   _____

Employee Name (Printed)   Employee Signature

_____

Date

Glossary of Electronic Business Communication, Legal, and Technology Terms

Amended Federal Rules of Civil Procedure (FRCP): In December 2006, the U. S. Federal Court System announced amendments to the Federal Rules of Civil Procedure (FRCP). The amended rules govern the discovery of "electronically stored information" (ESI), a new phrase that refers to e-mail and all other data that can be stored electronically. Enforced by the U.S. Supreme Court, the revised rules make it clear that all ESI is subject to discovery (may be used as evidence for or against your company) in civil lawsuits.

Archive: The use of reliable technology to store e-mail and instant messages that warrant neither immediate attention nor deletion from the system. Best practices call for the use of archiving technology that:

- automatically captures and stores internal and external e-mail in one central location;

- protects against malicious intruders intent on altering, deleting, or stealing your files;

- facilitates immediate access to archived data; and

- guarantees your ability to produce legally compliant, reliable evidence in the event of a lawsuit or regulatory investigation.

Attachment: A computer file sent with an e-mail or instant message. The file can be a word processing document, spreadsheet, database, photo, or graphic element. Attachments that are transmitted outside a company's firewall and security system, on the public Web via consumer-grade IM clients or personal e-mail accounts, put confidential company information and other valuable data at tremendous risk of theft, interception, and tampering.

Authenticity: For electronic business records, electronically stored information, and other evidence to be considered authentic and legally valid, the author and content must be verified as original. An authentic electronic document must, in other words, be what it claims to be.

Backup: A backup system is no substitute for automatic archiving technology. Designed solely for the recovery of critical data in the event of a man-made or natural disaster, backup is nothing more than the mass storage of electronic information in a known location. An archive, on the other hand, is a strategic record management tool that not only preserves corporate e-mail, but also facilitates the speedy search and reliable retrieval of the specific records you need, exactly when you need them.[1]

Blog: Short for "Weblog." The word "blog," which was coined in 1997, works as both a noun and a verb.[2] A blog is an online journal that contains written content, links, and photos, which are regularly updated. Blogs enable anyone with a computer and Internet access to publish their thoughts, ideas, and opinions for anyone else to read and comment on. Some blogs are business-related, while others are purely personal. Some highly influential blogs boast enormous public readerships, while other blogs are intended strictly for a limited audience of friends and family.

Blogosphere: The universe of blogs, or the community of bloggers.

Breach Notification Laws: As of 2007, 39 states had enacted breach notification laws, requiring companies to notify customers and other affected parties in the event of a data breach.[3] Sixty-nine percent of organizations in 2007 expressed concern for the safety of personal identity and financial privacy information.[4] Employers aren't alone in their concern for the security of electronic records and the impact data theft can have on individuals. The law takes data theft—and corporate compliance with security laws and procedures—seriously, too.

Business-Critical E-Mail: E-mail that rises to the level of a business record, as opposed to personal messages and other insignificant, nonbusiness-related e-mail. Business-critical e-mail must be strategically retained, reliably archived, and quickly produced for legal, regulatory, and business management purposes. Insignificant, nonrecord messages, on the other hand, may be purged from the system.

Business Record: Evidence of business-related activities, events, and transactions. Organizations are obligated to retain business record e-mail, IM, and other electronic information for their ongoing business, legal, regulatory, compliance, operational, or historical value.

Chat: Unlike e-mail, which allows the user to write a fairly lengthy message on a screen page, instant messaging lends itself to the ongoing exchange of short sentences, referred to as chat.

Client: The industry term for instant messaging software. For example, many users have downloaded the AOL Instant Messenger client for external conversations with customers and other third parties. Some employees download the three leading consumer-grade clients from AOL, Yahoo!, and MSN to ensure that they are able to send an instant message to just about anyone at any time without the software compatibility concerns that are typically associated with consumer-grade IM.

Comment Spam: Blogs often provide comment sections to allow customers and other readers to add their own opinions and reactions to a post. Blog spammers use tools to automatically flood a blog with advertising in the form of bogus comments. Anything that's been spammed about in e-mail is probably being spammed in the blogosphere. This is a growing and serious problem for bloggers and blog platforms.

Comments: Many blogs include a comment feature, which allows readers to easily and automatically respond to posts, ask questions, or inject their own point of view. Considered a vital element of a blog by blogging enthusiasts, many organizations fail to edit comments pre-post. Unedited comments can open an organization to claims of defamation, copyright infringement, and trade secret theft, among other risks.

Confidential Electronic Messaging: VaporStream Confidential Messaging is a new technology that is designed to send completely recordless eyes-only electronic messages. An alternative to corporate e-mail and instant messaging, VaporStream Confidential Messaging leaves no trace of being sent or received once it has been read. It is intended for the transmission of confidential messages that do not need to be retained as records for business, legal, or regulatory purposes.

Consumer-Grade IM: Free IM clients that are downloaded from the Internet. Consumer-grade, or personal, IM travels outside the organization's firewall, across public networks, and through servers controlled by providers such as AOL, Yahoo!, and Microsoft.

Copyright: The exclusive right granted to authors under the U.S. Copyright Act to copy, adapt, distribute, rent, publicly perform, and publicly display their works of authorship, such as literary works, databases, musical works, sound recordings, photographs and other still images, and motion pictures and other audiovisual works.[5]

Counterfeiting (Software): Making, distributing, or selling software that is faked to look like the real thing.[6]

Deleted File: E-mail messages or other electronically stored information that has been purged from the electronic media on which it resided.

Deletion Schedule: The systematic disposal of e-mail, IM, and other electronically stored information according to written rules and timelines that specify when business records have reached the end of their life cycle and may be purged from the system.

Destructive Retention Policy: The practice of retaining e-mail for a limited time, and then deleting it permanently from the company network. When it comes to destructive retention, preservation periods can range from months to years. Seven years is the most commonly applied corporate retention period for companies that practice destructive retention, according to ArcMail Technology.[7]

Discovery: The method by which information is garnered from legal adversaries and evidence is collected and produced for litigation. During discovery, parties on each side exchange documents, take depositions, answer questions, take testimony, and share information to help build their cases and prepare for the legal proceeding. Discovery prevents parties from being surprised by unexpected information, helps familiarize each side with facts and evidence prior to the proceeding, and helps prevent spoliation problems.[8]

Dooced: To lose your job for the contents of your blog. Typically employee-bloggers are dooced because of negative or unflattering comments they have posted about their employers or their companies' products or services. The term "dooced" was coined by blogger Heather B. Armstrong, who in 2002 was fired for writing about her job and colleagues on her site www.dooce.com.[9]

Electronic Communications Privacy Act (ECPA): The federal Electronic Communications Privacy Act of 1986 gives U.S. employers the legal right to monitor all employee computer activity and transmissions. The ECPA makes clear the fact that the organization's computer system is the property of the employer, and employees have absolutely no reasonable expectation of privacy when using company computer systems, tools, and technologies.

Courts in the United States have consistently ruled that employees should assume their computer activity is being watched—even if they have not been formally notified of monitoring. The courts generally support the position that informed employees neither would nor should assume that their e-mail transmissions are their own. Even in cases in which employers have told workers that incoming and outgoing e-mail is not being monitored, the courts have ruled that employees still should not expect privacy when using a company system.[10]

Electronically Stored Information (ESI): In December 2006, the U.S. Federal Court System revised the Federal Rules of Civil Procedure (FRCP) governing the discovery of electronically stored information (ESI). A new phrase, ESI refers to all data that can be stored electronically. ESI includes but is not limited to e-mail messages and attachments, instant messenger chat, text messages, blog posts, history of Web surfing, backup tapes, voice mail, and all other forms of created, retained, acquired, or archived data. Mindful of new and emerging technologies, ESI is intended to cover all current types of computer-based information plus future technology developments, as well.

Encryption: The process of scrambling text and other digital information to ensure privacy. Encrypted content can only be unscrambled and read by a person with the ability to decrypt. The scrambling process is called "encrypting," and the unscrambling process is "decrypting."[11]

Enterprise IM: An authorized enterprise system that the organization installs to enable internal IM conversations among employees. The system is closed to external communications. Enterprise IM offers security features that personal, consumer-grade IM can't match. Enterprise IM systems include antivirus software; encryption capabilities; and the ability to monitor content, purge messages, retain business records, and archive instant messages, among other capabilities.

Entry: See also "Post." The commentary that is written on a blog. Some bloggers write multiple entries every day. Most entries are relatively short. Entries often include external links, and offer readers the opportunity to comment.

Filtering: The act of scanning and blocking messages that may violate the organization's content policy or content-related regulations of government and industry. The recommended approach is to draft written rules and policy first, and then use policy-based content filtering technology to enforce your written guidelines.

Firewall: A piece of hardware or a software program that automatically examines network traffic and either blocks or allows it to pass based on predefined rules and security policies. Firewalls typically sit between a private internal network and the Internet and are one of the most common tools for protecting internal networks and users from harmful content and intrusion.[12]

When employees use personal e-mail accounts or consumer-grade IM tools, their messages travel across public networks, outside the organization's firewall. The result: The organization is open to security breaches, and messages may be intercepted by thieves and other malicious outsiders.

First Amendment: The First Amendment to the United States Constitution prohibits the government from restricting the freedom of speech.[13] Since the First Amendment only restricts government control of speech, in most states private employers are free to fire at-will employees who communicate unfavorable content electronically, provided the termination is not discriminatory or retaliation for whistle-blowing or union organizing.[14]

Freeware: Software, covered by copyright, that can be copied for archival and distribution purposes, but cannot be distributed for profit. Modifications to the software are allowed and encouraged. The public is allowed to decompile, or reverse engineer, the program code. Development of new works, or derivative works built on the package, is allowed as long as the derivative works are also designated as freeware. In other words, you cannot take freeware, modify or extend it, then sell it as commercial or shareware software.[15]

Gateway IM: Products that manage public IM traffic at the discretion of corporate IT. With gateway technology, employees are authorized to use personal IM clients, but all messages pass through the server-based gateway product. Management gains the ability to:

- determine what consumer-grade IM clients are being used
- control user IDs
- monitor use
- filter content
- retain, archive, and purge messages
- block attachments
- detect viruses

Gramm-Leach-Bliley Act (GLBA): Requires U.S. financial institutions to protect the privacy of customers and their nonpublic personal information. Under GLBA, financial services firms are legally obligated to safeguard e-mail messages and attachments that contain customers' private information.

Health Insurance Portability and Accountability Act (HIPAA): U.S. health care companies are legally required by HIPAA to safeguard e-mail messages and attachments that contain protected health information (PHI) related to patients' health status, medical care, treatment plans, and payment issues. HIPAA retention rules require the preservation of patient billing records and authorizations for six years, while preserving patients' e-mail conversations and other data for the life of the patient.[16]

Hidden Reader: An unintended e-mail reader. Includes persons to whom your intended reader forwards or copies your original message. Also may include your intended reader's employer, court personnel, regulators, law enforcement, and the media among others.

Intended Reader: The person(s) to whom an e-mail writer addresses and sends a message.

Instant Messaging: A combination of the telephone and e-mail, instant messaging facilitates conversations with multiple people in real time and combines the speed of online communication with a written record of your conversation. Instant messaging (IM) is turbocharged e-mail, offering all the features and capabilities of e-mail—and more—at lightning speed.

Legacy System: Any information system, including software and hardware, that may no longer be fully supported by its manufacturer, the user, or has been in use for a long time.[17]

Links: Successful bloggers strive to increase traffic and readership by incorporating incoming and outgoing links into their sites. Bloggers enhance the relevance of their blogs, and provide readers with a service, by including outgoing links to sites that contain relevant content or otherwise are likely to appeal to readers. High-quality content (a timely or controversial topic, compelling writing, and high search-engine rankings) helps motivate bloggers to create links into a site.

Litigation Hold: The process of identifying and preserving e-mail, electronic business records, and other information that may be relevant to current or pending litigation and regulatory investigations. Once a lawsuit is filed, or if you anticipate a claim will one day be filed, you must stop deleting relevant e-mail and other evidence. Failure to preserve e-mail and other electronic documents can lead to charges of "spoliation" or destruction of evidence.

Metadata: Data that describes other data such as an e-mail's body, header, attachments, and log files relating to its transmission and receipt. From a legal perspective, metadata is integral to electronic business records. To be accepted as legally valid, an e-mail message and its metadata or parts must be authentic—intact and unaltered.

MSM: Mainstream media. Through blogs, citizen journalists offer an alternative to the mainstream media.

Netiquette: Etiquette rules governing e-mail and other electronic business communication tools.

Permalink: Contraction of "permanent link." The permalink creates a unique Web address for every posting on a blog. Bloggers link to one another's posts, which typically remain accessible forever via the permalink (unlike Web pages, which are subject to change). The permalink creates a double-edged sword for business, giving blogs "a viral quality, so a pertinent post can gain broad attention amazingly fast—and reputations can get taken down just as quickly," according to *Fortune*.[18]

Post: See also "Entry." The commentary that is written by a blogger on a blog. Some bloggers post multiple times per day. Most posts are relatively short. Posts often include external links, and offer readers the opportunity to comment.

Renting: The illegal practice of renting software without permission of the copyright holder.

Sarbanes-Oxley Act (SOX): Designed by the Securities and Exchange Commission (SEC) to thwart fraud in public companies, SOX requires regulated companies to implement internal controls for gathering, processing, and reporting accurate and reliable financial information. Effective e-mail management is fundamental to SOX compliance. E-mail security breaches such as intercepted messages, corrupted files, and leaked, stolen, altered, or lost data can put an organization at risk of noncompliance.

Shareware: Software that is passed out freely for evaluation purposes only. The evaluation period typically is 30 days.[19]

Smartphone: A mobile phone, such as the BlackBerry, that offers advanced capabilities including wireless access to the Internet, e-mail, IM, phone, voice mail, and portable organizers among others.

Social Engineering: When hackers or other malicious intruders use human error to their benefit. It could involve a hacker talking an employee out of a password over the phone. Or it could be dumpster diving, rooting through trash containers for information to enable the hacker to crack the organization's computer system.

Social Networking Site: Online social networks are communities of people with shared interests, activities, or other connections. Every day, millions of people turn to MySpace, Facebook, and other popular social networking sites to post their own content, read others' posts, and stay in touch with online "friends" who can number in the hundreds, thousands, or more. Social networking sites increase the risk of confidentiality breaches and information leaks when employees and ex-employees—caught up in the unstructured, unfiltered, anything-goes culture of online sharing—discuss proprietary or private matters for all the world to read.

Softlifting and **Softloading:** In the workplace, "softlifting" occurs when extra copies of software are made for employees to use at the office or take home. If you purchase software with a single-user license, then load it on multiple computers or servers, you are guilty of "softloading,"[20] which violates intellectual property law.

Software Piracy: The unauthorized and illegal use of software.

Spim: The instant messaging equivalent of spam. Currently just an occasional irritant for users of consumer-grade IM, spim is likely to grow as spammers turn their attention to IM. Enterprise IM systems are immune from spim, since they limit outside access and prohibit delivery unless the recipient approves it.

Splog: Spam blogs. Spam blogs do not provide any real content for users. Sploggers use automated tools to create fake blogs that are full of links to specific websites (generally sites selling goods and services). The goal of splogging is to boost search engine results and send traffic to the linked-to sites. Blog search engine Technorati estimates that 5.8 percent of new blogs, or about 50,000 posts, are fake or potentially fake.[21]

Spoliation: The legal term to refer to the destruction of evidence, intentional or otherwise.

Trojan Horse: A term that refers to an apparently harmless software code that actually contains malicious code. Once installed, the malicious code within the Trojan horse can wreak havoc on your network.

Unbundling: Separating software from the products with which it was intended to be bundled or sold. Unscrupulous software distributors sometimes sell discount software that has been unbundled. If a deal seems too good to be true, it probably is.[22]

Unintended Reader. See "Hidden Reader." Includes persons to whom your intended reader forwards or copies your original message. Also may include your intended reader's employer, court personnel, regulators, law enforcement, and the media among others.

URL Block: Technology that prevents employees from accessing inappropriate, time-wasting, or otherwise off-limit websites. Employers have grown significantly less tolerant of employees who engage in nonwork-related Web surfing during business hours. Between 2001 and 2007, the number of employers who use URL blocking tools rose 27 percent, with 65 percent of employers using URL blocking technology in 2007 versus 38 percent in 2001.[23]

User ID: User ID is one of the biggest problems facing the IM industry and users. With consumer-grade IM, users are free to establish their own IM name and to use any domain they wish. Using AOL Instant Messenger, for example, a competitor could use your corporate domain to create an IM user name that reads JDoe@YourCompany.com. Another problem arises when employees using personal IM clients select inappropriate user IDs (HotMamma). The misuse and misappropriation of user names and domains raises concerns over authenticity (how do you really know who a message came from?) among other challenges. Employers are advised to combine written user ID policy with technology products that give the IT department some control over user IDs, enabling you to reserve your domain name and kick imposters off the system.

Vicarious Liability: A legal principle in which an employer may be held responsible for the accidental or intentional misconduct of employees including inappropriate e-mail, Internet, and cell phone use.

Video Site: Video sites give employees direct access to the public. Thanks to YouTube and other video sites, anyone whose cell phone is equipped with a video recorder can capture and upload potentially embarrassing or otherwise damaging videos of company executives, employees, facilities, and secrets—in a snap. Like social networking sites, video sites increase the risk of confidentiality breaches and information leaks when employees and ex-employees take and post unauthorized videos of a company's people, products, and proprietary information.

Video Snacking: Employees who surf the Web for personal reasons during their lunch breaks are engaged in "video snacking." A common practice within some organizations, unrestricted personal lunchtime surfing is an increasingly risky proposition for employers. Video snacking opens the organization to bandwidth waste and other risks as employees download and file large, nonbusiness-related videos. Systems can be damaged and security breached as spyware, viruses, and other malicious intruders enter your system via infected content. Employee productivity may be diminished as video snackers, hungry for more content, stretch the lunch hour into the afternoon.

Warez: Pirated or illegal software. In general, the standard in the Internet community is to make plural words describing illegal activity using the letter *z* instead of *s*. Software or sites labeled as warez usually contain illegal material and should be avoided and reported.[24]

Web Diary: See "blog." An online journal that contains written content, links, and photos, which are regularly updated.

Worm: A malicious code or computer virus that replicates itself on a computer, using up more of the computer's memory and system resources until the computer becomes sluggish or even inoperable.

Resources and Expert Sources

E-Mail Archiving and Management Solutions
ArcMail Technology
401 Edwards Street
Suite 1100
Shreveport, LA 71101
866-417-6495
www.arcmail.com

Founded in 2005, ArcMail Technology is a leading provider of simple, secure, and cost-effective e-mail archiving and management solutions for organizations of all sizes. ArcMail Defender was recently granted the Network Products Guide 2008 Product Innovation Award and Network Products Guide 2008 Best Products and Services Award for E-Mail Archiving. The ArcMail Defender solution is a self-contained, turnkey e-mail archiving appliance that is easy to buy, easy to install, and easy to use. The ArcMail Defender improves the end-user experience, reduces the load on IT resources, and safely and securely retains the business information contained in e-mail. ArcMail's scalable solutions are designed to meet the e-mail archiving and management requirements of organizations both large and small. ArcMail has a global channel program to help deliver its products to organizations worldwide. ArcMail is headquartered in Shreveport, LA, and has development groups in Washington and Arizona. For more information, visit www.arcmail.com.

Confidential Electronic Messaging
VaporStream, Inc.
247 S. State Street

Suite 350
Chicago, IL 60604
877-203-4980
www.vaporstream.com

Founded in 2005, VaporStream, Inc., is the creator of VaporStream™ Confidential Messaging, the world's first completely confidential and record-less electronic messaging system. By separating the message header from the message body, VaporStream, VaporStream Enterprise, and Vapor-Stream Mobile provide users with a private and confidential electronic messaging system that never leaves a record on any computer or server once the message is read. A complement to e-mail, VaporStream Confidential Messaging reduces the risks and costs associated with most e-mail and instant messaging systems. More information about VaporStream can be found online at www.vaporstream.com.

e-Policy Training, Consulting, and Expert Witness Services
The ePolicy Institute
Nancy Flynn, Executive Director
2300 Walhaven Ct.
Columbus, Ohio 43220
614-451-3200
nancy@epolicyinstitute.com
www.epolicyinstitute.com
epolicyinstitute.blogspot.com

The ePolicy Institute is dedicated to reducing employers' electronic risks, including litigation, through the development and implementation of effective e-Policies and employee training programs. ePolicy Institute services include on-site and online training seminars; expert witness services and litigation consulting; policy development and implementation; research surveys; and content development, including white papers and policy guides. An in-demand speaker and corporate trainer, Executive Director Nancy Flynn is the author of 10 books published in five languages. Her books include *Blog Rules* (AMACOM 2006), *E-Mail Rules* (AMACOM 2003), *Instant Messaging Rules* (AMACOM 2004), *The e-Policy Handbook* (AMACOM 2008 and 2001), *Writing Effective E-Mail* (Thomson Learning/ Crisp 2003 and 1998), and *E-Mail Management* (Thomson Learning/NETg 2007). Flynn is a popular media source who has been featured in *Fortune, Time, Newsweek, USA Today, Readers' Digest, US News & World Report,* the *Wall Street Journal, BusinessWeek,* and the New *York Times,* as well as on CBS, ABC, NBC, CNN, CNBC, MSNBC, FOX, NPR, and other media outlets.

NOTES

Chapter 1

1. Kim S. Nash, "E-Mail Retention: The High Cost of Digging Up Data," *Baseline* (August 2, 2006), http://www.baselinemag.com/index2.php?option=content& task=view&id=4044&pop=1&.

2. "2001 Electronic Policies and Practices Survey" from American Management Association and ePolicy Institute. Survey results available at www.amanet.org and www.epolicyinstitute.com.

3. Ibid.

4. "2006 Workplace E-Mail, Instant Messaging & Blog Survey" from American Management Association and ePolicy Institute. Survey results available at www.amanet.org and www.epolicyinstitute.com.

5. Ibid.

6. "2004 Workplace E-Mail and Instant Messaging Survey" from American Management Association and ePolicy Institute. Survey results available at www.amanet.org and www.epolicyinstitute.com.

7. "2006 Workplace E-Mail, Instant Messaging & Blog Survey" from American Management Association and ePolicy Institute. Survey results available at www.amanet.org and www.epolicyinstitute.com.

8. Ibid.

9. "2007 Electronic Monitoring and Surveillance Survey" from American Management Association and ePolicy Institute; "2001 Electronic Policies and Practices Survey" from American Management Association and ePolicy Institute. Survey results available at www.amanet.org and www.epolicyinstitute.com.

10. "2004 Workplace E-Mail and Instant Messaging Survey" from American Management Association and ePolicy Institute. Survey results available at www.amanet.org and www.epolicyinstitute.com.

Chapter 2

1. "2006 Workplace E-Mail, Instant Messaging & Blog Survey" from American Management Association and ePolicy Institute; "2001 Electronic Policies and

Practices Survey" from American Management Association and ePolicy Institute. Survey results available at www.amanet.org and www.epolicyinstitute .com.

2. "2006 Workplace E-Mail, Instant Messaging & Blog Survey" from American Management Association and ePolicy Institute. Survey results available at www.amanet.org and www.epolicyinstitute.com

3. Nancy Flynn and Randolph Kahn, Esq., *E-Mail Rules*, New York, AMACOM, 2003.

4. "2006 Workplace E-Mail, Instant Messaging & Blog Survey" from American Management Association and ePolicy Institute. Survey results available at www.amanet.org and www.epolicyinstitute.com.

5. Nate Leaf, "Survey: Most Businesses Lack Clear Email Retention Policy" (December 17, 2007), http://www.yourtv20.com/news/technology/12563691 .html. See also "Email Archiving vs. Destructive Retention Policies," ArcMail Technology White Paper (2007), www.arcmail.com.

6. Nancy Flynn and Randolph Kahn, Esq., *E-Mail Rules*, New York, AMACOM, 2003. See also Nancy Flynn, *Instant Messaging Rules*, New York, AMACOM, 2004.

7. "Fourth Annual Litigation Trends Survey Findings," Fulbright & Jaworski L.L.P. (2007), www.fulbright.com/litigationtrends.

8. Brett Burney, "State-Side Patchwork: Not All 50 States Are in Sync with Federal Rules," *LTN Law Technology News* (January 2008).

9. Nancy Flynn's telephone interview with ArcMail Technology's William T. Gates, President and CEO (October 24, 2008), www.arcmail.com.

Chapter 3

1. "Zurich American Insurance Company and Law Firms Get $1.25M Fine for Hiding 9/11 Insurance Claims Evidence," *InsuranceNewsNet* (June 22, 2007), http://enews.insurance-mail.net/print.asp?n = 1&id = 81228.

2. Eric J. Sinrod, "The New E-Discovery Burden," *CNETNews.com* (October 18, 2007), http://www.news.com/The-new-e-discovery-burden/2010-1030_3-6213845 .html.

3. "Fourth Annual Litigation Trends Survey Findings," Fulbright & Jaworski L.L.P., www.fulbright.com/litigationtrends.

4. Kim S. Nash, "E-Mail Retention: The High Cost of Digging Up Data," *Baseline* (August 2, 2006), http://www.baselinemag.com/index2.php?option = content& task = view&id = 4044&pop = 1&.

5. Eric J. Sinrod, "The New E-Discovery Burden," *CNETNews.com* (October 18,

2007), http://www.news.com/The-new-e-discovery-burden/2010-1030_3-6213845 .html.

6. Kim S. Nash, "Email Retention: The High Cost of Digging Up Data," *Baseline* (August 2, 2006), http://www.baselinemag.com/index2.php?option = content& task = view&id = 4044&pop = 1&.

7. *William T. Thomson Co. v. General Nutrition Corp.*, 593 F. Supp. 1443 (C.D. Cal. 1984). See also Nancy Flynn, *Instant Messaging Rules*, New York, AMACOM, 2004.

8. Michael Osterman, "E-Mail Retention," *Network World Messaging Newsletter* (January 28, 2002), http://www.nwfusion.com/newsletters/gwm/2002/01196628 .html. See also Nancy Flynn, *Instant Messaging Rules*, New York, AMACOM, 2004.

9. Kim S. Nash, "E-Mail Retention: The High Cost of Digging Up Data," *Baseline* (August 2, 2006), http://www.baselinemag.com/index2.php?option = content& task = view&id = 4044&pop = 1&.

10. *Zubulake v. UBS Warburg*, 02 Civ. 1243 (S.D.N.Y. Oct. 22, 2003). See also "Zubulake IV: Defendant Ruled Negligent for Destruction of E-Mail Evidence," *Kroll Ontrack Case Law Update and E-Discovery News* (November 2003) and "Case Law Update and E-Discovery News," vol. 5, issue 1, first quarter 2006, Kroll Ontrack, www.krollontrack.com. See also Nancy Flynn, *Blog Rules*, New York, AMACOM, 2006, and Nancy Flynn, *Instant Messaging Rules*, New York, AMACOM, 2004.

11. Ibid.

12. Kim S. Nash, "E-Mail Retention: The High Cost of Digging Up Data," *Baseline* (August 2, 2006), http://www.baselinemag.com/index2.php?option = content& task = view&id = 4044&pop = 1&.

13. Michael Osterman, "A Legal Guide to E-Mail Retention," *Network World Messaging Newsletter* (February 4, 2002), http://www.nwfusion.com/news letters/gwm/2002/01209344.html. See also Nancy Flynn, *Instant Messaging Rules*, New York, AMACOM, 2004.

14. Steve Ulfelder, "CSI: Lost E-Mails," *Network World* (September 8, 2003), http://www.nwfusion.com/research/2003/0908csi.html. See also Nancy Flynn, *Instant Messaging Rules*, New York, AMACOM, 2004.

15. "Email Archiving vs. Destructive Retention Policies," ArcMail Technology White Paper (2007), www.arcmail.com.

16. Marty Foltyn, "Getting Up to Speed on FRCP," *EnterpriseStorageForum.com* (June 29, 2007.) See also "Sarbanes-Oxley and Email Archiving," ArcMail Technology White Paper, (2007), www.archmail.com.

17. "Fourth Annual Litigation Trends Survey Findings," Fulbright & Jaworski L.L.P., www.fulbright.com/litigationtrends.

18. Nancy Flynn's telephone interview with ArcMail Technology's William T. Gates, President and CEO (October 24, 2008), www.arcmail.com.

19. Ibid.

20. Ibid.

21. Nancy Flynn and Randolph Kahn, Esq., *E-Mail Rules*, New York, AMACOM, 2003.

22. Ann Bednarz, "Electronic Records Policies Lacking, Firms Say," *Network World Fusion* (March 12, 2004), www.nwfusion.com/news/2004/0312records .html. See also Nancy Flynn, *Instant Messaging Rules*, New York, AMACOM, 2004.

Chapter 4

1. "Fourth Annual Litigation Trends Survey Findings," Fulbright & Jaworski L.L.P., www.fulbright.com/litigationtrends.

2. Ibid.

3. Nancy Flynn's telephone interview with Attorney Tamzin Matthew of Blake Lapthorn Tarlo Lyons (January 25, 2007). See also Tamzin Matthew, "E-mail Archiving and the Law," Blake Lapthorn Tarlo Lyons, PowerPoint presentation (March 27, 2007), www.bllaw.co.uk.

4. Kim S. Nash, "E-Mail Retention: The High Cost of Digging Up Data," *Baseline* (August 2, 2006), http://www.baselinemag.com/index2.php?option = content& task = view&id = 4044&pop = 1&.

5. Fourth Annual Litigation Trends Survey Findings, Fulbright & Jaworski L.L.P., www.fulbright.com/litigationtrends.

6. "NASD and NYSE Member Regulation Combine to Form the Financial Industry Regulatory Authority—FINRA," FINRA News Release (July 30, 2007), www.finra.org.

7. Kevin Burke, "SEC Fines Merrill $2.5 Million in Settlement Over Obstruction Charges," *Registered Rep*, March 15, 2006, http://www.registeredrep.com/ news/sec-fines-merrill/index.html.

8. "Electronic Discovery and Evidence," http://arkfeld.blogs.com/ede/2005/02/ jp-morgan-pays-html. See also Nancy Flynn, *Blog Rules*, New York, AMACOM, 2006.

9. Kim S. Nash, "E-Mail Retention: The High Cost of Digging Up Data," *Baseline* (August 2, 2006), http://www.baselinemag.com/index2.php?option = content& task = view&id = 4044&pop = 1&.

10. Kevin Burke, "SEC Fines Merrill $2.5 Million in Settlement over Obstruction Charges," *Registered Rep*, March 15, 2006, http://www.registeredrep.com/news/sec-fines-merrill/index.html.

11. Ibid.

12. Kim S. Nash, "E-Mail Retention: The High Cost of Digging Up Data," *Baseline* (August 2, 2006), http://www.baselinemag.com/index2.php?option = content& task = view&id = 4044&pop = 1&

Chapter 5

1. Ibid.

2. Rebecca Buckman, "The E-Mail Overload," *Courier Journal* (December 17, 2007), http://www.courierjournal.com/apps/pbcs.dll/article?AID = /20071217/Business/712170371. See also "Email Archiving vs. Destructive Retention Policies," ArcMail Technology White Paper (2007), www.arcmail.com.

3. Kim S. Nash, "E-Mail Retention: The High Cost of Digging Up Data," *Baseline* (August 2, 2006), http://www.baselinemag.com/index2.php?option = content& task = view&id = 4044&pop = 1&.

4. Marty Foltyn, "Getting Up to Speed on FRCP," *EnterpriseStorageForum.com* (June 29, 2007). See also "Sarbanes-Oxley and Email Archiving," ArcMail Technology White Paper (2007), www.arcmail.com.

5. Ann Bednarz, "Electronic Records Policies Lacking, Firms Say," *Network World Fusion* (March 12, 2004), http://www.nwfusion.com/news/2004/0312records.html. See also Nancy Flynn, *Instant Messaging Rules*, New York, AMACOM, 2004.

6. Kim S. Nash, "E-Mail Retention: The High Cost of Digging Up Data," *Baseline* (August 2, 2006), http://www.baselinemag.com/index2.php?option = content& task = view&id = 4044&pop = 1&.

7. Nancy Flynn and Randolph Kahn, Esq., *E-Mail Rules*, New York, AMACOM, 2003.

8. Best Buy Lawyer Alters Documents," *Associated Press* (June 5, 2007).

9. Nancy Flynn and Randolph Kahn, Esq., *E-Mail Rules*, New York, AMACOM, 2003.

10. *Williams v. Taser International*, 2007 WL 1630875 (N.D. Ga. June 4, 2007). See also Roger Matus, Sean True, and Chuck Ingold, "The New Federal Rules of Civil Procedure: IT Obligations for Email," (2007), www.inboxer.com. See also Conrad J. Jacoby, "E-Discovery Update: Understanding the Consequences of an Unsuccessful Meet and Confer Session," *LLRX.com* (August 27, 2007). See also Eric J. Sinrod, "The New E-Discovery Burden," *CNETNews*

.com (October 18, 2007), http://www.news.com/2102-10303-621384.html?tag = st.util.print.

11.   Roger Matus, Sean True, and Chuck Ingold, "The New Federal Rules of Civil Procedure: IT Obligations for Email," (2007), www.inboxer.com. See also Eric J. Sinrod, "The New E-Discovery Burden," *CNETNews.com* (October 18, 2007), http://www.news.com/2102-10303-621384.html?tag = st.util.print.

12.   Nancy Flynn's telephone interview with Attorney Tamzin Matthew of Blake Lapthorn Tarlo Lyons (January 25, 2007). See also Tamzin Matthew, "E-mail Archiving and the Law," Blake Lapthorn Tarlo Lyons, PowerPoint presentation (March 27, 2007), www.bllaw.co.uk.

13.   http://searchcio.techtarget.com/tip/0,289483,sid19gci1188687,00.html. See also "Sarbanes-Oxley and Email Archiving," ArcMail Technology White Paper (2007), www.arcmail.com.

14.   http://www.networkworld.com/news/2007/012307-wasted-searches.html. See also "Email Archiving vs. Destructive Retention Policies," ArcMail Technology White Paper (2007), www.arcmail.com.

15.   "Email Archiving vs. Destructive Retention Policies," ArcMail Technology White Paper (2007), www.arcmail.com.

16.   Nancy Flynn and Randolph Kahn, Esq., *E-Mail Rules*, New York, AMACOM, 2003.

17.   E-mail message from William T. Gates, ArcMail Technology's President and CEO, to author Nancy Flynn (October 24, 2008), www.arcmail.com.

18.   Mark Jewell, "Data Breaches Set Record," *Associated Press* (January 6, 2008).

19.   Nancy Flynn and Randolph Kahn, Esq., *E-Mail Rules*, New York, AMACOM, 2003.

20.   Lucas Mearian, "Sidebar: Regulations, Volume and Capacity Add Archiving Pressure," *Computerworld* (February 16, 2004). See also Nancy Flynn, *Instant Messaging Rules*, New York, AMACOM, 2004.

21.   E-mail message from ArcMail Technology's President and CEO William T. Gates, to author Nancy Flynn (October 24, 2008), www.arcmail.com.

Chapter 6

1.   "Trends in Student Use of Technology, Part II," *University of St. Thomas, Minnesota Bulletin Today* (February 6, 2008), http://www.stthomas.edu/bulletin/news/20086/Wednesday/WebWednesday2608.cfm.

2.   Press Release, "Steelcase Workplace Index Survey Examines 'Water Cooler' Conversations at Work" (August 9, 2007), http://www.steelcase.com/na/steel caseexamineswatercoolNews. See also Stephanie Armour, "Did You Hear the Story About Office Gossip?" *USA Today* (September 10, 2007).

3. Stephanie Armour, "Did You Hear the Story About Office Gossip?" *USA Today* (September 10, 2007).

4. Press Release, "Steelcase Workplace Index Survey Examines 'Water Cooler' Conversations at Work" (August 9, 2007), http://www.steelcase.com/na/steel caseexamineswatercoolNews. See also Stephanie Armour, "Did You Hear the Story About Office Gossip?" *USA Today* (September 10, 2007).

5. "NASD Fines Analyst $75,000 for Rumor-Mongering," *USA Today*, http:// usatoday.printthis.clickability.com/pt/cpt?action = cpt&title = USATODA Y.com + - + N.

6. Nancy Flynn, *Instant Messaging Rules*, New York, AMACOM, 2004. See also Nancy Flynn and Randolph Kahn, Esq., *E-Mail Rules*, New York, AMACOM, 2003. See also Jane Black, "Why Offices Are Now Open Secrets, *BusinessWeek Online* (September 16, 2003).

7. "2007 Electronic Monitoring & Surveillance Survey" from American Management Association and ePolicy Institute. Survey results available at www .amanet.org and www.epolicyinstitute.com.

8. *TBG Ins. Serv. Corp. v. Superior Court of Los Angeles County*, 96 Cal. App. 4th 443 (Cal. Ct. App. 2002).

9. *Smythe v. Pillsbury*, 914 F. Supp. 97 (ED Pa. 1996). See also Nancy Flynn and Randolph Kahn, Esq., *E-Mail Rules*, New York, AMACOM, 2003.

10. Nancy Flynn's telephone interview with Attorney Jonathan Naylor of Morgan Cole Solicitors (July 19, 2006). See also Nancy Flynn, "ePolicy Best Practices," MessageLabs White Paper (2006), www.messagelabs.com.

11. Nancy Flynn's telephone interview with Attorney Tamzin Matthew of Blake Lapthorn Tarlo Lyons (January 25, 2007). See also Tamzin Matthew, "E-mail Archiving and the Law," Blake Lapthorn Tarlo Lyons, PowerPoint presentation (March 27, 2007), www.bllaw.co.uk.

12. "2007 Electronic Monitoring & Surveillance Survey" from American Management Association and ePolicy Institute. Survey results available at www .amanet.org and www.epolicyinstitute.com.

13. T. Shawn Taylor, "E-Lessons," *Chicago Tribune* (February 14, 2001).

Chapter 7

1. *SC Magazine* (January 11, 2007). See also "Five Perils of Outbound Email," Sendmail Inc. (June 2007).

2. "Outbound Email and Content Security in Today's Enterprise, 2007," Proofpoint Inc., survey fielded by Forrester Consulting (July 2007).

3. "Aberdeen Messaging Security Benchmark Report 2006." Cited in "Five Perils of Outbound Email" Sendmail Inc. (June 2007).

4. "Outbound E-mail and Content Security in Today's Enterprise, 2007," Proofpoint Inc. survey fielded by Forrester Consulting (July 2007).

5. "2007 Electronic Monitoring & Surveillance Survey," from American Management Association and ePolicy Institute. Survey results available at www.ama net.org and www.epolicyinstitute.com.

6. Alex Berenson, "Lilly Considers $1 Billion Fine to Settle Case," *New York Times* (January 31, 2008), http://www.nytimes.com/2008/01/31/business/ 31drug.html. See also Ina Fried, "The High Cost of E-Mail Autocomplete," *CNETNews.com* (February 5, 2008), http://www.news.com/8301-138603-9865371-56.html. See also Katherine Eban, "Lilly's $1 Billion E-Mailstrom," *Condé Nast Portfolio.com* (February 5, 2008), http://www.portfolio.com/ news-markets/top-5/2008/02/05/Eli-Lilly-E-Mail-to-New-York-T.

7. Excerpted from Nancy Flynn's telephone interview with Attorney Stephen M. Fronk, Howard Rice Nemerovski Canady Falk & Rabkin (October 12, 2005), www.howardrice.com. See also Nancy Flynn, *Blog Rules*, New York, AMACOM, 2006.

8. Nancy Flynn, *Instant Messaging Rules*, New York, AMACOM, 2004. See also Jane Black, "Why Offices Are Now Open Secrets, *BusinessWeek Online* (September 16, 2003).

9. "2007 Electronic Monitoring & Surveillance Survey," from American Management Association and ePolicy Institute. Survey results available at www.ama net.org and www.epolicyinstitute.com.

10. Steve Fishman, "Inside Eliot's Army," *New York Magazine* (January 3, 2005), http://www.printthis.clickability.com/pt/cpt?action = cpt&expire = &urlID = 17 704273&fb.

11. Ibid.

12. *The People of the State of New York by Eliot Spitzer, Attorney General of the State of New York v. Marsh & McLennan Companies, Inc. and Marsh Inc.* See also Steve Fishman, "Inside Eliot's Army," *New York Magazine* (January 3, 2005), http://www.printthis.clickability.com/pt/cpt?action = cpt&expire = & urlID = 17704273&fb.

13. Joseph B. Treaster, "Insurance Broker Settles Spitzer Suit for $850 Million," *New York Times* (February 1, 2005), http://www.nytimes.com/2005/02/01/busi ness/01marsh.html?pagewanted = print&position.

14. Thor Valdmanis, "Marsh & McLennan Lops off 3,000 Jobs," *USA Today*, http:// usatoday.printthis.clickability.com/pt/cpt?action = cpt&title = USATODAY.com.

15. Bloomberg News, "Insurance Broker Wins Dismissal of a Customer Lawsuit," *New York Times* (September 29, 2007), http://www.nytimes.com/2007/09/29/ business/29insure.html?n = Top/News/Business/Com.

16. Liz Chong, "Two More Morgan Stanley Staff Quit Over Leaked E-Mail," *Times Online* (October 14, 2006), http://business.timesonline.co.uk/tol/business/indus trysectors/bankingandfinan cial/articl.

17. Ibid. See also Sundeep Tucker, "Morgan Star Quits After Email Blast," *The Australian* (October 5, 2006), http://www.theaustralian.news.com.au/story/ 0,20867,20526011-36375,00.html. See also "A Banking Star's Inconvenient Singaporean Truth," *Asia Sentinel* (October 4, 2006), http://www.asiasentinel .com/index2.php?option = comcontent&task = view&id = 199&pop.

18. Michael Osterman, "E-Mail Without a Trace," *NetworkWorld* (October 3, 2006).

19. "Outbound E-mail and Content Security in Today's Enterprise, 2007," Proofpoint Inc. survey fielded by Forrester Consulting (July 2007).

20. "2006 Workplace E-Mail, Instant Messaging & Blog Survey" from American Management Association and ePolicy Institute. Survey results available at www.amanet.org and www.epolicyinstitute.com.

21. "2004 Workplace E-Mail & Instant Messaging Survey" from American Management Association and ePolicy Institute. Survey results available at www.amanet.org and www.epolicyinstitute.com.

22. "2007 Electronic Monitoring & Surveillance Survey" from American Management Association and ePolicy Institute. Survey results available at www .amanet.org and www.epolicyinstitute.com.

23. Ibid.

24. Cara Garretson and Ellen Messmer, "Top 10 Security Companies to Watch," *NetworkWorld* (October 19, 2006).

Chapter 8

1. Robert Richardson, "2007 CSI Computer Crime and Security Survey," Computer Security Institute, www.gocsi.com.

2. Ibid.

3. Mark Jewell, "Data Breaches Set Record, Groups Say," *Associated Press* (January 6, 2008).

4. Ibid.

5. Ibid.

6. "Outbound E-mail and Content Security in Today's Enterprise, 2007," Proofpoint Inc. survey fielded by Forrester Consulting (July 2007).

7. Nancy Flynn's telephone interview with Attorney Jon Neiditz of Nelson Mullins Riley & Scarborough (November 15, 2007), www.NelsonMullins.com.

8. "NY Gets First Settlement Under Breach Notification Law," *Information Week* (April 30, 2007), www.darkreading.com/document.asp?docid = 122900& print = true.

9. Federal Trade Commission News Release, "ChoicePoint Settles Data Security Breach Charges; to Pay $10 Million in Civil Penalties, $5 Million for Consumer Redress" (January 26, 2006), http://www.ftc.gov/opa/2006/01/choicepoint.shtm. See also Bob Sullivan, "ChoicePoint to Pay $15 Million Over Data Breach," *MSNBC.com* (January 26, 2006), http://www.msnbc.msn.com/id/11030692/print/1/displaymode/1098.

10. Robert Richardson, "2007 CSI Computer Crime and Security Survey," Computer Security Institute, www.gocsi.com.

11. Press Release, "62% of Employees Report Incidents at Work That Put Customer Data at Risk for Indentity Theft" (June 2, 2003). Survey conducted by Harris International for Vontu, www.vontu.com.

12. "2007 Electronic Monitoring and Surveillance Survey" from American Management Association and ePolicy Institute. Survey results available at www.amanet.org and www.epolicyinstitute.com.

13. Ibid.

14. "2006 Workplace E-Mail, Instant Messaging & Blog Survey" from American Management Association and ePolicy Institute. Survey results available at www.amanet.org and www.epolicyinstitute.com.

15. Elron Software, "1999 E-Mail Abuse Study."

Chapter 9

1. "2007 Electronic Monitoring and Surveillance Survey" from American Management Association and ePolicy Institute; "2001 Electronic Policies and Practices Survey," from American Management Association and ePolicy Institute. Survey results available at www.amanet.org and www.epolicyinstitute.com.

2. Ibid.

3. "Fourth Annual Litigation Trends Survey Findings," Fulbright & Jaworski L.L.P., www.fulbright.com/litigationtrends.

4. Stanley M. Gibson, "Hit 'Delete' to Prevent EDD Disaster," JMBM/Jeffer Mangels Butler & Marmaro LLP (August 7, 2007), www.jmbm.com. Previously published on www.law.com.

5. "2007 Electronic Monitoring & Surveillance Survey" from American Management Association and ePolicy Institute. Survey results available at www.amanet.org and www.epolicyinstitute.com.

6. "2004 Workplace E-Mail and Instant Messaging Survey" from American Management Association and ePolicy Institute. Survey results available at www.amanet.org and www.epolicyinstitute.com.

7. Ralph Blumenthal, "Prosecutor, Under Fire, Steps Down in Houston" *New York Times* (February 16, 2008).

8. Ralph Blumenthal, "Houston Prosecutor Admits He Deleted E-Mail Messages," *New York Times* (February 2, 2008).

9. Dennis K. Berman, "Online Laundry: Government Posts Enron's E-Mail," *Wall Street Journal* (October 6, 2003), A1. See also Nancy Flynn, *Instant Messaging Rules*, New York, AMACOM, 2004.

Chapter 11

1. IM-related chapters excerpted from Nancy Flynn, *Instant Messaging Rules*, New York, AMACOM, 2004.

2. "Trends in Student Use of Technology, Part II," *University of St. Thomas, Minnesota Bulletin Today* (February 6, 2008), http://www.stthomas.edu/bulletin/news/20086/Wednesday/WebWednesday2608.cfm.

3. '2006 E-Mail, Instant Messaging and Blog Survey" from American Management Association and ePolicy Institute. Survey results available at www.amanet.org and www.epolicyinstitute.com.

4. Ibid.

5. Nancy Flynn's telephone interview with Jonathan Christensen, CTO, FaceTime Communications (October 21, 2003), *www.facetime.com*.

6. Dan Orzech, "Under IT's Radar, Instant Messaging Invades Corporate Desktops," *InstantMessagingPlanet.com* (July 14, 2003), http://*www.instant messagingplanet.com/enterprise/article.php/1120822348711*.

7. "2006 E-Mail, Instant Messaging and Blog Survey" from American Management Association and ePolicy Institute. Survey results available at www.amanet.org and www.epolicyinstitute.com.

8. Ibid.

9. Ibid.

10. "2004 Workplace E-Mail and Instant Messaging Survey" from American Management Association and ePolicy Institute. Survey results available at www.amanet.org and www.epolicyinstitute.com

Chapter 12

1. Dan Orzech, "Under IT's Radar, Instant Messaging Invades Corporate Desktops," *InstantMessagingPlanet.com* (July 14, 2003), http://www.instant messagingplanet.com/enterprise/article.php/1120822348711.

2. Christine Y. Chen, "The IM Invasion; Instant-Messaging Providers Are Targeting Corporations in a Big Way. Does Using IM Make Sense?" *Fortune* (May 26, 2003), 135.

3. "Fast and Furious: Instant Messaging Puts E-Mail into the Snail Mail Class," *The Guardian* (May 19, 2003), 5.

4. "2006 E-Mail, Instant Messaging and Blog Survey" from American Management Association and ePolicy Institute. Survey results available at www .amanet.org and www.epolicyinstitute.com

5. Dan Orzech, "Under IT's Radar, Instant Messaging Invades Corporate Desktops," *InstantMessagingPlanet.com* (July 14, 2003), http://www.instant messagingplanet.com/enterprise/article.php/1120822348711.

6. Kian Saneii, V.P. Marketing, Websense Inc., www.websense.com.

Chapter 13

1. "Lexicon: Video Snacking," Briefing Column, *Time* (January 21, 2008).

2. Nancy Flynn and Randolph Kahn, Esq., *E-Mail Rules*, New York, AMACOM, 2003.

3. "Nine D.C. Employees to Be Fired Over Porn at Work," *NBC4.com* (January 23, 2008).

4. "2007 Electronic Monitoring & Surveillance Survey" from American Management Association and ePolicy Institute. Survey results available at www .amanet.org and www.epolicyinstitute.com.

Chapter 14

1. Blog-related chapters excerpted from Nancy Flynn, *Blog Rules*, New York, AMACOM, 2006.

2. "One Blog Created 'Every Second,'" *BBC News* (August 2, 2005), http://news .bbc.co.uk/go/pr/fr/-/1/hi/technology/4737671.stm. See also "State of the Blogosphere, August 2005, Part 1, Blog Growth," Technorati Weblog, http:// www.technorati.com/weblog/2005/08/34.html.

3. "The State of Blogging," Pew Internet & American Life Project Data Memo (January 2005).

4. "Engaging The Blogosphere Survey," Edelman and Technorati (October 2005), www.edelman.com.

5. "Blogging in the Enterprise: Myths and Realities Survey" Guidewire Group and iUpload (October 2005), www.iupload.com.

6. "The State of Blogging," Pew Internet & American Life Project Data Memo (January 2005).

Chapter 15

1. "2006 Workplace E-Mail, Instant Messaging & Blog Survey" from American Management Association and ePolicy Institute. Survey results available online at www.amanet.org and www.epolicyinstitute.com.

2. "2007 Electronic Monitoring & Surveillance Survey" from American Manage-

ment Association and ePolicy Institute. Survey results available online at www.amanet.org and www.epolicyinstitute.com.

3. "2006 Workplace E-Mail, Instant Messaging & Blog Survey" from American Management Association and ePolicy Institute. Survey results available online at www.amanet.org and www.epolicyinstitute.com.

4. "2007 Electronic Monitoring and Surveillance Survey" from American Management Association and ePolicy Institute. Survey results available online at www.amanet.org and www.epolicyinstitute.com.

5. "2006 Workplace E-Mail, Instant Messaging & Blog Survey" and "2007 Electronic Monitoring & Surveillance Survey" from American Management Association and ePolicy Institute. Survey results available online at www.amanet.org and www.epolicyinstitute.com.

6. Excerpted from Nancy Flynn's phone interview with Attorney Stephen M. Fronk of Howard Rice Nemerovski Canady Falk & Rabkin (October 12, 2005), www.howardrice.com.

7. Ibid.

8. Nancy Flynn and Randolph Kahn, Esq., *E-Mail Rules*, New York, AMACOM, 2003.

9. Excerpted from Nancy Flynn's telephone interview with Attorney Stephen M. Fronk of Howard Rice Nemerovski Canady Falk & Rabkin (October 12, 2005), www.howardrice.com.

10. "No Longer Safe for Work: Blogs," *Wired News* (October 24, 2005), www.wired news.com.

11. "2007 Electronic Monitoring & Surveillance Survey," from American Management Association and ePolicy Institute. Survey results available at www .amanet.org and www.epolicyinstitute.com.

12. "Engaging the Blogosphere," An Edelman/Technorati Study (September 2005), http://www.extranet.edelman.com/bloggerstudy.

13. "2006 Workplace E-Mail, IM & Blog Survey" from American Management Association and ePolicy Institute. Survey results available at www.amanet.org and www.epolicyinstitute.com.

14. "Engaging the Blogosphere," An Edelman/Technorati Study (September 2005).

15. Daniel Lyons, "Attack of the Blogs," *Forbes* (November 14, 2005), www.forbes .com.

16. "Blogging in the Enterprise," A Guidewire Group Market Cycle Survey for iUpload (October 2005), www.iupload.com.

17. David Kirkpatrick and Daniel Roth, "Why There's No Escaping the Blog," *Fortune* (January 10, 2005).

18. Bradley Johnson, "What Blogs Cost American Business," *Advertising Age* (October 24, 2005), www.adage.com.

19. Dan Malachowski, "Wasted Time at Work Costing Companies Billions." Report on America Online/Salary.com's 2005 productivity survey, www.salary.com.

Chapter 16

1. "2006 Workplace E-Mail, Instant Messaging & Blog Survey" from American Management Association and ePolicy Institute. Survey results available at www.amanet.org and www.epolicyinstitute.com.

2. "2006 E-Mail, Instant Messaging & Blog Survey" from American Management Association and ePolicy Institute. Survey findings available at www.amanet.org and www.epolicyinstitute.com.

3. Ibid.

4. Ibid.

5. Paul Starkman, "Mixed Verdicts," *Law Technology News* (November 2005), www.lawtechnologynews.com.

6. Ibid.

7. Anna-Maria Mende, "US: 51% of Journalists Use Blogs," *The Editors Weblog* (August 26, 2005), www.editorsweblog.org.

8. Jo Best, "UK Staff in the Dark on Blogs," Silicon.com (September 27, 2005).

9. Paul Starkman, "Mixed Verdicts," *Law Technology News* (November 2005), www.lawtechnologynews.com.

Chapter 17

1. Steven Levy, "Facebook Grows Up," *Newsweek* (August 27, 2007).

2. Heather Havenstein, "Traffic to YouTube, Other Video Sites Doubled in 2007," *Australian PC World* (January 11, 2008), http://www.pcworld.idg.com.au/index.php/id;212345535;fp;4194304;fpid;1;pf;1.

3. Erika D. Smith, "Unauthorized," *Indianapolis Star* (June 11, 2007), http://www.indystar.com/apps/pbcs.dll/article?AID=/20070611BUSINESS/706110336&t.

4. Alex Berenson, "Lilly Considers $1 Billion Fine to Settle Case," *New York Times* (January 31, 2008), http://www.nytimes.com/2008/01/31/business/31drug.html. See also Ina Fried, "The High Cost of E-Mail Autocomplete," *CNETNews.com* (February 5, 2008), http://www.news.com/8301-138603-9865371-56.html. See also Katherine Eban, "Lilly's $1 Billion E-Mailstrom," Condé Nast Portfolio.com (February 5, 2008), http://www.portfolio.com/news-markets/top-5/20008/02/05/Eli-Lilly-E-Mail-to-New-York-T.

5. Erika D. Smith, "Unauthorized," *Indianapolis Star* (June 11, 2007), http:// www.indystar.com/apps/pbcs.dll/article?AID=/20070611BUSINESS/ 706110336&t.

6. Alex Berenson, "Lilly Waited Too Long to Warn About Schizophrenia Drug, Doctor Testifies," *New York Times* (March 8, 2008).

7. Erika D. Smith, "Unauthorized," *Indianapolis Star* (June 11, 2007), http:// www.indystar.com/apps/pbcs.dll/article?AID=/20070611BUSINESS/ 706110336&t.

8. Ibid.

9. "2007 Electronic Monitoring & Surveillance Survey" from American Management Association and ePolicy Institute. Survey findings available at www .amanet.org and www.epolicyinstitute.com.

10. Janet Kornblum, "Social, Work Lives Collide on Networking Websites," *USA Today* (January 18–20, 2008).

11. News Release, "Social Networking Sites Grow 47 Percent, Year Over Year, Reaching 45 Percent of Web Users, According to Nielsen/NetRatings" (May 11, 2006), www.nielsen-netratings.com.

12. "2007 Electronic Monitoring & Surveillance Survey" from American Management Association and ePolicy Institute. Survey findings available at www .amanet.org and www.epolicyinstitute.com.

13. Anick Jesdanun, "Recent Firings Raise Issues for Workers Who Publish Blogs," *Oregonian* (March 7, 2005), www.oregonian.com. See also Nancy Flynn, *Blog Rules*, New York, AMACOM, 2006.

14. "2007 Electronic Monitoring & Surveillance Survey" from American Management Association and ePolicy Institute. Survey findings available at www .amanet.org and www.epolicyinstitute.com.

15. Janet Kornblum, "Social, Work Lives Collide on Networking Websites," *USA Today* (January 18–20, 2008).

16. "Employee Blogging," Covington & Burling Technology & Software E-Alert, April 18, 2005, www.cov.com. See also Nancy Flynn, *Blog Rules*, New York, AMACOM, 2006.

17. Randall Stross, "How to Lose Your Job on Your Own Time," *New York Times* (December 30, 2007).

18. Theodore Decker, "Bigoted Videos Investigated," *Columbus Dispatch* (August 29, 2007), http://www.columbusdispatch.com/live/content/local_news/stories/ 2007/08/29/COPFOLO.ART_ART_08-29-07_B1_OP7OAIT.html?sid=101.

Chapter 18

1. The software piracy discussion in Chapter 18 is based on written material provided by the SPA Anti-Piracy Division of the Software & Information

Industry Association (SIIA). For more information about software piracy, visit www.siia.net. See also Nancy Flynn, *The ePolicy Handbook*, New York, AMACOM, 2001.

2. BSA News Release, "Worldwide Software Piracy Rate Holds Steady at 35%; Global Losses Up 15%," Washington, DC (May 15, 2007), http://www.bsa.org/ country/News%20andEvents/News%20Archives/Worldwide%20.

3. BSA News Release, "Use of Unlicensed Software Takes a Bite Out of Three Big Apple Companies," Washington, DC (January 8, 2008), http://www.bsa.org/ country/News%20and%20Events/News%20Archives/en-01082008-N.

4. BSA News Release, "BSA Conducts Record Global Anti-Piracy Enforcement Action: International Media Company Learns the Cost of Unlicensed Software," Washington, DC (September 18, 2007), http://www.bsa.org/country/ News%20and%20Events/News%20Archives/en-09182007-gl.

5. Software & Information Industry Association, *SIIA's Report on Global Software Piracy 1999*, Washington, DC, Software & Information Industry Association, 1999. See also Nancy Flynn, *The ePolicy Handbook*, New York, AMACOM, 2001.

6. SIIA News Release, "SIIA Settles with Florida Company Sued for Pirating Autodesk Software," Washington, DC (October 4, 2007), www.siia.net.

7. BSA News Release, "Financial Services Industry Settlements Help Deter Businesses from Using Unlicensed Software," Washington, DC (January 8, 2008), http://www.bsa.org/country/News%20and%20Events/News%20Archives/ en-0182008-Ge.

8. BSA News Release, "Use of Unlicensed Software Takes a Bite Out of Three Big Apple Companies," Washington, DC (January 8, 2008), http://www.bsa.org/ country/News%20and%20Events/News%20Archives/en-01082008-N.

9. BSA News Release, "Use of Unlicensed Software Takes a Bite Out of Three Big Apple Companies," Washington, DC (January 8, 2008), http://www.bsa.org/ country/News%20and%20Events/News%20Archives/en-01082008-N. See also "SIIA Settles with Florida Company Sued for Pirating Autodesk Software," Washington, DC (October 4, 2007), www.siia.net.

10. SIIA News Release, "SIIA 2006 Anti-Piracy Actions Reported," Washington, DC (February 21, 2007), www.siia.net.

11. Software & Information Industry Association, http://www.siia.net/piracy/pubs/ SoftwareUseLaw.pdf. See also Nancy Flynn, *The ePolicy Handbook*, New York, AMACOM, 2001.

12. Software usage checklist includes material excerpted in 2000 from the Software & Information Industry Association's website, www.siia.net. See also Nancy Flynn, *The ePolicy Handbook*, New York, AMACOM, 2001.

Chapter 19

1. "Cellphones and Driving," Insurance Information Institute (October 2007), http://www.iii.org/media/hottopics/insurance/cellphones. See also "'07 May Be Cell-Phone Spending Benchmark." *Columbus Dispatch* (December 19, 2007), C8.

2. W. David Gardner, "AT&T to Hang Up on Pay Phone Business," *Information-Week* (December 3, 2007), www.informationweek.com.

3. Mike Tierney, "Hang Up and Drive: Firms Take a Look at Liability," *Atlanta Journal-Constitution* (February 28, 2005).

4. Tom Hester, Jr., "New Jersey Bans Cell Phone Use, Texting While Driving," *Associated Press*, November 2, 2007.

5. "Cellphones and Driving," Insurance Information Institute (October 2007), http://www.iii.org/media/hottopics/insurance/cellphones.

6. Ibid.

7. Frank Drews, David Strayer, and Dennis Crouch, *Human Factors: The Journal of the Human Factors and Ergonomics Society*, June 29, 2006. See also "Study: Drivers Using Cellphones as Bad as Drunks," *Consumer Affairs.com*, June 30, 2006, www.consumeraffairs.com.

8. "Cellphones and Driving," Insurance Information Institute (October 2007), http://www.iii.org/media/hottopics/insurance/cellphones.

9. Ibid.

10. Mike Tierney, "Hang Up and Drive: Firms Take a Look at Liability," *Atlanta Journal-Constitution* (February 28, 2005).

11. Ken Belcon, "Four Score and . . . Mind If I Take This?" *New York Times* (September 30, 2007).

12. *Yoon v. Wagner et al.* See also "Civil Rights, Personal Injury, and Wrongful Death," Bode & Grenier, LLP, www.bode.com/civilrights.htm.

13. Mike Tierney, "Hang Up and Drive: Firms Take a Look at Liability," *Atlanta Journal-Constitution* (February 28, 2005). See also "Cellphones and Driving," Insurance Information Institute (October 2007), http://www.iii.org/media/hottopics/insurance/cellphones.

14. Tracey Wong Briggs, "Book's Not Closed on Texting," *USA Today* (September 4, 2007).

15. Ibid.

16. Ibid.

17. Jim Suhr, "Lawsuit Alleges Cardinals Negligent In Posting Text Message on Scoreboard," Associated Press (November 8, 2007).

18. Tracey Wong Briggs, "Book's Not Closed on Texting," *USA Today* (September 4, 2007). See also Katie Thomas, "On Texting, a Question of Access or Invasion," *New York Times* (January 12, 2008).

19. Pat Olsen, "Up on Teen Text Lingo?" ParentSmart Column, *USA Weekend* (January 11–13, 2008).

20. Corey Williams, "Detroit Mayor Sends Steamy Text Messages," *Associated Press* (January 24, 2008).

21. Nick Bunkley, "Mayor's Amorous Texts Lead to Perjury Inquiry," *New York Times* (January 26, 2008).

22. Jeff Karoub, "Texting Remains Relatively Private," *Associated Press* (January 25, 2008).

23. "2005 Electronic Monitoring & Surveillance Survey" from American Management Association and ePolicy Institute. Survey results available at www. amanet.org and www.epolicyinstitute.com.

24. Randy Cohen, The Ethicist, "Cellphone Naughtiness," *New York Times Magazine* (September 16, 2007).

25. "2005 Electronic Monitoring & Surveillance Survey" from American Management Association and ePolicy Institute. Survey results available at www .amanet.org and www.epolicyinstitute.com.

26. "How Americans Use Their Cellphones," *Pew/Internet Reports: Technology & Media Use* (April 3, 2006), www.pewinternet.org/report.

27. Ken Belson, "Four Score and . . . Mind if I Take This?" *New York Times* (September 30, 2007).

28. "How Americans Use Their Cellphones," *Pew/Internet Reports: Technology & Media Use* (April 3, 2006), http://www.pewinternet.org/report.

29. Ibid.

30. Ken Belson, "Four Score and . . . Mind if I Take This?" *New York Times* (September 30, 2007).

Chapter 20

1. "2006 Workplace E-Mail, Instant Messaging & Blog Survey" from American Management Association and ePolicy Institute. Survey results available at www.amanet.org and www.epolicyinstitute.com.

2. "2007 Electronic Monitoring & Surveillance Survey" from American Management Association and ePolicy Institute. Survey results available at www .amanet.org and www.epolicyinstitute.com.

3. J. Lynn Lunsford, Andy Pasztor, and Joann S. Lublin, "Boeing's CEO Forced to Resign over His Affair with Employee," *Wall Street Journal* (March 8, 2005). See also Nancy Flynn, *Blog Rules,* New York, AMACOM, 2006.

4. "2006 Workplace E-Mail, Instant Messaging & Blog Survey" from American Management Association and ePolicy Institute. Survey results available at www.amanet.org and www.epolicyinstitute.com.

5. "2004 Workplace E-Mail and Instant Messaging Survey" from American Management Association and ePolicy Institute. Survey results available at www.amanet.org and www.epolicyinstitute.com.

Chapter 21

1. "2007 Electronic Monitoring & Surveillance Survey" from American Management Association and ePolicy Institute; "2001 Electronic Policies and Practices Survey" from American Management Association and ePolicy Institute. Survey results available at www.amanet.org and www.epolicyinstitute.com.

2. "2007 Electronic Monitoring & Surveillance Survey" from American Management Association and ePolicy Institute. Survey results available at www .amanet.org and www.epolicyinstitute.com.

3. Ibid.

Chapter 22

1. *Smythe v. Pillsbury*, 914 F. Supp 97 (ED Pa. 1996). See also Nancy Flynn and Randolph Kahn, Esq., *E-Mail Rules*, New York, AMACOM, 2003.

2. Nancy Flynn's telephone interview with Attorney Jonathan Naylor, Morgan Cole Solicitors (July 19, 2006), www.morgan-cole.com.

3. "2007 Electronic Monitoring & Surveillance Survey" from American Management Association and ePolicy Institute; and "2001 Electronic Policies and Practices Survey" from American Management Association and ePolicy Institute. Survey results available at www.amanet.org and www.epolicyinstitute.com.

4. Ibid.

5. "2006 Workplace E-Mail, Instant Messaging & Blog Survey" from American Management Association and ePolicy Institute. Survey results available at www.amanet.org and www.epolicyinstitute.com.

6. "2007 Electronic Monitoring & Surveillance Survey" from American Management Association and ePolicy Institute. Survey results available at www .amanet.org and www.epolicyinstitute.com.

7. Ibid.

8. Ibid.

9. Ibid.

10. Ibid.

Chapter 23

1. "2007 Electronic Monitoring & Surveillance Survey" from American Management Association and ePolicy Institute. Survey results available at www .amanet.org and www.epolicyinstitute.com.

2. "2006 Workplace E-Mail, Instant Messaging & Blog Survey" from American Management Association and ePolicy Institute. Survey results available at www.amanet.org and www.epolicyinstitute.com.

3. Ibid.

4. *Smythe v. Pillsbury*, 914 F. Supp 97 (ED Pa. 1996). See also Nancy Flynn and Randolph Kahn, Esq., *E-Mail Rules*, New York, AMACOM, 2003.

5. Ben Westhoff, "Attack of the Blog," *Riverfront Times* (December 22, 2004), www.riverfronttimes.com.

6. Charles Toutant, "Blog's Demise May Chill Other Federal Lawyers' Online Comments," *New Jersey Law Journal* (November 21, 2005), www.law.com.

7. Ibid.

8. Matt Villano, "Write All About It (At Your Own Risk), *New York Times* (July 24, 2005).

9. Paul Starkman, "Mixed Verdicts," *Law Technology News* (November 2005), www.lawtechnologynews.com.

10. "Employee Blogging," Covington & Burling Technology & Software E-Mail Alert, April 18, 2005, www.cov.com.

11. Ian Shapira, "When Young Teachers Go Wild on the Web," *WashingtonPost .com* (April 28, 2008), http://www.washingtonpost.com/wp-dyn/content/article/ 2008/04/27/AR2008042702213.

12. Anick Jesdanun, "Recent Firings Raise Issues for Workers Who Publish Blogs," *Oregonian* (March 7, 2005), www.oregonline.com.

13. Matt Villano, "Write All About It (At Your Own Risk), *New York Times* (July 24, 2005).

14. Alorie Gilbert, "FAQ: Blogging on the Job," *CNETNews.com* (March 8, 2005), www.news.com.

15. "Employee Blogging," Covington & Burling Technology & Software E-Mail Alert (April 18, 2005), www.cov.com.

16. Ian Shapira, "When Young Teachers Go Wild on the Web," *WashingtonPost .com* (April 28, 2008), http://www.washingtonpost.com/wp-dyn/content/article/ 2008/04/27/AR2008042702213.

17. Stephanie Armour, "Warning: Your Clever Little Blog Could Get You Fired," *USA Today* (June 15, 2005).

18. Ian Shapira, "When Young Teachers Go Wild on the Web," *WashingtonPost .com* (April 28, 2008), http://www.washingtonpost.com/wp-dyn/content/article/2008/04/27/AR2008042702213.

19. Ibid.

Chapter 24

1. "2006 Workplace E-Mail, Instant Messaging & Blog Survey" from American Management Association and ePolicy Institute. Survey results available at www.amanet.org and www.epolicyinstitute.com.

2. "2007 Electronic Monitoring & Surveillance Survey" from American Management Association and ePolicy Institute. Survey results available at www .amanet.org and www.epolicyinstitute.com.

3. Anick Jesdanun, "Recent Firings Raise Issues for Workers Who Publish Blogs," *Oregonian* (March 7, 2005), www.oregonline.com.

4. Matt Villano, "Write All About It (At Your Own Risk), *New York Times* (July 24, 2005).

5. *Smythe v. Pillsbury*, 914 F. Supp 97 (ED Pa. 1996). See also Nancy Flynn and Randolph Kahn, Esq., *E-Mail Rules*, New York, AMACOM, 2003.

6. Ian Shapira, "When Young Teachers Go Wild on the Web," *WashingtonPost .com* (April 28, 2008), http://www.washingtonpost.com/wp-dyn/content/article/2008/04/27/AR2008042702213.

7. "2007 Electronic Monitoring & Surveillance Survey" from American Management Association and ePolicy Institute. Survey results available at www .amanet.org and www.epolicyinstitute.com.

8. Ibid.

9. "2005 Electronic Monitoring and Surveillance Survey," from American Management Association and ePolicy Institute, Survey results available at www.amanet.org and www.epolicyinstitute.com.

10. Jeff Karoub, "Texting Remains Relatively Private," *Associated Press* (January 25, 2008).

11. "2007 Electronic Monitoring & Surveillance Survey" from American Management Association and ePolicy Institute. Survey results available at www .amanet.org and www.epolicyinstitute.com.

12. Ibid.

13. Janet Kornblum, "Social, Work Lives Collide on Networking Websites," *USA Today* (January 18–20, 2008).

Glossary

1. Nancy Flynn and Randolph Kahn, Esq., *E-Mail Rules*, New York, AMACOM, 2003.

2.   Lev Grossman, "Meet Joe Blog," *Time.com* (June 21, 2004).

3.   Nancy Flynn's telephone interview with Attorney Jon Neiditz of Nelson Mullins Riley & Scarborough (November 15, 2007), www.nelsonmullins.com.

4.   "Outbound E-mail and Content Security in Today's Enterprise, 2007," Proof-Point Inc. survey fielded by Forrester Consulting (July 2007).

5.   Thomas J. Smedinghoff, ed., *Online Law: The SPA's Legal Guide to Doing Business on the Internet,* Reading, MA, Addison-Wesley Developers Press, 1996, 510.

6.   Software & Information Industry Association, Washington, DC, Software & Information Industry Association, 2000, www.siia.net/piracy.

7.   Nancy Flynn's telephone interview with ArcMail Technology's William T. Gates, President and CEO (October 24, 2008), www.arcmail.com.

8.   Nancy Flynn and Randolph Kahn, Esq., *E-Mail Rules,* New York, AMACOM, 2003.

9.   Steve Johnson, "When Blogs Bite Back," SignOnSanDiego.com (November 14, 2005), http://signonsandiego.com. See also Matt Villano, "Write All About It (At Your Own Risk)," *New York Times* (July 24, 2005).

10.   *Smythe v. Pillsbury,* 914 F. Supp 97 (ED Pa. 1996). See also Nancy Flynn and Randolph Kahn, Esq., *E-Mail Rules,* New York, AMACOM, 2003.

11.   Nancy Flynn and Randolph Kahn, Esq., *E-Mail Rules,* New York, AMACOM, 2003.

12.   Ibid.

13.   "Legal Overview: The Electronic Frontier and the Bill of Rights," *Electronic Frontier Foundation* (April 4, 2005), www.eff.org/legal.

14.   The Associated Press, "Firms Taking Action Against Worker Blogs," *New York Lawyer* (March 7, 2005), www.nylawyer.com.

15.   Software & Information Industry Association, Washington, DC: Software & Information Industry Association, 2000, www.siia.net/piracy/programs/share.

16.   Kim S. Nash, "E-Mail Retention: The High Cost of Digging Up Data," *Baseline* (August 2, 2006), http://www.baselinemag.com/index2.php?option = content& task = view&id = 4044&pop = 1&.

17.   Nancy Flynn and Randolph Kahn, Esq., *E-Mail Rules,* New York, AMACOM, 2003.

18.   David Kirkpatrick and Daniel Roth, "Why There's No Escaping the Blog," *Fortune* (January 10, 2005).

19.   Software & Information Industry Association, Washington, DC, Software & Information Industry Association, 2000, www.siia.net/piracy.

20. Ibid.

21. "State of the Blogosphere" report from Technorati, (August 2005), www.tech norati.com.

22. Software & Information Industry Association, Washington, DC, Software & Information Industry Association, 2000, www.siia.net/piracy.

23. "2007 Electronic Monitoring & Surveillance Survey" and "2001 Electronic Policies and Practices Survey" from American Management Association and ePolicy Institute. Survey results available at www.amanet.org and www .epolicyinstitute.com.

24. Software & Information Industry Association, Washington, DC: Software & Information Industry Association, 2000, www.siia.net/piracy.

INDEX

ABOUT THE AUTHOR

Nancy Flynn is founder and executive director of The ePolicy Institute, an organization dedicated to reducing employers' electronic risks, including litigation, through the development and implementation of effective ePolicies and employee training programs. An in-demand speaker and corporate trainer, she is the author of ten books published in five languages. Her books include *Blog Rules (AMACOM 2006), E-Mail Rules (AMACOM 2003), Instant Messaging Rules (AMACOM 2004), The ePolicy Handbook* (AMACOM 2008 and 2001), *Writing Effective E-Mail,* and *E-Mail Management.* Flynn is a popular media source who has been featured in *Fortune, Time, Newsweek, USA Today, Readers' Digest, US News & World Report, The Wall Street Journal, Business-Week,* and *The New York Times,* as well as on CBS, ABC, NBC, CNN, CNBC, MSNBC, FOX, NPR, and other media outlets.

ePolicy Institute services include on-site and online training seminars; expert witness services and litigation consulting; policy development and implementation; research surveys; and content development, including white papers and policy guides.

To schedule a training seminar or speaking engagement, book a consultation, or conduct a media interview, contact:

Nancy Flynn
Executive Director
The ePolicy Institute
614-451-3200
nancy@epolicyinstitute.com
www.ePolicyInstitute.com